GROWING UP IN BOSTON'S GILDED AGE

For Francie —
I suspect your grandmother, Ethel Washam Lowe, shared similar characteristics with Alice — love of books, strength of purpose, perceptiveness, & an ability to write very well. I'm eager to read yours & Barbara's book! Good luck in these final stages of getting everything published! With warm regards,

Verily Terrill

December 2, 1991

GROWING UP IN
BOSTON'S GILDED AGE

The Journal of
Alice Stone Blackwell, 1872–1874

Edited by Marlene Deahl Merrill

Yale University Press
New Haven & London

Published with assistance from the foundation established in memory of William McKean Brown.

Designed by Nancy Ovedovitz and set in Century Expanded type by The Composing Room of Michigan, Inc. Printed in the United States of America by Edwards Brothers, Inc., Ann Arbor, Michigan.

Library of Congress Cataloging-in-Publication Data

Blackwell, Alice Stone, 1857–1950.
  Growing up in Boston's Gilded Age : the journal of Alice Stone
Blackwell, 1872–1874 / edited by Marlene Deahl Merrill.
      p.   cm.
  Includes bibliographical references.
  ISBN 0–300–04777–0
    1. Blackwell, Alice Stone, 1857–1950—Diaries.   2. Boston
  (Mass.)—Social life and customs.   3. Women—Massachusetts—
  Boston—History—19th century.   4. Boston (Mass.)—
  Biography.   I. Merrill, Marlene.   II. Title.   III. Title: Gilded Age.
F73.5.B53   1990
974.4'61041'092—dc20   90-34019
                            CIP

The paper in this book meets the guidelines for permanence and durability of the Committee on Production Guidelines for Book Longevity of the Council on Library Resources.

10   9   8   7   6   5   4   3   2   1

Title page illustration: Alice at about the time she began her journal. (Library of Congress)

To Dan,
for always being there

CONTENTS

CONTENTS

PREFACE

Documentary editors frequently encounter tedious work in transcribing and editing old manuscripts. The lively Boston journal of Alice Stone Blackwell, however, was an absolute joy to edit from beginning to end. I have chosen to present her in a straightforward way—just as she presents herself in her journal writing—with the addition of notes, an introduction to provide background on her family, friends, and Boston environment, and an afterword to characterize her later life. Alice has much to say in her journal about political, social, and gender issues that specialists should find of interest and may wish to interpret. I have refrained, as much as possible, from categorizing her or interpreting her either as a developing adolescent (during the time she kept her journal) or later as an adult. My intention, as Alice's editor, has been to let her speak for herself and to make her world more accessible to twentieth-century readers.

Editing decisions were simplified by Alice's clear handwriting. She was already a fine writer when she began the journal, with a thorough understanding of grammar, spelling, and punctuation, and she took care to compose lively, readable entries. The few misspellings that slipped by her (as well as some words that she deliberately misspelled and appear as puns) have not been altered. I have occasionally silently corrected punctuation, most often by inserting single or double quotation marks around quoted material or sections of dialogue, and I have, on a few occasions, silently corrected jarring phrases (such as "a apple") or filled out Alice's confusing shorthand (ditto marks have been changed into the words they stand for). I have struck successive repeated words but retained her crossed-out words if they provide added meaning. Interlineations have been integrated into the regular text where indicated. Square brackets enclose editorial insertions; most commonly these supply missing words of book and periodical titles when she first refers to them.

Because Alice mentions so many titles, I have not footnoted each one individually, supplying instead (in appendix 1) an annotated and alphabetized list, by title, of all books and periodicals mentioned in the journal.

Because there is a proliferation of names in Alice's journal, as well as some duplication of first names, I have provided a dramatis personae, which appears immediately before the introduction. This list briefly identifies individuals who figure significantly in her entries and should make it easier for readers to keep track of the many people in her life. Except for Alice's schoolmates and teachers, most of the individuals on this list are usually more fully annotated when Alice first introduces them in her journal.

Journal entries have been formatted to resemble as closely as possible the original entries, including Alice's style of setting off her dateline and her use of superscripts. Because Alice chose a relatively narrow book for her journal writing, she seldom wasted space by indenting paragraphs. That format has been retained, except in a few cases of unusually long paragraphs that I have broken into more readable sections. The only sections of text that I have deleted are a few jarring and meaningless asides or phrases; their omission is indicated by ellipses.

In keeping with the tone of the journal, and to create a sense of intimacy with Alice and her family, I have referred to both her parents by their first names. This is a departure from my usual preference for last names. In this case, however, I feel readers will enjoy approaching them more familiarly as Alice's parents and less as leaders in the woman suffrage cause.

The journal is deposited with the Blackwell Family Papers at the Library of Congress, along with a number of Alice Stone Blackwell's later journals, running from 1889 to 1937. Alice refers in this journal to a previously kept diary, but no earlier volume or volumes have been located among her papers at either the Library of Congress or the Schlesinger Library at Radcliffe College. These two repositories house the substantial manuscript collections of the Blackwell family (available on microfilm), including the sixty-seven-year correspondence between Alice and her cousin Kitty Barry Blackwell. Their correspondence often provided additional information and background to Alice's journal entries and was utilized in footnotes to her text as well as in the accompanying introduction and afterword.

All but three engravings used to illustrate Alice's journal are from the 1872 edition of *Boston Illustrated* (Boston: James R. Osgood and Co.). Engravings of the ruins of the Boston fire (page 126) and of the Statehouse (page 231) are from the 1878 edition of *Boston Illustrated* (Boston: Houghton, Osgood and Co.). The engraving of the scenes from Boston Common (page 106) is from *King's Hand-Book of Boston* (Cambridge: Moses King, 1878).

The journal was brought to my attention as a publishable work by Geoffrey Blodgett, professor of history at Oberlin College. He came across it in the late 1960s while preparing to write the entry for Alice Stone Blackwell for *Notable American Women*. He shared with me an early transcription of the journal, as well as his considerable knowledge of nineteenth-century Boston. For this, for his reading of an early draft of the manuscript, and for his belief in and enthusiasm for the project, I am deeply grateful.

I also wish to thank Walter and Jean Reeves, longtime friends now living in Boston, for providing me with guided walking tours, research assistance, books, and warm hospitality as I sought to place Alice in her Boston and Dorchester settings. They also generously shared their knowledge and love of Boston in many other ways, including reading a final draft of the manuscript.

Anthony Sammarco, director of the Dorchester Historical Society (located in the carefully restored William Clapp House in Dorchester), shared his knowledge of the area and provided me with many important documents relating to Dorchester, Alice, and her family and friends. There I had the great pleasure of reading scrapbooks kept by Mary Fifield—Alice's Harris School chum and dueling partner—who is mentioned many times in her journal. These scrapbooks (put together some fifty years after Alice wrote her journal) were full of references to Alice's old friends and favorite Dorchester places. Mr. Sammarco also graciously read the final draft of the manuscript and kept me supplied with maps of Dorchester and Boston.

I am indebted to the Blackwell family, especially George and John Blackwell, for their support of this project as well as their help in trying to locate early pictures of Alice and her family.

Carol Lasser, associate professor of history at Oberlin College and my coeditor of *Friends and Sisters: Letters Between Lucy Stone and Antoinette Brown Blackwell, 1846–1893*, suggested several important articles on female friendships, read an early draft of the manuscript, and offered welcome Blackwell camaraderie.

Joanna Walters assisted in proofreading my first transcription of the journal against a photocopy of the original. As we worked together in the shadow of the Teton Mountain Range, nineteenth-century Boston often seemed far away. But her memories of growing up in the Dorchester area made the journal entries take on extra meaning; her parents, Eddie and Edie Walters, also contributed important information and a lively interest in the project.

Robert Longsworth, professor of English at Oberlin College, found Alice's phonetic spelling of Gaelic words intriguing and graciously provided me with his lexical expertise and resulting English translations.

Various staff members at the Oberlin College Library provided both knowledgeable and efficient services. Valerie McGowen-Doyle, interlibrarian loan supervisor, arranged for a number of obscure and difficult-to-locate books and periodicals to find their way to Oberlin; Cynthia Comer, head of reference, used unflagging detective skills while tracking down seemingly irretrievable bits of information; Kerry Langan and Anne Zald also graciously assisted me with reference questions. Dina Schoonmaker, curator of special collections, made the reading of the *Women's Journal*, as well as other nineteenth-century newspapers, both pleasurable and comfortable. Fred Zwegat, director of audio-visual services, provided carefully done photoduplications from old periodicals. Special thanks also go to other library staff members: Marjorie Henderson, Sharon Fenton, Bill Ruth, Shelby Warren, Shirley Williams, and Julie Weir. Jeffrey Weidman, Oberlin College art librarian and Helen Black, administrative assistant, helped me locate information on nineteenth-century dress and Boston buildings. William A. Moffett, director of Oberlin College libraries, Ray English, associate director, Allison Gould, head of circulation, and Roland Baumann, Oberlin College archivist, also provided me with institutional courtesies and an interest in my work that was greatly appreciated.

Kevin Weidenbaum, director of academic computing, and Anne Pearson, library technician, calmly provided solutions to several distressing computer problems. I also wish to thank Thelma Kime and Terri Mitchell for additional computer services.

My work at the Boston Athenaeum was made pleasurable and efficient by Jill Erickson and Jan Malcheski, reference librarians, Sally Pierce, curator of print and photographs, and Harry Katz, also of the print department. Similarly, reference librarian Katharine Dibble at the Boston Public Library assisted me in a number of helpful ways, as did Eugene Zepp, curator of rare books and manuscripts, and Ralph Montilio, of the print department. I also wish to thank Katherine Cain, rare books selector and archivist at Boston University; Elizabeth Swaim, archivist at Wesleyan University; Susan Halpert, reference librarian at the Houghton Library at Harvard University; Mary Wolfskill, of the manuscript department, and Yvonne Brooks, of the photoduplication office, at the Library of Congress; Susan Boone, curator of the Sophia Smith Collection at Smith College; Jane Knowles, Roberta Kovitz, and Marie-Hélène Gold at the Schlesinger Library at Radcliffe College; Lee Davison at the MIT Archives; Marcella Flaherty, reference librarian at the Education Library at Harvard University; and Louis Tucker, director, and Ross Urquhart, of the print department, at the Massachusetts Historical Society.

Elizabeth M. Furdon, assistant archivist for the Episcopal Diocese of Massachusetts, provided me with information on Agnes Winny's wedding. Elibet

Moore Chase, director of marketing at the Chapel Hill–Chauncy Hall School, supplied important material relating to the history of Chauncy Hall and arranged for the school's photographer, Alice Solorow, to reproduce an original print of the school.

I am indebted to scholars in the relatively new field of material culture, especially Ellice Ronsheim, supervisor of collections and textile curator at the Ohio Historical Society; Claudia Kidwell, curator of American costume at the National Museum of American History at the Smithsonian Institution; Kasey Grier, historian, Strong Museum in Rochester, New York; Susan Swan, curator at the Winterthur Museum in Winterthur, Delaware, and Virginia Gunn, assistant professor of clothing, textiles, and interiors at the University of Akron.

I am especially indebted to Ricky Clark and Laurel Sherman, fellow affiliate scholars at Oberlin College, as well as to Karan Cutler, Martha Merrill Pickrell, and Cary Reich for their suggestions and support. Clayton Koppes, Heather Hogan, and Larry Buell, all on the Oberlin College faculty, along with former Oberlin archivist Bill Bigglestone and London scholar Richard DuPuis, provided me with welcome information and encouragement. Mary Louise Van-Dyke, project director of the *Dictionary of American Hymnology*, helped me identify old hymns, the Reverend Leah Matthews helped me locate several important biblical passages, Dr. Bart Saxbe loaned me a number of his books and articles related to nineteenth-century medicine, and Joelle Runkle generously shared her research on Lucy Stone's suffrage associate Margaret Campbell.

As an editor herself, Alice Stone Blackwell would be pleased to know that her girlhood diary was placed in the capable and caring hands of Charles Grench, Karen Gangel, and Leslie Nelson at Yale University Press.

Most of all, I am grateful to my family. The twentieth-century urban partnership of my son and daughter-in-law, Steve Merrill and Corie Swanberg Merrill, provided special insights to my nineteenth-century enterprise. Their enthusiasm for Alice's journal also confirmed its contemporary relevance. My daughter, Karen Merrill—a continuing source of encouragement to me in my work as an editor—generously contributed her skills as a writer and historian to the project, in spite of the pressures of her graduate studies. Dan Merrill's day-to-day enthusiasm for and interest in the project kept me from ever feeling I was working in isolation. He enriched my perspective and knowledge on many journal-related topics and provided thoughtful suggestions for changes and additions to drafts of editorial material. The blessings of such familial support contributed significantly to this work and happily reflected a similar tradition found within the Stone Blackwell family.

ABBREVIATIONS

Personal Names
ASB Alice Stone Blackwell
KBB Kitty Barry Blackwell
LS Lucy Stone

Repositories (Unless otherwise indicated all correspondence
    is from the Blackwell Family Papers.)
LC Library of Congress
SL Schlesinger Library

Newspapers
WJ *Woman's Journal*
BDET *Boston Daily Evening Transcript*
BDG *Boston Daily Globe*

Biographic Dictionaries
DAB *Dictionary of American Biography*
DNB *Dictionary of National Biography* (British)
NAW *Notable American Women*
NCAB *National Cyclopedia of American Biography*
OCEL *Oxford Companion to English Literature*

Organizations
AWSA American Woman Suffrage Association
NWSA National Woman Suffrage Association
MWSA Massachusetts Woman Suffrage Association
NEWSA New England Woman Suffrage Association

DRAMATIS PERSONAE

Alice refers to many people in her journal, often by first names, nicknames, or her relationship to them (e.g., "Aunt Nettie"). The following list briefly identifies individuals who figure significantly in the journal: Alice's special friends, teachers, relatives, and household servants (with the approximate beginning dates of their service in parentheses). They are listed alphabetically, according to their relationship with Alice and her usual way of referring to them in her journal.

CHS = Chauncy Hall School
HS = Harris School

Agnes—Agnes Blackwell: younger cousin, youngest daughter of Sam and Antoinette.
Agnes—Agnes Reed/Reid: HS classmate.
Agnes—Agnes Winny: an English domestic (July 1872).
Alice—Alice Earle: older teenaged friend then living in Europe.
Anna—Anna Lawrence: younger cousin who became ill, daughter of Lucy's sister, Sarah.
Annie—Annie McLeod: a Scottish domestic working for the family when the diary begins.
Annie—Annie Phips: HS classmate.
Arthur Chamberlain: CHS schoolmate.
Aunt Elizabeth—Dr. Elizabeth Blackwell: Henry's sister, then living in England with her adopted daughter, Kitty Barry.
Aunt Ellen—Ellen Blackwell: Henry's sister, an artist living in New York City with her brother George and sister Dr. Emily Blackwell.
Aunt Emily—Dr. Emily Blackwell: Henry's sister, who was practicing medicine in New York City.

Aunt Marian—Marian Blackwell: Henry's then-itinerant sister, who was in the process of moving to Europe.

Aunt Nettie—Antoinette Brown Blackwell: wife of Henry's brother Sam and Lucy's close friend from college days.

Aunt Sarah—Sarah Stone Lawrence: Lucy's sister who was married to Henry Lawrence and lived in Gardner, Mass.

C.B.—Charley Bradley: HS student in class ahead of Alice.

Cushing/that Cushing boy: [Harry] Cushing: CHS schoolmate.

Eddy Jenkins: HS classmate.

Edie—Edith Blackwell: ASB's young cousin, daughter of Sam and Antoinette.

Emma—Emma Adams: HS classmate.

Emma—Emma Lawrence: older cousin, daughter of Lucy's sister, Sarah. She frequently stayed at Pope's Hill and assisted at the offices of the *Woman's Journal*.

Etty—Everett Sharp: HS student in the class ahead of Alice.

Fanny—Fanny Benedict: HS classmate.

Florence/Floy—Florence Blackwell: slightly older cousin, daughter of Sam and Antoinette.

Florence—Florence Schenck: CHS classmate.

Frank—Frank Fellows: chore boy who also helped with the garden and stables (April 1872).

Georgie Townsend: CHS classmate.

Guild—Curtis Guild, Jr.: CHS schoolmate.

Grace—Grace Blackwell: younger cousin, daughter of Sam and Antoinette.

Hannah—a domestic. (June 1873).

Harry—Harry Spofford: teenaged son of old friends of Alice's parents; he worked at Pope's Hill in the summer of 1872.

Hattie—Hattie Burditt: HS classmate.

Hattie—Hattie Mann: HS classmate.

John—chore boy for the family when the journal begins.

Josie Jones: HS friend in the class ahead of Alice.

Kitty—Catherine Barry (alias Capt. Kidd): adopted daughter of Dr. Elizabeth Blackwell, and Alice's "betrothed."

Lucy—Lucy Chadbourn: a domestic (October 1872).

Lulu—Louise Mann: HS classmate.

Mamie—Ada Marie Molineux: CHS classmate.

Mary—Mary Fifield: HS friend in the class ahead of Alice.

Mary—Mary Hooper: the daughter of neighbors when Alice and her parents lived in Roseville, N.J., and part of the Pope's Hill household from the time the journal begins until April 1872.

Mary Emma—Mary Emma Ryder: HS classmate.

Mike—a yard and stable man (October 1872).

Miss Bass—a domestic (February 1873).

Miss Jones—a domestic (May 1873).

Miss Ladd—Emily Ladd: an older student at CHS.

Miss Lily/Miss Lilla—Lilla Morse: Alice's and Edie's piano teacher.

Miss Newhall—Lucy Newhall: assistant teacher at CHS.

Miss Rand—Lizzie Rand: CHS classmate.

Miss Smith—Sarah Smith: mathematics teacher at CHS.

Miss Titcomb—dressmaker.

Miss Tolman—Ann Tolman: Alice's teacher at HS..

Miss Tucker—a domestic (April 1872).

Miss Turner—Harriet Turner: CHS schoolmate.

Mr. Cushing—Thomas Cushing: proprietor and senior principal at CHS.

Mr. Demerit—Edwin DeMerritte: Latin teacher at CHS.

Mr. Herbert—Herbert Cushing: assistant principal and Latin teacher at CHS.

Mr. Horne—Edwin Horne: principal at HS.

Mr. Ladd—William H. Ladd: proprietor and head of rhetoric and elocution at CHS.

Mrs. Coe—a domestic (May 1873). Her small daughter Annie lived in the household as well.

Mrs. Spear—a domestic (February 1873).

Nannie—Hannah Blackwell: adopted baby daughter of Dr. Emily Blackwell.

Neelie/Neenie/Nina—Cornelia Blackwell: adopted baby daughter of Ellen Blackwell.

Phebe—Phebe Stone: ASB's older cousin, daughter of Lucy's brother Bowman.

Ruth Swan: HS classmate.

Sadie/Sadi—Sadie Wilson: a HS friend from the class ahead of Alice.

Sam King: in the class ahead of Alice at HS.

Uncle George—George Blackwell: Henry's youngest unmarried brother, living with his sisters Emily and Ellen, in New York City.

Uncle Henry—Henry Lawrence: husband of Lucy's sister, Sarah, living in Gardner, Mass.

Uncle Sam—Samuel Blackwell: Henry's brother, husband of Antoinette Brown, from Somerville, N.J.

Uncle Stone/Uncle Bo—Bowman Stone: Lucy's brother, from West Brookfield, Mass.

INTRODUCTION

On the evening of February 1, 1872, fourteen-year-old Alice Stone Blackwell felt a compelling need to start another journal. This was not the first time she would begin a journal, nor would it be the last.[1] She did not wait to purchase a special notebook, however, but instead found something that suited her purpose: an old, barely used account ledger of her father's. With sturdy and straightforward writing, she began her first entry.

Alice speaks to this journal as if it were a person, albeit a passive one who only receives and accepts her impressions and reactions. In her first entry she introduces herself and her "situation," then cuts short the formality, saying: "That is about enough introduction, and if Posterity wants more, Posterity will have to do without. Not that I mean to have P. read it—at least not miscellaneous Posterity." This kind of direct communication with her journal (and ultimately her journal reader) characterizes the entire document. In it, Alice's writing is so immediate that she often seems to be speaking directly to us today.

Her lively, candid accounts of Boston events and people come alive as we watch the British actress Charlotte Cushman perform at the Music Hall, or we meet "unpleasant looking" Louisa May Alcott and learn she "laces" (wears a corset) and is thus on the wrong side of the dress reform issue. The notable friends of Alice's parents, seen through her eyes, become less than legend and

1. Alice began her first (and now missing) journal on 1 May 1870, according to an entry made on 1 May 1872.

take on human qualities: William Lloyd Garrison's warmth and love of cats appeal to Alice so much that she turns to his poetry to know him better; and Theodore Weld's crusty encouragement that she "Be thyself . . . don't be any-body else" elicits her undaunted reply that she "couldn't be two people at the same time"—a response that must have pleased the eccentric old reformer.

Alice's school times also engage us as we listen to her banter with classmates and teachers, react to examinations, and compete on the playground. Her journal entries also capture the home routines of a young Victorian girl, emp-tying slops, making pie tarts and chemises, and coping with cramps by drink-ing tansy tea. Alice's nineteenth-century world becomes real on an everyday basis, in the same way that she emerges from her writing as someone we can know on a personal level.

Unlike most adolescents, she was a voracious reader who took weekly trips to Boston's Athenaeum and the Boston Public Library to check out books. In the course of the next twenty-six months of daily journal writing she refers to over 130 books, magazines, and newspapers—most of which she had read or was reading.[2] Not surprisingly, she was blessed with a splendid vocabulary and a lively literary style far in advance of her years. Alice's pen served her well in writing this journal—just as it would later in her life when she became an outspoken reformer and a noted editor and writer.[3]

As the only child of prominent woman suffragists Lucy Stone and Henry Blackwell, Alice experienced an exceptional homelife.[4] For instance, on the eve-ning that Alice wrote her first journal entry her parents, typically, were away from home, this time spending their second full day at an annual woman's

2. See Appendix 1 for an annotated list of these books and periodicals, arranged alphabetically by title.

3. See Afterword. There is no full-length biography of Alice Stone Blackwell. The most recent biographical summaries of her life are by Geoffrey Blodgett in *Notable American Women*, v. 1, 156–58, and by Gail Thain Parker in *DAB*, suppl. 4, 1945–50, 85–87.

4. For full-length biographies of Lucy Stone, see Alice Stone Blackwell, *Lucy Stone: Pioneer of Woman's Rights* (Boston: Little, Brown, 1930), and Elinor Rice Hays, *Morn-ing Star: A Biography of Lucy Stone, 1818–1893* (New York: Harcourt, Brace and World, 1961). Stone's lifetime reform interests, as well as her domestic and family concerns, are chronicled in Carol Lasser and Marlene Deahl Merrill, *Friends and Sis-ters: Letters Between Lucy Stone and Antoinette Brown Blackwell, 1846–1893* (Urbana: University of Illinois Press, 1987). There is no full biography of Henry Blackwell, but he is featured in Elinor Rice Hays, *Those Extraordinary Blackwells* (New York: Harcourt, Brace and World, 1967), as well as in Hays, *Morning Star*. Leslie Wheeler explored the Stone Blackwell marriage in *Loving Warriors: Selected Letters of Lucy Stone and Henry B. Blackwell, 1853–1893* (New York: Dial Press, 1981). Alice fondly recalled her father in Sydney Strong, ed., *What I Owe to My Father* (New York: Henry Holt, 1931), 35–48.

Alice's parents, Lucy Stone Blackwell (Dorchester Historical Society) and Henry Blackwell (Schlesinger Library, Radcliffe College), c. 1872.

suffrage convention in Boston.[5] As leaders of three suffrage organizations—the Massachusetts, the New England, and the American Woman Suffrage Associations—they had numerous responsibilities. Added to this was Lucy's virtually full-time job as editor of the *Woman's Journal*, the suffrage paper of the AWSA. Although Henry assisted with some editorial work, Lucy carried the full burden of producing this nationally distributed eight-page weekly.

Alice's parents were part of a circle of prominent Boston reformers, many of whom Alice knew personally. She had, in fact, always been surrounded by strong and motivated people. Two of her aunts were Elizabeth and Emily Blackwell, pioneering women physcians. Another aunt, Antoinette Brown Blackwell, was the first woman ordained as a minister.[6] They, like Alice's mother, were powerful examples of ambitious and achieving women.

5. The Massachusetts Woman Suffrage Association (MWSA), was in the midst of its annual convention, held at Tremont Temple (*BDG*: 1 Feb. 1872).

6. Numerous works describe the lives and medical achievements of Elizabeth and Emily Blackwell. Their professional and personal lives are described in Hays, *Those Extraordinary Blackwells*; and their complex relationships within the Blackwell clan are explored in a major study of the family in Margo Horn, "Family Ties: The Blackwells, a Study in the Dynamics of Family Life in Nineteenth Century America" (Ph.D. diss., Tufts University, 1980). A shorter version of this appears as "'Sisters Worthy of Re-

INTRODUCTION

Lucy Stone had been one of the first women to lecture on antislavery and woman's rights. A devoted follower of radical abolitionist William Lloyd Garrison, she both spoke and wrote on behalf of his organization, the American Anti-Slavery Society, during her four years as a student at Oberlin College (from 1843 to 1847). While there, she also taught a number of free black adults, who made up an expanding Afro-American community in the town. Her deep commitment to work on behalf of human rights extended not only to the antislavery cause but also to the cause of woman's rights. Because Garrison's society was one of the few reform organizations endorsing the public speaking of women, she found its work especially attractive, and in June 1848 she became an agent and lecturer for the society.

By this time she had also spoken publicly on behalf of woman's rights, preceding (by at least six months) the first woman's rights convention held in Seneca Falls, New York, in July 1848.[7] One of only a dozen or so women with a college degree, Stone believed that by working together, women could advance their right to legal and political equality, as well as their right to equal higher education. Beginning in 1850, she helped organize and lead the earliest national conventions on woman's rights. At the same time, she continued to address large public audiences on women's issues and petitioned several state legislatures to reform laws that subordinated a married woman's civil identity to that of her husband. For nearly ten years she submerged herself in these causes, supporting herself from salaries and fees and earning both respect and ridicule from large sectors of the American public.

Although resistant to the idea of marriage, she married British-born Henry Blackwell, a Cincinnati hardware merchant and abolitionist, after a long courtship. The couple prepared and read a statement at their wedding ceremony, protesting existing marriage laws that left wives with little legal protection and personal autonomy and resolving to live as equal and independent partners. A year later, Lucy made the even more unconventional announcement that henceforth she would be known only by her maiden name. For many years, women who followed her example were known as Lucy Stoners.

In spite of her strong need for personal independence, Lucy discovered that

spect': Family Dynamics and Women's Roles in the Blackwell Family," *Journal of Family History* 8 (Winter 1983): 369–82. The above books and articles also treat Antoinette Brown Blackwell at length. For her full-length biography, see Elizabeth Cazden, *Antoinette Brown Blackwell: A Biography* (Old Westbury, N.Y.: Feminist Press, 1983). See also Lasser and Merrill, *Friends and Sisters*.

7. Stone gave her first public woman's rights lecture in Gardner, Mass., late in 1847 (Lasser and Merrill, *Friends and Sisters*, 11–12).

Lucy and Alice in 1858. (Library of Congress)

her needs changed with the birth of Alice in the fall of 1857. She soon abdi-
cated most of her public roles in favor of full-time motherhood. Settling in
northern New Jersey, she devoted herself to Alice for the next eight years,
while Henry held various jobs and energetically pursued business and real
estate ventures around the country. Although Lucy occasionally reinvolved
herself in women's issues, this period was often a time of extreme loneliness
and conflict for her. In 1858 she confessed that she wished she could feel "the
old impulse and power to lecture, both for the sake of cherished principles and
to help Harry with the burdens he has to bear." After one occasion when she

thought it possible she might resume her work, she returned home and "looked into Alice's sleeping face and thought of the possible evil that might befall her if my guardian eye was turned away. I shrank like a snail into its shell, and saw that for these years I can only be a mother—no trivial thing either."[8]

"These years" lasted until the end of the Civil War when reconstruction of the Union held the promise of suffrage for both blacks and women. If anything could bring Lucy Stone out of retirement, it was the combination of these two causes. The time was also right: Alice was becoming less dependent, and Henry had built up enough income to allow them the luxury of devoting their combined energies to political and social reform.

Lucy began taking a leading role in two new organizations she had helped found: the American Equal Rights Association, designed to press for both black and woman suffrage, and the New England Woman Suffrage Association. By 1869 she found herself embroiled in a bitter ideological and personal conflict with her old friends and woman's rights associates Susan B. Anthony and Elizabeth Cady Stanton. Their resulting schism led to the formation of two separate suffrage organizations, with differing tactics and temperaments: Stanton and Anthony founded and led the National Woman Suffrage Association (NWSA); Lucy and Henry helped found and lead the American Woman Suffrage Association (AWSA).[9]

Alice's parents almost immediately moved to Boston, where they established a broad base of suffrage operations among such like-minded reforming friends as William Lloyd Garrison, Thomas Wentworth Higginson, Julia Ward Howe, and Mary Livermore. They purchased a seventeen-room house on Boutwell Street in the historic and newly annexed suburb of Dorchester—just a fifteen-minute train ride from downtown Boston and the offices of the *Woman's Journal*. They named their new home Pope's Hill, for the high wooded hill on which it had been built. Here they put down roots that would last the rest of their lives.

Such a feeling of permanence, however, was far from Alice's experience on the night she began her journal. Uprooted too many times in the past several years, she did not feel much at home anywhere. Beginning in 1867, her parents frequently began to leave her with relatives. That year (her longest separation from them), she was deposited in New York City for several months with her

---

8. Lasser and Merrill, *Friends and Sisters*, 150.

9. There are various accounts of this division, often reflecting the loyalties of the authors. See *History of Woman Suffrage*, ed. Elizabeth Cady Stanton, Susan B. Anthony, Matilda Joslyn Gage, et al. (Rochester: Susan B. Anthony, 1881–1902 [vols. 1–4]; New York: National Woman Suffrage Association, 1922 [vols. 5–6]); Alice Stone Blackwell, *Lucy Stone*; Hays, *Morning Star*; and Wheeler, *Loving Warriors*.

physican aunts, Drs. Elizabeth and Emily Blackwell, while Lucy and Henry stumped for equal suffrage in Kansas. Later, as her parents settled into their busy new lives in Boston, Alice attended Jane Andrew's progressive school for girls in Newburyport, Massachusetts, where she lived intermittently from October 1869 until probably the early spring of 1871. Alice's most traumatic upheaval occurred in December 1871—shortly before she began her journal—when a fire destroyed so much of the Pope's Hill house that the family was forced to move into a smaller house on an adjacent lot until substantial repairs could be made and the household furnishings replaced. Lucy and Henry were away when Alice and Annie McLeod, the young Scottish domestic Alice adored, discovered the fire and managed to escape, attempting to save what they could of important valuables. Characteristically, Alice first tried to save her favorite books.

As full-time working parents, Lucy and Henry were alert to Alice's disloca-tions and her need for continuity and company. As middle-aged parents (Hen-ry was forty-six and Lucy fifty-three), they also recognized that their spirited daughter needed more activity than they could provide. Consequently, they carefully selected women for their two positions of cook and housekeeper so that at least one was young enough (usually in her late teens or early twenties) to be good company for Alice. In addition, they frequently invited young family friends or Alice's cousins for extended visits. During the period of the journal, Alice's headstrong, preadolescent cousin Edith ("Edie") spent several months at Pope's Hill and proved to be a challenging distraction but, as Alice confesses in her journal, also a "thorn" in her side.

In spite of the complexities of a busy household and crowded schedules, Alice enjoyed comfortable routines as well as special times together with her parents. Henry, an avid reader and lover of books, often read to the family in the evenings. They would gather in the library and listen to him read from a carefully selected and on-going book (usually a British novel), while Lucy and Alice sometimes sewed or mended. During hot summer evenings, they moved these readings to the cooler environment of their high mansard roof with a widow's walk. Here, while Henry read, they were refreshed and invigorated by the salty breezes from nearby Dorchester Bay.

Lucy enjoyed taking her daughter to meetings and lectures in Boston. Alice would take the train in to meet her mother at the *Journal* office, and the two might then shop or have dinner or supper together before attending an after-noon or evening program. Mother and daughter also shared a great love of nature. Whether observing a sunset (which Alice called "the Glories") or working side by side in their garden, the two enjoyed a warm camaraderie out-of-doors. Raised on a large working farm in the rolling hills of West Brook-

Pope's Hill, 45 Boutwell St., Dorchester.
(Library of Congress)

field, Massachusetts, Lucy felt most at home in rural settings with abundant trees, a sweeping view, and ample space for a garden. Pope's Hill satisified all such longings, offering spacious grounds and a splendid view of Boston to the north and of the ocean to the east. Alice once counted over 160 trees on their grounds, yet there was ample room for fruit, flower, and vegetable gardens— even for a cow and chickens. Alice raised the chickens, a job she took seriously and enjoyed for the most part, except when told to choose one for dinner. Lucy taught Alice many gardening skills, and they enjoyed consulting seed catalogs together as they planned the garden for the new season.

In spite of Henry's high levels of nervous energy, he let others, including a hired yardman and stable boy, tend to such outdoor activities as gardening. He did, however, enjoy making various kinds of jelly from their homegrown fruits and took special pleasure in producing each year, near the Fourth of July, a big batch of clear, deep-red currant jelly. Henry delighted in teaching Alice jelly-making skills, and the two often preserved and canned other homegrown products, which also ended up in the family larder.

Public and private agencies supplied Dorchester residents with the conveniences of water and gas, as well as waste disposal services.[10] Alice's house, like most of the large Victorian homes in the vicinity of Pope's Hill, came equipped with such household conveniences as double windows, a coal furnace connected to a system of floor radiators, and a number of rooms with fireplaces. The lighting fixtures used gas, but the family also relied on freestanding kerosene lamps for table and reading light. Because their house was situated at the top of one of Dorchester's highest hills, water pressure was a problem; they had, however, at least one indoor pump and several water faucets on the first floor. A year before beginning her journal, Alice wrote that her father intended to abolish their "very bad smelling privy" and make an earth closet.[11] Many thought that earth closets would reduce the risk of contaminated drinking water, the cause of typhoid fever. This latest but short-lived sanitary reform was similar to a water closet, except that it used dry earth to cover waste and had the advantage of being portable and easily installed. It is not clear, however, whether or not Henry made such an installation.

Typical of upper-middle-class Victorian families, the Blackwells relied on live-in servants. As working parents, Lucy's and Henry's reliance on such help was dictated not by a sense of entitlement or social status but by a very real need for assistance in running their large house. Lucy's farm upbringing instilled in her a devotion to thrift and making do. In 1871 she wrote of her need for a "suitable woman" to help, saying that "though I have a good cook . . . there is so much waste that I cannot prevent, that a whole family might be kept on it. A thrifty Yankee woman would be invaluable, and at $200 a year and her board, might lay up money. I *must* have some one, or I must leave all Woman's rights work, or I must leave my family—Do duties ever conflict?"[12]

She and Henry rarely spent money on luxuries, coming closest, perhaps, when refurnishing their house after the fire. Alice disapproved even of this: she found the new French roof "hideous," the new furnishings lacked the comfortable "homey" quality of the old, and she concluded that "the whole house now seems almost too splendid to use. . . . I don't think splendid agrees with me."[13]

10. Sam Bass Warner, Jr., *Streetcar Suburbs: The Process of Growth in Boston*, 1870–1900 (Cambridge: Harvard University Press and MIT Press, 1962), 29–31.

11. ASB to KBB: 9 Apr. 1871, LC.

12. LS to Margaret Campbell: 22 Aug. 1871, LC.

13. ASB to KBB: 3 Mar. 1872, LC; and ASB to KBB: "1873", LC. (Another hand has incorrectly identified the latter letter; it was undoubtedly written in late June 1872.)

In matters of dress, however, even Alice could not accuse her parents of indulging in high fashion. As a leader in the dress reform movement, Lucy believed in the healthful benefits of loose and comfortable attire for women. She and Alice were always well dressed but never stylish compared to many Boston mothers and daughters of a similar social position. Because the ready-to-wear clothing industry was just developing, nearly all women's clothing had to be custom-made.[14] Lucy was an able seamstress and made clothes for Alice and herself during her early years as a full-time homemaker. Because of her increased commitments outside the home, however, she now had to rely on dressmakers for most of their wardrobe. Mother and daughter enjoyed picking out material for their dresses, usually making such purchases in downtown Boston, at C. F. Hovey's large dry goods store on Summer Street or at department stores that offered dressmaking services.

Although Boston offered many richly stocked stores, Dorchester residents could supply their more ordinary needs in smaller, nearby shops clustered around a number of villages or neighborhoods located within the suburb. The village of Harrison Square was closest to Alice and her family, located less than half a mile north of their home on Boutwell Street. Here stood the Harris Grammar School, which Alice attended until 1873, several churches, a variety of shops, and a number of picturesque homes and stables on small tree-lined lots. It was a lush area, full of shade trees and hedges, expansive lawns and gardens, and stretches of yet unoccupied land. In this setting, Alice walked to and from school six days a week, including Saturday mornings.[15] A two-hour noon recess allowed her time for a relaxed noon dinner at home or even a quick trip into Boston. After school she could shop for needed household items in nearby Harrison Square stores, visit the homes of school friends, or enjoy a leisurely uphill walk back home.

Most Harrison Square residents did not go away for the summer; in fact, because of the hills, shade trees, and proximity to the ocean, the area was

14. Women's undergarments as well as overcoats and mantles (called "outer sacks") had been available on a ready-made basis in big cities for some time. But it would not be until the 1890s that more difficult-to-fit clothes, such as dresses, skirts, blouses, and suits, would be produced. When Alice speaks of shopping for a dress, she means she is buying the material from which a dressmaker would make it. See Claudia Kidwell, *Cutting a Fashionable Fit* (Washington, D.C.: Smithsonian Publication, 1979); and Claudia Kidwell and Maggie Christman, *Suiting Everyone: The Democratization of Clothing in America* (Washington, D.C.: Smithsonian Publication, 1974).

15. From Alice's diary, it appears that the Harris Grammar School dismissed its Saturday classes at noon. Some schools, however, held classes until 1 P.M. Homework assignments were not given out over the weekend (Annual Report of the School Committee of Boston for 1872, appendix).

10

considerably cooler than Boston and regarded as a summer resort. A thriving yacht club was located on Dorchester Bay, and Tenean Beach (a protected sandy strip on the bay along Commercial Point) provided bathhouses and pleasant bathing for residents. Alice frequented the beach in summer and enjoyed meeting her friends there as well as bathing in the cool waters. It is worth noting, however, that her journal often reveals that she suffered bouts of diarrhea a day or two after these occasions. It is unclear whether Alice connected this malady with contaminated water; if so, she does not acknowledge it in her journal. Alice and her friends also enjoyed boating on the Mill Pond, "a lovely little sheet of water," located near the beach, where one could safely learn to row, and when sufficiently expert, venture out into Dorchester Bay and bigger water.[16]

Harrison Square was one of several locations between Quincy and Boston that provided a depot for the Old Colony Railroad. Service to Boston cost twenty cents, with trains following a scenic route along the shoreline to the city. Because the passenger station on Kneeland and South streets was a number of blocks from central Boston, the family counted on a long walk after they arrived, and depending on weather and time constraints, they sometimes relied on horse-drawn streetcars ("horsecars") or cabs to deliver them to their destination. Lucy, overweight and suffering from rheumatism, found it difficult to walk long distances and almost always relied on cabs and carriages. When she returned to Dorchester from the city, she rarely walked home but was met by the family carriage.

Field's Corner, adjacent to and west of Harrison Square, was a more recently developed village center with stores, a post office (where the family kept a mail box), and a small horsecar station. Alice and her parents often took horsecars from Field's Corner to Boston and back, especially in nice weather. The route to Boston took them directly into the business and shopping center of the city, terminating on Summer Street. Because the cars stopped frequently along the way, they were convenient for shopping, although the trip took considerably longer than by train.

Other nearby neighborhoods also held attractions for the family. Meeting House Hill was the location of Dorchester's historic First Parish Church, which Alice sometimes attended. Right next door to it was Lyceum Hall, an attractive Greek Revival building and the site of many school exhibitions and community programs. The village of Neponset (at the convergence of the Neponset River and Dorchester Bay) was the next stop on the train beyond

16. This quotation as well as the characterization of the Harrison Square area is from an unpublished recollection, "Harrison Square As It Used To Be," by Alice A. Burditt (paper delivered at the Dorchester Historical Society, March 23, 1926).

Harrison Square, a little over half a mile south of Alice's house. She would sometimes ride the extra distance just to enjoy the change in scenery on her walk home. Lower Mills (situated still further south and inland along the Neponset River) was still another favorite walking place for Alice because of the dramatic hilly terrain; there she enjoyed visiting the Baker Chocolate Factory and a small Episcopal chapel.

Dorchester supplied all the suburban convenience and country charm Alice's family required. But Lucy and Henry derived their greatest satisfactions in Boston, which was not surprising, given Henry's long attraction to the advantages of big cities. Less than a month after his marriage to Lucy, he described the kind of permanent home he desired: something with "a garden, a second Eden with a house upon it, somewhere in the vicinity of a large city, on a railroad affording access to lectures and society. . . . I am . . . determined . . . never to live very far from a city."[17] He clearly fulfilled all these desires by moving to the Boston suburb of Dorchester.

Boston was in the midst of its most dramatic period of growth when Lucy and Henry moved there. Between 1850 and 1900 the city grew from a tightly compressed seaport of two hundred thousand to a sprawling metropolitan area covering a ten-mile radius and encompassing thirty-one cities and towns, with over one million inhabitants. Foreign immigration greatly increased the population; by 1875 there were sixty thousand foreign-born Irish in Boston, swelling the labor pool and contributing to the industrial prosperity of the city.[18]

Responding to the need for further expansion, the city developed the old Back Bay, and by the time of Alice's diary, this western area had changed significantly, as new row houses and large buildings began appearing on Commonwealth Avenue and adjacent streets. Copley Square was still, however, "a desert of dirt, dust, mud and wind." [19] Alice visited this area whenever she attended lectures at the Massachusetts Institute of Technology, then located in one building at the western outskirts of the city on Boylston Street.

Alice found her greatest attractions in the old west end and central sections of Boston. Once or twice each week she walked a regular route around or through the Boston Common as she visited the Athenaeum, the Public Library, and the office of the *Woman's Journal*. The latter was at 3 Tremont Place, a short street off Beacon Street (and just east of the Athenaeum) and adjacent to the Old Granary Burial Ground. This multistoried building also housed the quarters of the New England Woman's Club, as well as several other apart-

17. Henry Blackwell to Augustus Moore: 26 May 1855, LC.

18. Sam Bass Warner, Jr., *Streetcar Suburbs*, 1.

19. Walter Muir Whitehill, *Boston: A Topographical History* (Cambridge: Harvard University Press, 1959), 168.

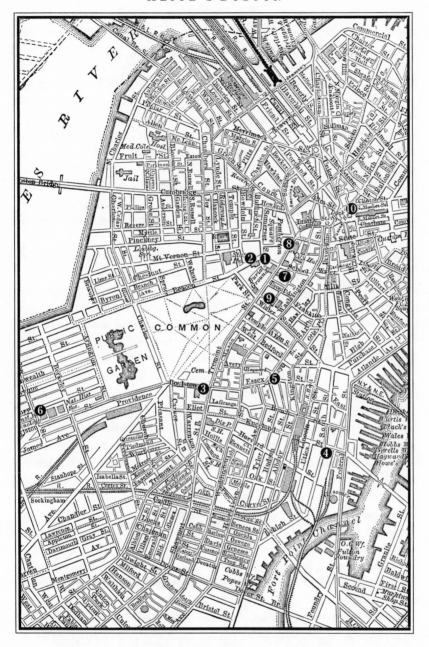

(1) *Woman's Journal* office and New England Woman's Club; (2) Athenaeum;
(3) Public Library; (4) Old Colony Railroad Depot; (5) Chauncy Hall School
(temporary quarters, 1873–74); (6) Massachusetts Institute of Technology;
(7) Tremont Temple; (8) Boston Museum; (9) Music Hall; (10) Faneuil Hall. City
of Boston, *King's Hand-Book of Boston* (Cambridge: Moses King, 1878).

ments. In fact, Henry and Lucy had lived in one of the apartments for several months when they first moved to Boston.

The Boston Athenaeum, an elegant freestone Italianate building completed in 1849, was a proprietary library for shareholders and members but granted liberal privileges to guests. Henry's membership permitted Alice to check out books there. In 1872 the Athenaeum offered its members a choice of nearly 100,000 volumes in its library, a gracious reading room, and four art galleries that exhibited their fine collection of paintings and sculpture. During the time of Alice's journal, the Museum of Fine Arts (organized in 1870) occupied two of the four Athenaeum galleries while its own quarters were being completed. When the museum finally moved, in 1876, to its new building on Copley Square, it took not only its own new acquisitions but the gift of a large portion of the Athenaeum's impressive collection.[20]

The Boston Public Library was, in 1872, the largest free circulating library in the world, containing close to 200,000 volumes. During its fourteen-year existence, the collection of books had burgeoned, necessitating a major remodeling effort. Situated on Boylston Street (on the present site of the Colonial Theater), the library boasted a handsome redbrick and sandstone facade with huge arched windows looking out on the Boston Common. Inside, the Bates Hall reading room was even more impressive with its high Corinthian columns, tile floor, and handsome furniture. British author Matthew Arnold found the elegance of this hall so incongruous with the democratic lending policy of the library that he inquired shortly after entering, "Do you let barefoot boys in this reading room?"[21] Alice did not comment on the opulence of either the Public Library or the Athenaeum and seemed unintimidated by either; undoubtedly she was more interested in books than in her surroundings.

Alice's many trips between these buildings took her either through or around the Boston Common. Set aside in 1634 as a public reservation, the forty-eight-acre site had been used as a grazing area for cattle, as well as a place for public executions. For Alice, it was much as it is today—a spacious public park offering her the pleasures of shade trees, soft expanses of grass, charming paths rather than sidewalks, and benches for reading, resting, and contemplation.

Boston offered many other attractions for Alice in addition to her enjoyable library excursions. She attended several churches and frequented a number of

20. Mabel Munson Swan, *The Athenaeum Gallery, 1827–1873* (Boston: Boston Athenaeum, 1940), 171–75.

21. Jane Holtz Kay, *Lost Boston* (Boston: Houghton Mifflin, 1980), 16.

public halls and theaters: Tremont Temple, the Music Hall, and the Boston Museum—all located on Tremont Street. The latter, built in 1846, housed several art galleries but was best known for its large, comfortable theater, which had a history of fine dramatic productions performed, at the time of Alice's journal, by a resident stock company.

Such Boston landmarks provide an ever-present background in Alice's journal, but they are of only secondary importance to her. The opulent buildings and ostentatious displays that characterized the Gilded Age meant little to Alice. Instead, she found her gold in books and ideas and in the vast array of people who touched her life and affected her development.

One person who deeply impressed her bears special mention. Robert Collyer (1823–1912), a popular Unitarian minister, began lecturing and preaching in Boston after the Chicago fire of 1871 destroyed his New Unity Church—one of the largest Protestant churches in that city. Born in England to workhouse parents, he was deeply affected by his early experiences of poverty and worked to improve the lot of poor and working class people after he moved to the United States. Preaching on the accessible and simple themes of a personal religious life, he attracted large followings from all classes of people. Sincere, enthusiastic, and eloquent, he was an impressive speaker and writer. Alice not only heard him whenever she could but frequently read his published sermons.[22]

This was a time of sporadic but nevertheless intense religious questioning for her, and she vacillated between a yearning for a personal God whom she could love and trust and bouts of frightening skepticism. She observed, and was probably influenced by, the importance that religion played in the lives of the Irish Catholic and English Anglican domestics who worked in the household and attended church regularly. Deep issues of faith also surfaced for her as she helplessly watched her cousin Anna Lawrence (just two years her junior) gradually weaken from what proved to be a terminal illness. As lukewarm agnostics, her parents offered little help in spiritual issues, whereas Robert Collyer did.

Religion was complicated for her by a need to belong to a group of friends her own age. Many of her schoolmates attended Dorchester's First Parish, a Unitarian church served by Nathaniel Hall, who had been its minister for nearly forty years. Alice sometimes attended Sunday school and church services there, and although she enjoyed being with her friends, she seems to have derived little spiritual benefit from these occasions. She became more attracted to Sunday services at Episcopal churches largely because of Agnes Winny, a

---

22. For a more detailed biography of Robert Collyer (1823–1912), see *DAB*.

young English domestic in the household, who was Anglican. In fact, Alice was her bridesmaid when Agnes was married in an Episcopal ceremony in Dorchester. Soon after this occasion Alice began attending (often by herself) a small Episcopal chapel in Lower Mills.

Like several other young women who served as domestics for the family, Agnes Winny was a kind of big sister for Alice, as were her older cousins Emma Lawrence and Florence Blackwell. Certainly no shortage of women existed in either Alice's household or in her more extended family, for a female domestic, aunt, or cousin was almost always close at hand. Conversely, with no male cousins and no boys or young men as neighbors or family friends, Alice enjoyed no brother substitute. She encountered boys her own age at Harris School but had enrolled there too recently to feel comfortable with them. The only young men she knew worked for the household, and even with them she was often ill at ease.

Her mother may have recognized Alice's need to have young male companionship, for she arranged for Harry Spofford, the teenaged son of old family friends, to assist in the outdoor work at Pope's Hill. Alice liked him but did not know how to show it. Unaccustomed to typical boy-girl banter she overreacted to his teasing by becoming verbally sharp-edged and assertive, hiding her uncertainty behind a facade of bravado. She thought Harry would take her remarks as a joke, but, according to Alice, he took her seriously, and "got it into his head [goodness?] knows how, that I hated him and was abusing and insulting him." He soon left, and Alice ended up feeling disgusted with him and with herself "for not being more careful with my tongue."[23]

Similar kinds of bravura appear in Alice's journal as rhetorical poses. Such flourishes are, of course, transparent attempts to mask her own insecurities. In fact, Alice recognized that she was different, both physically and socially, from other girls her age. Unusually tall, she was awkward and sharp-featured; her weak, sensitive eyes also embarrassed her, because they often watered and seemed resistant to any treatment except rest and abstinence from reading. She was, however, much too competitive and exhuberant a person to become preoccupied for long with either her appearance or her lack of popularity. As her journal also reveals, her many interests helped prevent her from becoming overly self-absorbed.

During her early teenage years, another complication distracted her. Interaction between boys and girls no longer involved just play; these times had become fraught with intriguing and somewhat frightening sexual overtones. Claiming to abhor the flirting she observed around her, Alice removed herself as much as possible from girls who indulged in this activity. Two such girls,

23. ASB to KBB: 29 Oct. 1872, LC.

---

referred to in her journal only as "The Serpent" and "The Duchess," became her absolute nemeses. Yet despite her frequent disclaimers, boys and the idea of romantic love fascinated her, and she began learning ways to indulge her own romantic fantasies, as well as to create make-believe substitutes for her apparent lack of boyfriends.

Reading became one acceptable way of satisfying her romantic imagination. She especially enjoyed adventure stories with romantic heroes and heroines. When she selected novels by such well-known authors as Sir Walter Scott, she received parental approval. But when she read stories published in the *New York Ledger*, an eight-page weekly "Devoted to Choice Literature, Romance, the News, and Commerce," her mother objected. As editor of the *Woman's Journal*, Lucy subscribed to this paper (along with many others) as a way of keeping up with news about women. But she apparently disapproved of its romantic short stories and tried (usually unsuccessfully) to prevent Alice from picking up copies at the office or reading it at home.

Real-life romance intrigued Alice even more, and she watched with great interest the courtships of two young domestics who lived with them. She also indulged herself in several crushes on pretty and popular older girls in school.[24] The year before she began her journal, she had become infatuated with Alice Earle, an older schoolmate and the daughter of acquaintances of her parents. She became so completely immersed in Alice Earle's life that she secretly read the girl's diary—an event so traumatic that she frequently recalled it in her own journal. The Earle saga continued to play a part in Alice's journal entries of 1872 and 1873, as the Earle family whisked their two daughters off to Europe to impede several suitors. Convents and a runaway marriage also figured in this real-life drama and fed Alice's preoccupation with romance and adventure.

---

24. Such schoolgirl crushes for other girls were fairly common during this time. Alice later recalled the "wild unreasonable fancies which I used to take for older girls" when she reported in a letter to Kitty in 1881 her objections to similar attentions she was receiving from a young girl, saying she didn't know how to deal with the problem. One year later she confessed to Kitty her even greater dismay at hearing reports of "smashing"—a more violent variation of adolescent flirting—then occurring at women's colleges. "Smashers," according to Alice, "write each other the wildest loveletters, & send presents, confectionary, all sorts of things. . . . If the 'smash' is mutual, they monopolize each other & spoon continually, & sleep together & lie awake all night talking instead of going to sleep; & if it isn't mutual the unrequited one cries herself sick & endures pangs unspeakable." Alice reports she reacted with "undisguised curiosity & amazement. . . . I could hardly have believed that the things they told were not exaggerations" (Nancy Sahli, "Smashing: Women's Relationships Before the Fall," *Chrysalis* 8 (1979): 17–27.

Alice indulged in another schoolgirl crush soon after beginning her journal—this time on Sadie Wilson, a bright and popular girl in the class ahead of her. This crush became a minor obsession for a brief period but happily resulted in something of a friendship between the two before Sadie graduated in June 1872. By this time Alice's popularity had increased. Sadie, like many of her schoolmates, had learned to appreciate Alice's wit and originality, her academic achievements, and her fierce loyalty to the issues and people she cared about.

Alice's relationships with both Alice Earle and Sadie Wilson paled, however, in comparison to that with her cousin Catherine ("Kitty") Barry, the adopted daughter of Dr. Elizabeth Blackwell. Ten years older than Alice, Kitty had been her closest older friend and confidant for as long as Alice could remember. The two visited for extended periods in each other's homes, as well as at Martha's Vineyard, where the two families often summered. In 1869, when Kitty and Elizabeth Blackwell moved to England, the two cousins began a regular and spirited correspondence that revealed their unusually close and imaginative relationship.

What marked it as imaginative was their intriguing and persistent role playing around the myth that they were engaged to be married. For Alice, Kitty was her "betrothed." Their so-called engagement began when Alice was four and Kitty fourteen but still flourished at the time of Alice's journal, when their respective ages were fourteen and twenty-four. The idea for their engagement may possibly have derived from the then-current practice of "Boston marriages"—the long-term monogamous relationships that existed between New England women who were often feminist reformers and dedicated to social betterment.[25] Given the difference in age between Kitty and Alice, however, the family saw their betrothal as a joke, as did the participants probably. But the joke gave full play to Alice's lively imagination when she composed creative letters to her future "husband." And the provocative stories she told her classmates gave her a unique sense of status, especially since Kitty had taken on the identity of the swashbuckling English pirate Captain Robert Kidd. It was all done tongue in cheek, but the ruse did serve several important functions. For Alice, it was another way she could indulge in romantic fantasies. At the same time, the engagement story compensated for her lack of male attention.[26]

25. See chapter 4, "Boston Marriage", in Lillian Faderman, *Surpassing the Love of Men: Love Between Women from the Renaissance to the Present* (New York: William Morrow, 1981), 190–203.

26. Although Alice and Kitty's friendship and correspondence at this time can be characterized as nurturing, their "betrothal" was based more on a jovial childhood fantasy than any intense emotional dependence characteristic of the deep female friend-

Alice's and Kitty's correspondence ranged far beyond their pose as an engaged couple. They exchanged family news, reactions to books, and accounts of important happenings around them. Kitty also served as Alice's "private escape valve,"[27] and Alice's confidences in letters often illuminate journal entries written about the same time. The journal, on the other hand, includes many private concerns that are not conveyed to Kitty, such as Alice's unsettled religious feelings. Although the two exchanged diaries during this time (Alice sent Kitty a special diary kept while on a month's vacation in the White Mountains in the summer of 1873), it is unlikely that Alice ever sent this Boston journal to Kitty. She sometimes copied sections from it verbatim in her letters to Kitty, suggesting that she had no intention of sharing all the personal experiences recorded in it.

This journal became Alice's primary window on the world and also served as a window on herself. At one point she writes of her need to "sift myself out, and find what there is of me." Her journal writing did just that, although it never became a self-conscious exercise. By writing about her experiences and her reactions to them, she began to know herself.

Alice kept this diary for over two years. Besides family and household concerns, her long early entries (comprising the largest portion of the diary) often described activities relating to the Harris Grammar School and her friends there. But in September 1873, despite her protests, she was sent to the Chauncy Hall School, a private school founded in 1823 in downtown Boston.[28] The school advertised that their upper level prepared young men for Harvard and young women for the newly coeducational Boston University. Alice found only a handful of girls in her upper-level courses, however, and a slew of boys everywhere. Despite her anxieties, she soon discovered she could enjoy some of her new male schoolmates, even though she towered over most and felt "like

---

ships recently examined by feminist scholars. Certainly Alice and Kitty were aware of such friendships, whether within their family (as with Lucy's and Antoinette Brown Blackwell's deep and abiding friendship) or among their family friends. See Carol Lasser, "'Let Us Be Sisters Forever': The Sororal Model of Nineteenth-Century Female Friendship." *Signs: Journal of Women in Culture and Society* 14 (1988): 158–81; and Carroll Smith-Rosenberg, "The Female World of Love and Ritual: Relationships between Women in Nineteenth-Century America" *Signs: Journal of Women in Culture and Society* 1 (1975): 1–29.

27. ASB to KB: 23 June 1874, SL.

28. For background on the Chauncy Hall School, see Thomas Cushing, *Historical Sketch of Chauncy Hall School: With Catalogue of Teachers and Pupils* (Boston: David Clapp, 1895); Elibet Moore Chase, "Chapel Hill–Chauncy Hall School: An Historical Perspective," *The Chronicle* (publication of Chapel Hill–Chauncy Hall School) 4 (Fall 1987): 3–12.

---

a watermelon amongst peaches." Most important, she found that the strong emphasis on serious academic work suited her extremely well. She thrived on the scholarly competition yet made friends with her new schoolmates and teachers.

Alice even enthusiastically accepted the school requirement that she participate on the girls' military drill team, with the result that she learned precision marching and how to handle a gun—a far cry from her activities at the Harris Grammar School. Drill teams had become popular around the time of the Civil War, and all-male city and school teams competed for coveted yearly prizes. Chauncy Hall organized one of the first school drill teams in Boston, and by the time Alice enrolled, its teams had won a number of competitions. Apparently Chauncy Hall officials believed that girls would also benefit from drill training, although girls' teams never became highly competitive.

Chauncy Hall's tougher, more serious atmosphere agreed with Alice. Increasingly self-confident, she took special pleasure in new challenges and moving beyond the expected. She had predicted this of herself at the time of her graduation from Harris School. Acclaimed for her clever and highly original valedictory address, she delighted in the fact that she had not made the traditional kinds of commencement remarks and confessed to her journal that she had every intention to break through more "old fences."

Such journal confidences, however, appear less frequently as the spring term of her first year approached. Alice's life became fuller and more complex, and her time was more at a premium. Her journal entries dwindle into shorter, even misdated, accounts, often written several days after the entry date. Finally, after her entry for April 27, 1873, they stop altogether. Alice tucked inside the journal's remaining blank pages little scraps of paper on which she had written one-line reminders of events that she undoubtedly intended to write up later as complete entries.

Brief as her last entries are, the journal Alice left richly documents a time, a place and, most of all, her own young life. Now, well over one hundred years later, her writing acts like a wondrous time machine, drawing us back into a nineteenth-century world in which we watch her develop from a precocious, rambunctious adolescent into an accomplished and determined young woman.

THE JOURNAL OF
ALICE STONE BLACKWELL,
1872–1874

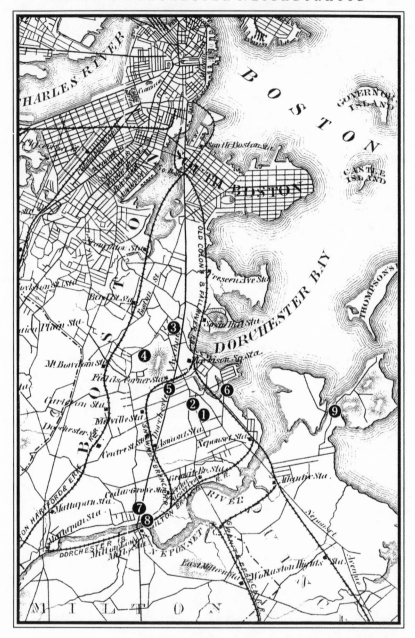

(1) Alice's house, 45 Boutwell St.; (2) Harris Grammar School; (3) First Parish
Church and Lyceum Hall, Meeting House Hill; (4) St. Mary's Church; (5) Field's
Corner Horsecar Depot; (6) Tenean Beach; (7) St. Mary's Chapel, Lower Mills;
(8) Baker Chocolate Factory, Lower Mills; (9) Squantum. Municipality of Boston,
Strauss' Atlas of Boston and Vicinity: 1874–75 (Boston: F. A. Strauss, 1874).

THE JOURNAL FOR 1872

FEBRUARY

Feb. 1ˢᵗ

Thursday. Beginning a new volume of my diary, I may as well begin by stating my situation. I, Alice, Elsie or Alsette, am living in the small house at the foot of the hill, waiting till our large burnt house is built up. Papa and Mama and Mary are generally away all day in Boston, Mary Hooper[1] in an Architect's office, and my parents at the *Journal* Office. I am at school from 9 till 12, and from 2 till four; am aged 14, and my chief associate, at least while I am at home, is Annie Mᶜ Leod, our pretty Scotch girl. I am head and Monitor of the 2ⁿᵈ Class, and sit next [to] Hattie Man[n], a pretty, fair haired girl who is No. 2. That is about enough introduction, and if Posterity wants more, Posterity will have to do without. Not that I mean to have P. read it—at least, not miscellaneous P. I spent the time before breakfast in copying the Ode to Kitty, which must go today if she is to get it by the 14ᵗʰ.[2] At school Miss Tolman came down upon Ellen Mᶜ Laughlin in a very severe way, for asking a question about the Arithmetic lesson which Hattie and I were just trying to decide which should ask, and said some things about copying questions which made her cry. I caused a violent commotion in part of the second class by showing Hattie the

1. Mary Hooper and her family had been neighbors of the Stone Blackwells when they lived in Roseville, N.J. Alice explained her presence in the household shortly before beginning this journal, saying she was "acting as housekeeper, and elder sister generally" (ASB to KBB: 15 Oct. 1871, LC).

2. Alice knew it would take about two weeks for her Valentine greeting to reach her cousin Kitty in England.

"Dear Betrothed," at the beginning of one of Kitty's letters. The way it came about was this. Hattie and Mary Fifield were violently disputing for the ownership of the Grand Duke Alexis,[3] and I told them "I had been engaged for 10 years; that they needn't talk," and to prove it produced the letter to Hattie. Such a commotion as she, Fanny Benedict and Emma Adams raised, that I saw what a high opinion of my sense and discretion they must have had, and was decidedly scared lest my character for steadiness was gone forever. Hattie kept trying to pick my pocket of the letter, and exchanging significant looks with me, till we both nearly went into convulsions of suppressed laughter, and I felt twice as well aqquainted with her. After school two or three set upon me at once to steal the letter, but I beat them, and bore it off in triumph. Papa had a caller in the evening, so I spent it reading with Mary.

Feb. 2nd

Friday. At recess, during the game, Annie Phips and I got to fighting, a real wrestling match, and the girls joined hands and formed a ring round us, watching our evolutions with interest, and Mary Fifield called out that she bet on me; I suppose she felt justified in doing so, having herself felt some specimens of my strength. Annie Phips pulled me down upon the bank, but she was undermost, and I kept her so, and the girls crowded round and offered me their congratulations, to the huge disgust of A. Phips, who protested that she was the victor. M. Fifield told me she had betted on me, and I crushed her by answering that I did not approve of betting. At cross tag I crossed Sadie Wilson, with whom I am in love, and of course was caught at once, and she gave me "her warmest gratitude" which I was happy to receive. I confided to her the secret about my "dear Betrothed," and she whispers those magic words to me with eyes brimful of fun and mischief. Took Hattie in to History with me, and raised her curiousity much, by showing her bits of several letters that I had raked up at noon. Mama, Mary and I spent the evening over the register. I made one outrageously rude remark to Mary, who aggravated me, till I [told] her to hold her tongue.

Feb. 3d

Saturday. It is said a scalded child fears cold water; I am sure I do fear being inveigled into a second tea kettle like that with which I burnt myself on June 14th, yet I have walked into one nearly as bad. Annie yesterday got the long

3. The Grand Duke Alexis (son of Russia's czar, Alexander II) was visiting America in the winter of 1872. A dashing bachelor, he had just visited Boston and attracted much attention.

expected letter from Ronald Campbell,[4] and this morning I teased her about it, and ended by telling her I should go to her room and hunt up the letter. I found a box full, and brought them down to the kitchen, where I opened each and looked at the signature, Annie laughing, remonstrating, and every now and then making a grab at the letters. At last I came to the one I wanted, on lace edged paper, and gave her the rest. I looked at the beginning and end, and took one little peek at the middle, where I saw a most desperate remark, and then Mama interfered, and made me give the letter to Annie, who promised to let me read it, but changed her mind and refused. Mama told me I had never done so naughty a thing since I was borne; and then that other transaction suddenly came into my mind, and upset me utterly.[5] Went to school in a very low state of mind though Annie had made some attempts at fun before I left. Hattie had set her mind upon showing me some trick with strings, and I told her if she could do it I would tell her the name of my Betrothed. She did it, and I told her the name was Catharine Barry. At first she refused to believe it, but when convinced laughed and shook her fist at me. Before noon a great snow storm rose, but as I had foreseen something of the kind and worn my water-proof, I was all right. It was really a splendid storm, quite equal to the last, but I spent the afternoon indoors. At Mama['s] instigation I sorted and fixed the huge mass of twine and woorsteds which has been lying in the cupboard, and then rooted Mrs. Browning's Poems out from the library.[6] Mary came home in the middle of the afternoon, when it was just the least little bit beginning to grow dark, and as I was groaning out a wish that I was out, with not quite energy enough to get up and go there, she laughed and said if I went up to the top of the hill I should have enough of it, or something of the sort. Of course that set my back up at once, and I rushed away, put on my things, and set out despite all remonstrances. It really was a very wild storm, and I enjoyed it extremely, of course. On the very top of the hill I got a few breaths of salt air, which the storm had brought from the sea; that was the best of the whole. But my Beserker fit was fairly on me, and I did not mean to go home yet, by any means. Down I went past the school house, down through Mill St. and across the railroad; I turned around and came back the same way. On the top of our hill, in the gateway of our yard, was a great drift nearly as high as the tops of the posts, and I flung myself backward into it, lay there a moment, then rose and went down the hill at a splitting pace. But that my leggings would keep

4. Ronald Campbell was Annie McLeod's suitor.
5. The previous year, Alice had surreptitiously read the diary of her friend Alice Earle.
6. Elizabeth Barrett Browning (1806–61), English poet (*DNB*).

coming down, it would have been almost perfect bliss. Papa got home soon after, wet and cross, but after supper he grew much more amiable. The storm still kept on into the night. I made my peace with Annie after I got home from school, and she actually let me read the letter, in which I found ample material for no end of teasing.

Feb. 4th

Sunday. Wrote out the first rough draft of my composition, and read. The storm kept on part of the morning, and then cleared up very brightly. Did up newspapers in packages at Mama's bidding, and stowed them in the back chamber. As I lay in bed after taking my bath I happened to open my eyes and look at the window. Great was my surprise to see the sky all red. First I thought of fire; but it was not like fire; then that something was the matter with my eyes; and I sat up and stared; but it did not change. I jumped out of bed and looked through the window, and soon made up my mind that they were northern lights. I went down and notified the folks, but they had heard it from Annie, who had been much scared by them, thinking it was the day of judgement, and is still uneasy regarding them. Really they were wonderfully beautiful; a deep dark rose tint, th[r]ough which the stars shone, but perfectly steady, not flashing and quivering like those at Roseville.[7] Mary and I stood at my window and watched them, till sleepiness and conscience sent me to bed.

Feb. 5th

Monday. Witnessed the idiotic behavior of Maggie Whitton and Carrie Thayer. The boys door, as often happens, was not opened as soon as ours, and just after I had got in, Charley Bradley came up the steps and in through our door, for which he might have had a check, and went up the boys stairs while I was proceeding up the girls'. Maggie W. and Carrie T. came hurrying up past me, Maggie two stairs at a time, plainly wishing and intending to get to the dressing room at the same time he did, in which they succeeded. I got in there about the same time too, and heard him making sweet remarks to Carrie Thayer, to my great edification. His presence was inconvenient, as I wanted to pull up my stockings, which I could not do while he was there; but he went at last, and I got them pulled up. But I was fairly disgusted with the sight of Maggie's and Carrie's and C. Bradley's idiocy. Isn't there a girl in school who can keep idiocy out of her head? Not to my knowledge! I fight my best against it, and keep my self pretty well free of idiotic ideas; at least as much as I can; and wholly out of my actions. And their idiocy really disgusts me. Ugh! There

7. Alice had last seen northern lights when she lived with her family in Roseville, N.J., in the 1860s.

was a great fuss in the afternoon, because of the swooning of Miss Fisher, a teacher in one of the other rooms. M[iss] T[olman] and Mr. Horne[8] hearing of it, left precipitately, and did not come back. Mary Fifield was also drafted as an assistant, probably for her strength. The school, our room of it, being left minus their lawful guardians and rulers, began to fidget, and at last to cut up dreadfully. All the scholars almost were either whispering, laughing, or making demonstrations of some sort; some spoke out loud; some cried silence; a fight arose between George Cook and Winny Tilden, Eddy Jenkins now and then joining in, and the confusion rose to such a height that I had two minds to jump up and say "I exert my authority as monitor; 2nd Class, behave!" but I didn't. Thus far I knew nothing of the cause of the commotion, but in the dressing room Saidi flung up her arms and made believe swoon; and going down stairs told me about it.

Feb. 6th

Tuesday. Drawing lesson of course. About as bad walking as ever I knew of. A perfectly dreadful history lesson, which I studied with Hattie, at her request, expressed in dumb show.[9] We spent too much time in groaning over the lesson, and too little in studying, and shook in our shoes at every question, but got through somehow. *Ivanhoe* in the evening.[10] Made some poetry about Saidi Wilson, my present beloved. She has a "cold and clear cut face" which reminds me of the picture of the North Wind in George McDonald's book,[11] and when she smiles it suddenly sparkles out all over. She dresses beautifully too; I dont mean richly, but everything hangs together so. Also she is head of the school, and a splendid scholar; a much better one than I am, though only my age; all which are excellent reasons for adoring her.

Feb. 7th

Wednesday. As I gave my hair a hasty combing before going into school, my comb snapped in two, and I was obliged to tuck my hair behind my ears, and put the bits of comb in my pocket. All of them stared, and Miss T. nearly laughed as I gave in my words.[12] Of course I felt very uncomfortable, but it was

8. Edwin T. Horne (b. 1842) graduated from Harvard University in 1864 and was principal of Harris School from 1866 to 1881.

9. "Dumb show" is pantomime, or action without speech.

10. Henry was reading to the family from Sir Walter Scott's *Ivanhoe*. This and subsequent books referred to by Alice are annotated (when possible) in Appendix 1.

11. George MacDonald (1824–1905), Scottish novelist and poet, and one of Alice's favorite authors, wrote the immensely popular children's book *At the Back of the North Wind* in 1871 (still in print today), illustrated by Arthur Hughes (*OCEL*).

12. Alice and her classmates were sometimes assigned a list of words to define as part of their homework.

the best I could do. Maggie Whitten signed to me to study my definitions with her, which I accordingly did, and sat with her on the platform, to my no small discomfort when I thought of my hair; but luckily it did not last long, for we were soon called back. Nevertheless, I came home in a state of utter and exulting happiness, having walked with Sadi a[s] far as our ways lay together. I took the opportunity of asking her about the little bit of conversation I heard between her and C. Bradley the day after we spoke our pieces. She said if I had heard my name (which I had told her) that most likely they were speaking of my piece, for they had been discussing the different pieces, and C. B. had been repeating "My sonne's faire wife, Elizabeth." We then spoke of that piece, and as we separated I told her that I had asked, not liking to be slandered behind my back without knowing what it was, and she called after me, laughing, that it was not that, but the opposite; which I told her I did not believe, and went home on air. Went in to Boston in the afternoon, and had another added to my stock of proofs that all boys are not unmitigated scoundrels. I had hunted in vain for an unused catalogue,[13] and had just resigned myself to my fate and engaged one from the owner, when a black eyed boy who was standing near and heard me, pointed out one on a bench, which I straightway seized upon. Drew *Ravenshoe* and *Annals of a Quiet Neighborhood* at the Public, and went up to the Atheneum, where I selected one of Cooper's,[14] being attracted by a picture of a romantic looking pirate, who had just climbed in at a window, and was holding a moonlit conversation with a lady; but found afterward to my disgust that he disapproved Womans Rights and called Queen Bess a Monster because she was strong minded. Also *The Pilot* and *Battles at Home*. At the office neither Mrs. Hinckley[15] nor I could find the letter of directions which Mama, (who has gone to Maine) told me to expect, so I waited for Papa, who said it had doubtless been picked up, and took me down to a tea store, loaded my satchel with tea, and bid me good-bye. I bought two loaves at H[arrison] S[quare] and walked up well loaded with five books, 2 loaves and a satchel full of tea. My first writing out of composition has been put in the waste paper basket, and I wrote out another, sitting over the register with Mary and Annie, our lawful guardians being away.

13. Boston's Public Library had begun using a card catalog system at this time; however, Alice may have been more used to the two-volume bound catalog of the library's holdings printed in 1866.

14. James Fenimore Cooper (1789–1851), American novelist. (*DAB*).

15. Mrs. Hinkley assisted at the *WJ* office.

Boston Athenaeum.

Feb. 8ᵗʰ

Thursday. Saidi's first words to me across the room were that "what I told her I didn't believe yesterday was true." After our noon waiting she came up half the hall to me, and we went on together, comparing notes and grievances as Monitors, and telling which were our worst cases. She expressed the same feeling I have had as to our duty of reporting, and proposed making lists of the order of the files. When I left her at the gate, and went hurrying home, I was in such a state of happiness I had to hug myself to keep from bursting. Made my list in the afternoon. In the evening, my parents being away, I was reading *The Water Witch*, and when I was sure it was between 7 and 8, Mary told me it was 20 to 9, and pointed to the clock, which said the same; so I soon after tore myself from my book, went to bed in a hurry, "lay awake and rolled."

Feb. 9ᵗʰ

Friday. My confidence in my species was much weakened. Annie promised me not to tell Mary what Olack[16] meant, and after I had gone to bed she coaxed her

16. Annie was teaching Alice Gaelic; "olack" is Gaelic for eunuch.

into doing it by threats of asking John. This Mary confessed while getting ready to go, and also that when she told me it was 20 minutes of 9 she had just set the clock an hour forward, thinking I was over reading myself; which if not a lie was a first cousin to one. I felt very much vexed, remembering how I tore through the last part of the story without enjoying it, and lay awake afterward; also this second lie of Annie's made me feel as if the world was all lies. But Mary and Annie lie to me like all the rest, and I went to school feeling miserable. After 4 I hurried home, finding Mama had got back from Maine, got some money, and started off for Fields Corner to get paper for my composition, as we have none unstamped.[17] Also I had a hope of way laying Sadi, and walking home with her. I caught sight of her coming through the school yard, and turned slowly down Mill St. Presently she came trotting up behind me, and I went on with her in a state of bliss. She said it was rather a long way to Fields corner, and I confessed it was in hopes of having her company, of which she wished me joy as we parted at the gate. She said I could get paper at Parkers, and need not go to the Corner; so I got 5 sheets for five cents, (not very good paper). Met S[am] King and G[eorge] Cook and went home hugging myself. Papa corrected my composition, which I began to copy, but it hurt my eyes and they made me stop and hear *Ivanhoe*.

Feb. 10th

Saturday. Heard Saidi say she was going in on the 1.11 as several of the other girls were too, and I got leave and marched off, with 2 books to return at the Atheneum. The serpent, the Duchess, Carrie and Lulu, were there, and others came afterward. Presently some one said "Here's Sadie," and in she came, as beautiful as ever, and more so. She spoke to me a little, and in the cars she sat down by me. She talked mostly to Josie and another girl on the next seat, but leaned her elbow on me, and I was happy. As we walked through the station she asked me which way I was going, and finding it was hers, said she would walk with me, unless a car came along, and then she supposed she must take it. She was going to the Museum, to see "Gold Dust,"[18] so we talked about Theaters, and I found she had seen "Little Em'ly," over which we went into raptures. Then we got upon the subject of flirting—she started it—and sat in judgement on Ruth Swan and others. I told her my scrape with the Serpent, and she told me what a bad character the same was getting. I said I didn't see how it was possible for anyone, even those boys themselves, to respect such

17. Alice's family frequently used writing paper stamped with a *Woman's Journal* heading.

18. "Gold Dust" was written by the Irish-American actor and playwright John Brougham (1810–80), who specialized in comic writing and impersonations (*DAB*).

girls, and she said, "Oh, they dont! I've stood by that door with Charley Bradley for two months now, and I know. I'll give you one specimen, just for an example. You know when Mr. Horne asked for a word ending in silent e today, Ruth gave 'love', and he said that it was just the word that would be likely to come into her head first. Now would you like to have that said of you?" I answered "Of course not", and we walked on talking till we came to the door of a resteraunt where she was going to get some lunch, and there she bade me good bye and left me. (My state of mind all this time may be imagined.) I went on to the office, but got no letters; to the Atheneum, and drew *Neighbors Wives*, but decided to keep *The Pilot*. Came out on the 3.35 train. My diary has come to be more a record of Saidie's proceedings than mine; but she is fast taking Annie Mac Phail's place with me. Lately she has tried to scurry out of the dressing room before me, and today I reproached her for trying to leave me in the entry while the boys come out; and she begged pardon. *Ivanhoe.*

Feb. 11

Sunday. Put a new band on my drawers, and read Henry Kingsley. A story by him in every Saturday, which Papa handed over to me, and *Ravenshoe.*[19] Every thing of his gives me the same feeling, though in a less degree, that *The Boy in Grey* did. Walked over to North Quincy, with the mud flats looking drearier than I ever saw them, crusted with ice, and felt gloomy. Mama is getting to be just like Aunt Sarah, snarling all the time. I could stand it well enough, though not half as sweetly as Anna,[20] but that Papa looks so tired and worn that I think I should cry if I didn't feel so much like swearing. Annie was shocked at my sewing, and read me the 4th commandment, to which I replied by directing her attention to the 14th Romans, and quoting Christ, and the corn.[21] Made buttonholes, picked up papers, and Read a little of Amy as Leigh.

19. Henry Kingsley (1830–76) was a British novelist much admired by Alice. His work was distinguished for its humorous and well-sustained character sketches, as well as fine descriptions of English landscape (*OCEL*). A check of the periodicals normally read by the Stone Blackwells does not reveal where his stories were appearing at this time.

20. Sarah Witt Lawrence (b. 1821), Lucy's younger sister, lived in Gardner, Mass., with her husband, Lawrence (a schoolteacher), and their two daughters, Emma and Anna.

21. The Fourth Commandment, "Remember the Sabbath day, to keep it holy," was often quoted by those who set aside Sunday as a day of prayer and rest. Alice and her family did not subscribe to this practice, and she cites the two biblical verses to support her argument. Romans 14 treats the need to suspend judgment of those who differ from us. The parable of "Christ and the Corn"(Matt. 12:1–8) reveals Christ's approval of his disciples plucking ears of corn on the Sabbath.

I think that will always be the story of stories for me, as John Brown is the song.[22]

Feb. 12ᵗʰ

Monday. A report was started that some of Miss T[olman]'s relations were sick, and she would not be there, and the girls began a jubilee; but Mr. H[orne] squashed their hopes by saying she would be in presently. Sadi stood by me at recess, spoke of the play (Gold Dust) and offered to chase me. At noon when I came up before the doors were open she came up to me and said she had got there first; talked of "Gold Dust," touched on flirting, and after we were let in came and sat by me and questioned me about *Our Mutual Friend*, which she has never read. After school [s]he signed to me to look at the clock, and I talked a few minutes with her waiting in the entry. Mary having broken the chimney of the big lamp, which Annie has hunted through Dorchester to replace, despairingly appealed to me to [go to] H[arrison] S[quare] through the mud and get some small chimneys, which I did. My feather was taken in to be curled. Took Hattie Mann into the closet for History. G. Cook was in the dressing room and we could hear him hemming and hawing and getting the hiccups. *Ivanhoe*.

Feb. 13

Tuesday. At recess Sadie asked me the name of Mortimer Lightwood, and the boys threw hard snowballs, none of which hit me. The walking is horrible, and when I had got half way back to school I stepped into the mud and splashed my stockings very badly. Back I rushed, changed my socks faster than I ever did before in my life, and sped back, meeting Mr. Horne, also late. <u>MISSED IN GEOGRAPHY!</u> Bit myself going down stairs with Sadie, went home and swore at Annie in Gaelic, at Mary in French, and at Mama in English. (I think it necessary to my reputation to mention that I only said "The Deuce," in English.) Papa had the jaw-ache, but read *Ivanhoe* part of the evening nevertheless. He has bought a new horse, a successor to poor Billy, and a very pretty creature. He has also suspended the white lamp chimney from the ceiling with two strings, our best lamp chimney being broken, and the other lamp being minus a shade. Took Fanny Benedict into the closet, where we found Sadie's Geography, which I returned, and was rewarded by a smile. Mem[o]: <u>never</u> to let Posterity get this. A letter from Kitty.

22. This reference is to *Westward Ho! or the Voyages of Sir Amyas Leigh* by Charles Kingsley. The song Alice likes is the popular Civil War song "John Brown's Body," set to the tune of a Negro spiritual. Julia Ward Howe later used the same tune for the "Battle Hymn of the Republic."

Feb. 14th

Wednesday. A gray day. Sadie did not come out at recess, but as she passed me in her carriage going home, she looked through the window, smiled and shook her fist at me. Walking vile. A great thaw. Our front yard is completely filled with water; the hens cannot get out of the hen house, and I can't get in; John has to wade through to feed them. Went to Boston with my waterproof hood over my head; found my way along the streets Papa goes through to the Atheneum, where I got *Elsie Venner, A History of Wales*, and another book the name of which I have forgotten. Mama then took me shopping, and bought me a pair of gloves and 10 yds Scotch plaid for a dress. Came out alone and supped with Mary and Annie. *Elsie Venner* in the evening.

Feb. 15th

Thursday. I have caught a Tartar.[23] Positively the most frightful story I ever read. Oliver Wendell Holmes ought to be indicted for writing it. I mean *Elsie Venner*. No wonder Mama told me I had better not read it. Still, I went to it with my eyes open, and if I have brain fever and rave about rattlesnakes, it is my own fault. But I had no idea how frightful it was. I have just finished the first volume. I shan't begin the other tonight; its not safe. That scene where she saves him from the rattlesnake has utterly upset me; I am so nervous I cant even write decently. I must finish this entry tomorrow, and read Amyas Leigh to compose myself. That will do it if anything can. What would Sir Richard Grenville[24] have done with such a creature as Elsie, I wonder?

When I wrote that last I was too much excited to put down the days events. There weren't many. Went down to Fields Corner, and inquired for letters, but there were none. I walked with Hattie as far as our ways lay together, and stopped in with her at Fanny Benedicts. Fanny had a headache, and had not been at school. Her house is full of plants, and smells like a green house. There came a letter from Kitty threatening to hang me at the yard arm if I were faithless, as I didn't write to her often enough, while I was in the midst of that terrible *Elsie Venner*. *Ivanhoe*, the trial of Rebecca, and to bed to dream of the inquisition, and coming back at the risk of my life to save this diary. Sadie gave me an apple, and I saved the skins. Mama let me have a *[New York] Ledger* for a few minutes, and then lit the fire with it.

---

23. "To catch a tartar" is to grapple with an unexpectedly formidable opponent.

24. Sir Richard Grenville (1797–1861), the second Duke of Buckingham, was a historian and author of many books on Great Britain (*DNB*).

Feb. 16th

Friday. Forgot what day it was, and went out to History with Emma Adams, but no one said anything. Scurried out of the dressing room with Sadie, who rushes away rubbers in hand and things half on, but cant get down before me. I am afraid our disorderly proceedings will get us into disgrace. When Hattie Burdett came down I knew Sadie would wish to go, so looked at the clock, announced the news, and was rewarded by a brilliant smile. If Posterity ever get this, I am a flirt! and I couldn't make that any stronger. Sadie borrowed my knife, and we got reproved for speaking by the basket after the bell had struck. We drew a background for the first time, and I made bad work of mine. Valiantly resisted the temptation to read *Elsie Venner* till the lamps were lighted; then read, and stopped just before I got quite upset. *Ivanhoe.*

Feb. 17th

Saturday. I had forgotten all about my definitions, and hurried off to school, overtaking Miss Gilbert.[25] As I came through the yard, an angel stood up at an open window and called to me through it. It was Sadie looking like a living sunbeam, and after I got in, she exultingly said she had got there first. As I hastily copied out my words, she bade me apply to her for definitions if I needed; which I did. After recess as she hurried past me in the dressing room she said she wanted to speak to me after school; she had a new plan. After our usual scurry down I asked her what it was, and she told me she had written down the names of her worst girls, and told them she would report them, and it had the best possible effect. She waited at the foot of the stairs till she had told me. As I afterward walked along with her and Hattie Burditt. Sadie was in great vexation because her side had been beaten in the spelling match; we had not chosen sides, but Mr. Horne had put me on hers. Sewed on my chemise in the afternoon, and nearly finished it.

Feb. 18th

Sunday. Made a fool of myself. It is not my habit to behave idiotically,—over a story, at least—but I did it over *Ravenshoe*. Finding myself crying, I went up to my room and onto my bed, where I lay reading, and winking away my tears when I was crying too hard to see the words. Henry Kingsley will certainly make an end of me sooner or later. First *The Boy in Grey*, and then *Ravenshoe*! Went up to the house with Papa, who went up a ladder, and then came down and let me in. It was pleasant an[d] sunny and blue and breezy, but I disap-prove of all the alterations but Mama's bow window. Mama went off to lec-

25. Annie Gilbert was a teacher at the Harris School.

ture,[26] and I, having promised her the chemise should be finished, finished it, while Papa read *The Geography of the Sea*, and I tried to seem interested, though I hardly heard what he said.

Feb. 19*th*

Monday. Sadie called to me from the window again, and we made an agreement to see which would get there first in the afternoon. I was victorious, and deserved to be so, as I started at 5. of 1, and read *Ravenshoe* under the trees till she came. I had told her of my making an idiot of myself over *Ravenshoe*, and she sat down by me on the wall and asked to be shown the "crying part". I showed, and she sat by me reading and asking questions till a teacher came, when we made a rush for the door, and I got in first, she holding onto my skirts. After school Hattie Mann and [I] walked to Milton Lower Mills, and back by Dr. Means' church.[27] I had horrified her dreadfully while we were supposed to be properly learning History, by letting her know I sewed on Sunday. I did not enjoy the walk much, but on the home way I happened to mention "Woman's Rights," and she answered by asking if I stood up for them. I said of course I did; she said she didn't; I said so I supposed; she said she didn't want to be a lawyer; I said that was no reason I shouldn't; she said she didn't want to vote, anyway; I said she would not have to; she was under the idea every man had to vote unless he could get a substitute, which I convinced her was not so. Soon after we separated on our winding ways, a carriage came up behind me, containing Sadie, Hattie Burditt, and the two young ones with roses in their bonnets.[28] She stopped, asked if I knew where Mr. Silas Hopkins lived, and invited me to get in. We rode on, joking about her "fiery steed," and she drove me to the brow of the hill, asked how far my house was, apologised, let me out, and drove to her own place. My eyes hurt so in the evening that I sat with a wet cloth over them, while Papa read *Ivanhoe*.

Feb. 20*th*

Tuesday. Saw Sadie go into the yard, but came up later. Was a few minutes before her in the afternoon. The girls have got up what they call "Mystic Albums," in which you are to write, fold and seal the leaf down, and write on the outside your name, and when it is to be opened. Read in the afternoon, and

26. Lucy preached in the pulpit of the Reverend Cudworth in East Boston, on "The Bible Position of Women" (*WJ*: 24 Feb. 1872).

27. The Reverend James H. Means was pastor of Dorchester's Second Church located at the corner of Washington and Centre streets.

28. The "two young ones" were Sadie's sisters.

darned stockings at night. Went out to the stable and held the lantern while Papa fed and watered Billy.

Feb. 21st

Wednesday. There was a sort of a celebration which I had hardly known of, in honor of Washington's birthday being tomorrow; singing, playing, declamations and a reading by Charley Bradley of W[ashingto]n's address. A villainous lot of horrid little boys from the lower rooms sat on settees ranged round behind us on purpose, and aggravated me beyond endurance. When they sang "America" I sang "God Save the Queen," through the two first verses, which are really idiotic. I dont think anyone found me out, though. I got there before Sadie, and called to her from the window, but she did not hear, and Mr. Horne came down upon me, asking me to think how it would look to the people outside. A battle royal took place at recess between us girls, each having taken the name of some English or American General of the Revolution. Those who had muffs used them as weapons; Sadie had none; she was Burgoyne; Hattie Burditt was Howe; I was Clinton, to be on their side; Maggie Whitton was Washington.[29] The fight ended with a general stampede at the end of recess. Mary Fifield and I practice calling one another all the bad names we can string together. Yesterday she sent me two notes in school calling me villanous ones, and after school I sent her one by Sadie. I called Hattie Mann a bad girl while we were in the closet, and she said I was the bad one as I sewed on Sunday, and I replied by telling her she was worse, as she didn't believe in Womans Rights. "Why Alice Blackwell!" cried she, "do you mean to say you think it's as wicked not to believe in Womens Rights as to sew on Sunday?" I said "I think its quite as much of a mistake," and bade her not turn it into a Womans Rights meeting, but learn her lesson. Went in on the train with Josie Jones, drew *The Guardian Angel*, a swindle, I think, from the Public, and renewed *Ravenshoe* for Mary. At the Atheneum I got *Geoffrey Hamlyn*, *Magdalen Hepburn*, and *Zerub Throop's Experiment*. Came out on the same train as Mama, but not with her. Drove up. I am afraid the new horse is very nervous by the way he acts. *Ivanhoe*.

Feb. 22nd

Thursday. Washington's Birthday! The bells rang before I was down in the morning, and afterward they fired guns. No school, of course, and grumblings because we can't have the rest of the week also. I made a lemon pie in honor of the day, while Mary made molasses candy, Mama something else, and Annie

29. John Burgoyne, William Howe, and George Clinton were British generals.

helped generally. After my pie was in we all set to work and pulled the candy with much mirth. Read, and mended my green nightgown. Made some poetry to Toby;[30] very dripping. Papa finished *Ivanhoe.*

Feb. 23ᵈ

Friday. Chiefly devoted to hostilities between Mary Fifield and myself. We exchanged various notes of vituperation, and Sadie, who espoused my cause with interest, told me of a place in the reading book where I could find names, and brought her book to me in school to show me the page. The consequence was a stunning epistle which I presented to Mary when she came down stairs. She also had one in readiness; we exchanged, and she took up her station in the dressing room, and we mutually read, laughed, and shook our fists malevolently at each other. My note was much the worst though, thanks to Sadie, and she, Hattie Burditt and I supported her along her homeward way, while she rolled about and butted her sleek round head into us in convulsions of laughter. I devoted recess to composing a thunderbolt, and set off to school with it in my pocket. Sadie and I mutually caught sight of each other from a long distance, waved our hands, and she set out to meet me. We afterward met Mary Fifield with whom I exchanged notes, and we went on, reading. She had gathered up a quantity of long words; but if her's were the longest, mine were the worst. In the evening Mary and Annie went off, and I spent the evening alone with Mama, composing a note for M. Fifield.

Feb. 24ᵗʰ

Saturday. Put my note under M. Fifield's inkstand. She found it, and read it to Sadie. We were examined in Arithmetic, and I got 100, for the first time. I worked very hard at it, and deserved to succeed. Mended my muff, sewed new ends onto my sash, sewed up the sides of my chemise, and read *Geoffrey Hamlyn.* Went over to the house beyond Mr. Putnam's for cider and vinegar with Annie, and when I came back I found that someone who from the description I am sure must have been Sadie and her fiery steed, had enquired for me apparently to take me out riding. Felt very uncomfortable and cross, it being a warm day, and thawing. Late in the afternoon I was fired with a project; namely, to go and look at Sadie's windows after dark. I asked Mama if I might borrow Annie, and Annie if she would be borrowed. Mama was doubtful, but Annie was willing, and after supper I was brought into the sitting room, where my parents sat in solemn conclave, and requested to tell my purpose. This I declined to do, protesting however that it was harmless, and after a great deal

30. Toby is Alice's cat.

---

of badgering, and an emphatic charge to Annie not to let me do anything bad, I was allowed to go. So Annie and I set out through the bright moonlight, she on thorns to know what was going on, for though I had exacted the deepest promises of secrecy I had told her nothing. When we came to the place I passed and repassed several times, stopping when I dared, for the moon was very bright. The blind was up, and I could catch glimpses of what was inside, and of a young lady, whether Sadie or not I could not make up my mind, who scared me by looking out at me. If she has recognized me, I shall emimgrate to Australia. Then we came home, Annie making frantic guesses as to my reasons for such conduct. We got home safely, and went to bed unquestioned.

Feb. 25th

Sunday. Bathed, studied my grammar, recited my history to Mama, and sewed on my chemise. I am really living upon the remembrance of my sight of Sadie in that bright warm elegant room. Did up the dishes with Mary and at Mama's request practiced ladylike behavior at table. It was a success.

Feb. 26

Monday. Examined in grammar in the morning. I got 98, and Hattie 80. I feel pretty sure of my Monitorship. I wish I was as sure of Sadie's keeping hers. Examined in History in the afternoon. Mary Fifield said she had left my last note on the dining table, and that her father had got it, read it, and told her that "the young lady who wrote that must have hated her pretty bad." Bad grammar! I struck consternation into her soul by telling her I had shown her's to Mama. She asked what Mama said, and I told her I believed she didn't say anything; only laughed. Asked Sadie if she had read *Our Mutual Friend* yet, and she said she had begun it, but could not read much at a time as the print was small. We compared our eye troubles, and when I told of my having sat a whole evening with a wet cloth over my eyes, she grunted, and said I might think myself lucky to get off with only one evening of it. She borrowed my knife. A glorious day, with a cloudless sky and a furious wind, which sends the dust whirling along the road and covers the sea with white caps but frightfully cold. Read *Magdalen Hepburn*.

Feb. 27th

Tuesday. Annie threatens to go. A false alarm. Various corrections in the morning, and Geography examination in the afternoon. Sadie did not get on her things as soon as I did, and as I passed her I whispered that I should be down first. I heard a scurry of foot steps behind me, and before I reached the bottom Sadie had whisked down the boys' stairs, laughing and silently clapping her hands. After school I wrote out a petition for the loan of Annie in the evening, and presented it at head quarters. I was to be allowed to go on condition that the wind went down. Papa sat with his feet on the top of the stove, saturated with laziness, and rated me for enjoying stories, and formed plans to give me a taste for instructive literature, and ended by making me bring *Plutarch's Lives*,[31] and beginning to read them aloud. Annie came in to have me start, and interrupted this delightful species of entertainment. We set out together through the splendid, cold, windy, starlight night, and went down Mill St. to Sadie's. I was bolder than before, as the moon was not up, and actually ventured to creep into the yard, but quickly hurried out again. We went up into the Carter's yard, and looked through a side window with plants, but could get no satisfactory views. However, we made out that there were two males in the room, and I was so scared when I saw one with a moustache glaring right at me as I stood on tip toe looking over the hedge, that Annie and I straightway departed home, not to say fled. Having heard Sadie invite Hattie Burditt to come over and study spelling with her, I was in hopes to have caught them at it. Annie made me promise to tell her what I came out for, but I put her off by telling her it was to look at someone's windows, which she knew before, but at last I told her the whole story. I can see she doesn't know what to make of it.

Feb. 28

Wednesday. Examined in spelling. Mine all right, I think. Was tormented all day, especially in school, by an odd, but most distressing feeling in my nose, as if someone was tickling the inside with a feather. Went into the city and to the Public with Josie, and got *Hide and Seek* and *Shirley*. I don't think I shall like either of them. At the Atheneum I got a book which I so like, a fairy story of George Macdonald's called *The Princess and the Goblins*. I read it through in the evening. Papa had brought out and left a minister and a small boy. The minister had a funny hooked nose and reminded me of Jack Brimblecombe.[32] The boy was small and fat and pretty and unpleasant, and Annie and I rated him in the best of Gaelic over his innocent and unconscious head. At supper the minister—Mr. Sterritt, I think his name is—said he hoped I should lecture, or to that effect, and I answered that I had not brass enough; that I could not bear being stared at. I found afterward that this was a double edged thrust, as the

31. Plutarch (A.D. 46?–120?), Greek biographer and philosopher, was the author of *The Parallel Lives*.

32. Jack Brimblecombe is the schoolmaster and curate in Charles Kingsley's novel *Westward Ho!*

brass reflected on Mama, and the staring on him, as he was looking at me, and then looked out of the window. They departed after supper, and Papa came home, and was fed, to my envy and admiration. I finished the jar of cider.

Feb. 29

Thursday. I waited with my heart in my mouth for the list of places. I was first, then Agnes, then Fannie, then Hattie, then Jenkins. The first class places are not given out yet, but Sadie seems sure she shall not be Monitress. She went down the boys stairs again, and got down first, though I hopped down two steps at a time; but she got a reproof from Mr. Horne, and came near having a check, so she says she does not mean to try it again. The whole school was in a state of excitement over a surprise party to be given to Arthur Carter that evening, to which most of them were invited. I wish I was invited to things sometimes. After school I went down to Fields Corner for a darning needle, as Mama says I must buy her one in place of the one I broke. Emma Adams, Ruth Swan and Hattie Mann were escorting Charley Bradley home, and they were having some dispute about a letter, which Emma protested she would show C. B. while Ruth declared she should not. They were all struggling together when I passed them and making noise enough for ten murders. When I passed the spot going back the ground was strewn with bits of paper, so I judge they tore it up at last. There were no letters. Read and darned.

M A R C H

March 1st

Friday. The second class left the room just before the first changed their seats. When we came back Sadie had got the seat next mine! My bliss is indescribable. Wrote notes to Mary Fifield. Mama wanted some cloth from Boston, and bade me get excused a few minutes before 4, and go in for it on the 4.10 train. I did so, and had the pleasure of finding that Mama had mistaken the time, and waiting an hour in the depot. Josie went in on the same train, and directed me on a nearer way to Summer St. and Hovey's.[1] It was quite dark when I got back, and I was horribly scared on the way home by a boy sitting on a fence and hooting, whom my fancy magnified into three drunken men. Bought 1/4 lb. chocolate drops.

March 2nd

Saturday. 20 past 8 P.M. Sadie was away from school all day, and I heard nothing of her, so I felt it really necessary to go and look at her windows. I gave

1. C. F. Hovey and Company, on Summer St., was a dry goods store.

notice to Annie, and also to Mama, who said nothing whatever, either then or when I referred to it in the course of the day. I took the chococlate drops to school, meaning to offer Sadie some, but she being absent, ate them. Mr. Horne announced that a prize of $5.00 for the best composition on "Kindness to Animals," and the Animals paper for one year for the next best, would be given, the compositions to be given in by March 15th.[2] Also a notice of our declamations, which are to be on the last half day before the vacation. Oliver Optic, otherwise Mr. Adams, Emma's father,[3] examined us in various things. He is short, dark and square, and she certainly does not inherit her prettiness from him; but he seems good natured. I made candy, and tried to bear the fitting of my dress and sack by Miss Everett like an angel, but felt rather nervous as to my oonyacking[4] from Mama's persistent silence. It was a gray day, and late in the afternoon a wild storm of wind and snow rose. Papa came, bringing me a letter from Kitty, and Annie two, one from Ronald Campbell. Mama decidedly forbid my stirring from the house, and as I saw her mind was made up, I retired to the library and sat down on the floor to be miserable. With the darkening gloom and storm and leafless woodbine outside the window, I felt almost ladylike. Felt unhappy all the evening. Read *Magdalen Hepburn.*

March 3ᵈ

Sunday. My head felt very bad all day; not aching, but tired and sick. Read some, looked over pieces, and got my list down to two. Made candy, and wrote to Kitty and Aunt Elizabeth.[5] Confided some of my woes and worries to Mama, who proposes stopping some of my lessons. Washed at night.

2. The Massachusetts Society for the Prevention of Cruelty to Animals was sponsoring this essay contest for Boston Public Schools; their monthly paper, *Our Dumb Animals*, was given as a prize to winners.

3. William T. Adams (1822–97), a prolific writer of children's books and short stories for periodicals, wrote under the pseudonym Oliver Optic. He also edited *Oliver Optics Magazine*, a monthly that claimed to be "the leading Juvenile Magazine of America." Representing the Dorchester ward on the Boston School Committee, he was a frequent visitor at Harris School and for many years was superintendent of the First Parish Sunday School (*DAB*).

4. "Oonyacking" is Alice's phonetic rendition of the Gaelic word "uinneag," meaning window. She is using it to mean "windowing" or "window peeping."

5. Elizabeth Blackwell (1821–1910), Henry's sister, was the first woman to graduate from a regular medical school, obtaining her degree in 1849 from Geneva College. With her sister Dr. Emily Blackwell she later opened the New York Infirmary for Women and Children. In 1869 she moved to London where, at the time of the journal, she was engaged in a large and successful medical practice. Kitty is Catherine Barry, her adopted daughter (*NAW*).

March 4ᵗʰ

Monday. Had a dreadful time, with no clean socks. Hastily washed the cleanest pair, and put them over the register, but had to go at 20 of 9 with one damp one. Mama sent a note to Miss Tolman by me to give her notice I should come only in the morning. When I brought up my sums she said laughing that she was sorry I was to leave off, but of course did not want me to have headaches. The girls to whom I mentioned it lamented and remonstrated. It seemed so very queer not to go back after dinner! Made a good deal of candy, which turned out very well. Went sliding in the yard with Mary and Annie, and cleared some snow off to lengthen the slide. Mary had to go in soon, and Annie had a bad fall, hitting her head. Papa began to read *The Antiquary* aloud.

March 5ᵗʰ

Tuesday. Composed and sent Mary Fifield three verses of poetical abuse, after showing it to Sadie, who said it was the best yet. Mary said first that she couldn't come up to that; then that she would fix me. Distributed my home-made candy in my usual awkward way, to Sadie and others. Sadie asked how I made it, expressed surprise at the spoon part, and said it was good. That minx Emma Adams sent some to Bradley, and Hattie said she had told him it was from me; but when I quoted the 9ᵗʰ commandment[6] at Emma, she protested she had only said it was my making. It is the coldest day this year; thermometer 3 below 0; one boy at school had a thumb frozen, another his ears. Bright and sunny though, and I was vexed that no one went out at recess. In the afternoon ironed the towels and handkerchiefs, read *The Princess and the Goblins* to Mary, cut out and basted the lining of my dress, under Mama's supervision, and made a lot more candy after supper. One of my poor hens, who has been ailing ever so long, had her feet frozen, and was kept before the fire most of the day. Cold!!

March 6ᵗʰ

Wednesday. Sadie was absent, but some books of hers, among them two stories, were on my desk, and I regaled myself with *In School and Out* during the intervals of lessons. The authorities in Boston say it is the coldest weather there has been for 45 years. I was bundled up the feet deep to go to school, yet my feet were nearly frozen. In the afternoon I made mincemeat for pies, also candy, and read *Hide and Seek*. Also, I feel very miserable. I wish I had been

6. The Ninth Commandment is "Thou shalt not bear false witness against thy neighbor."

Alice Lauder or Dunbar, or Marjorie, or Jean Bowman, or Magdalen herself![7] They believed something then, and seemed to feel it so close and real, and knew what they did believe, above all.

I have been roused out of a most gloomy and theological state of mind by Mamma's telling me there is a surprise in store for me tomorrow, and Mary and I asked questions and got ourselves thoroughly puzzled; but as we did up the dishes an idea occurred to Mary, and she gave me hints, and at last confessed that last evening she overheard what makes her suppose that they have laid hands on one of my pieces, and are going to have it come out in the *Journal*! I beat myself flat against the door, put my piecebook up my back, and spent the evening sewing and reading. Papa left for N.Y. after Breakfast.

March 7

Thursday. School in the morning. The ruling excitement at present is Mary Fifield's party, to take place tonight. I am not invited. I wish I was. Of course Mary has a perfect right to choose her own guests; but I was quite well aqqcuainted with her, and I do wish I could sometimes have a little fun like other girls, and live something as they do. The serpent and several others had their hair in papers, wherefore I rightly judged that they were going. In the afternoon Mama brought home my surprise. It actually is that Toby thing, altered and put on the first page of the *Journal*, with A. S. B. at the bottom.[8] I was prepared for it, yet sat down on the floor and shrieked, after my usual style. Mama seems rather disgusted that I am not pleased, and showed signs of turning blue; so I decided to be pleased, and abated my wrath.

March 8ᵗʰ

Friday. Sadie has a bad sore throat, Hattie Burditt says, and will not be at school for several days. I wanted to go oonyacking, but Mama forbade, and gave me a lecture on drunken men. She proposes to buy a large dog for my escort, as I have confessed the whole matter. I took too much mince pie and cider at dinner, and became slightly intoxicated, to the great eddification of Mary and Annie. Went over to Mrs. Mudie's with Mary, taking some work, and I finished a pair of crochetted white mats for which Mama has furnished materials. Slid very successfully in the yard. Mama had a terrific headache, and I nursed her and put her to bed, and tucked her in.

7. All the people named are from the book Alice was then reading, *Magdalen Hepburn: A Story of the Scottish Reformation* by Margaret Oliphant.
8. Alice's "Ode to Toby" appeared in print as "Pussy Cat" in the February 22 issue of the *WJ* (see Appendix 2).

March 9th

Saturday. Went out into the recitation room with Fanny Benedict for spelling. Annie has a whitlow on her finger, which is making trouble.[9] Mary has received an idiotic proposal from an invalid gentleman, who had advertized for a companion to an invalid, which advertisement she had answered, supposing him to be a lady. We had the "Widow of Glencoe" for the reading lesson, and the last 4 lines fell to Charley Bradley's share. I managed to live through it. In the dressing room he twice remarked that it was a fine piece, in a sneering way. Went into Boston, and did lots of errands. Got the letters and papers at the office, and my pin at Mr. Gardiner's. Had bad luck at the Atheneum, for they had neither Macdonald's poems nor Whittier's *Home Ballads*. I got *[Mosses from an] Old Manse* and *Story of a Bad Boy* instead, returning the Welsh History and *Magdalen Hepburn*, and went to the Public, which was crowded, and I had to wait 35 m[inutes] but got both the books I wanted, *Zaidee* and *In School and Out*.

March 10th

Sunday. I determined that I would make out the first rough draft of my composition of "Kindness to Animals" today, and did it, with much trouble, and by no means to my satisfaction. And I have one more to add to my list of dreadful bathing adventures. I was washing in the dining room, and John pumping in the kitchen. I had charged Mary to make him go round to the cellar the other way, but she went into the closet, and he took the opportunity— unconsciously, I hope—of starting for the furnace. He cast one glance at me as I stood horror stricken in my long green nightgown, and discreetly inspected the floor for the rest of the way. I was as completely covered as if I had been dressed, yet I wished myself in Australia, which Mr. Horne says is the Antipodes of New England. Mary and Mama consoled me afterwards. Papa got home from N.J. bearing a letter from Florence,[10] which I answered. A miserable dripping day. Annie's whitlow was very painful, and she went down to her uncle's. A boy came up afterward to say she was not coming back till her finger was better. *Antiquary.*

March 11

Monday. Sadie still absent. Miss T. asked me if I was any better, and I told her I thought my head did not ache so much; but that very afternoon, though I

9. A whitlow is an inflammation of the area of a finger or toe around the nail.

10. Florence Blackwell (1856–1937) was Alice's fifteen-year-old cousin, who lived in Somerville, N. J., with her parents, Samuel and Antoinette Brown Blackwell.

spent it very reasonably in crochetting and helping Mary roll up, sprinkle and take in the clothes, I had the most frightful sick headache, almost, that ever I had in my life, which made me utterly useless, and awfully cross, as far as my misery would let me.

March 12ᵗʰ

Tuesday. Snowing. Sadie gone. Only one session, but I was let out at 12. Mary Fifield most brazenly came and sat by me in school, and tormented me after her usual fashion. By way of vengance I wrote some verses descriptive of her personal appearance, and pinned them to the inside of her cap as I passed through the dressing room. Annie made a call here yesterday, looking prettier than ever, but says she is not coming back till her finger is well. She had it cut by Dr. Fifield last night, and squealed till he said "Hut tut, dont make such a noise in a man's house." Just like her, mo grarge![11] My head did not ache, but I felt generally miserable. Made some candy, which did not turn out well at all. *Antiquary*. Wrote out my composition for the second time.

March 13ᵗʰ

Wednesday. Hattie Burditt and I chased one another most of recess. I asked her about Sadie, and she said she had not seen her that day; believed she was a little better, but had been much troubled by fainting fits. I had a letter from Kitty last night. Her writing gets worse and worse, and I suspect she is faithless. She enclosed a letter from my little cousin Lily Rogers,[12] speaking of me very pleasantly. To my great delight, I found Annie at work with Mary just as usual when I came home from school. She gave me some Gaelic and read *Ossian* and *Mountain Adventures*, and crochetted. There was a regular rebellion in school. Miss T., being slightly savage, bade several of the boys who were convicted of writing instead of studying their grammar, write out the whole exercise. Upon which Audway disputed, I forget in what words, but ended by flatly saying that he would not write the exercise if she told him to. She told him very quietly and sternly that he should not recite with the class till he had apologised for that remark in some way, and bade him go into the other room to Mr. Horne. He sat still with an insolent smile on his face. She told him that his parents were at liberty to take him away from school whenever they pleased, but while he was scholar, and she was teacher, he should

11. Dr. William Fifield was the father of Alice's friend Mary. His office, in his home, was located near Field's Corner. "Mo grarge" is Alice's phonetic spelling for the Gaelic "mo gradh," meaning "my dear."

12. Lily Rogers and her family were relatives of Henry's who lived in Abercarne, Wales.

obey; she had never yielded to a scholar yet, and did not mean to now; she would bid him once more to go into the other room before she sent for Mr. H. to take him. He should not sit in her presence till the matter was settled. He sat a minute or two, then rose and sauntered out. The girls who sat nearer the front than I all say she was perfectly white, and her hands shook; but her voice and manner were perfectly stern and decided all the while. When Audway was out and the recitation was going on she bade Cook stand on the platform; he said he had not been doing anything; she repeated her order several times, and he finally exploded with "What was I doing?" and went. Mr. H. broke off Carrie L. in the middle of a verse and gave it to Charley Alexander. We had the "Widow of Glencoe" again, and I got horribly nervous. *Antiquary.*

March 14

Thursday. Papa looked over my punctuation etc. in my composition (I'm sure his punctuation isn't right; it may be grammar, but its not reason or common sense either) and I copied it. Took it to school and was bribed by the Serpent by a piece of candy to let her see it. Agnes Reed and I exchanged and read, and those who had seen mine said I was sure to get the prize, and quite raised my spirits. Agnes' was moral, and seemed to relate chiefly to the creation of the world. As I squabbled with Mary Fifield to see hers C. B. who sat by watching said admonishingly "Alice! that's disorderly!" or to that effect. I then insulted him; for which my conscience pricks me a little, as it was needless; but his patronizing tone aggravated me awfully, and I was flustered. I told him it was none of his affair, and retired to my seat. Pinned another note into M. F.'s cap. Oh, wasn't she furious when she came down? At recess there was snow balling. The boys formed a line and flung balls. One hit Jenny Reed's mouth and she went in crying. I felt like going and expressing my opinion of them to their faces. We got a lecture after recess from Mr. H. on snow balls. Went in to convoy out Phebe,[13] and found she had appointed to meet me at the 5.5 train; got *Our Mutual Friend,* 1 vol. from the Atheneum, and *Estelle Russel[l]* from the Public. Read in the station till Phebe came, and went out with her. Told and heard news and after supper Annie told me what I have been expecting and dreading; that she was going in a few days. I left; then thought of how lonely I should be and came back and cried, much to Annie's distress. Mary aggravated me by inquiries and I fled, and sobbed on the back stairs till Annie begged me

13. Phebe Stone (1849–1913), Alice's twenty-two-year-old cousin, was the daughter of Lucy's brother, Bowman, who lived with his family on the old family farm in West Brookfield, Mass. Phebe, then attending Wesleyan University, was one of the first four women admitted there, graduating in 1876.

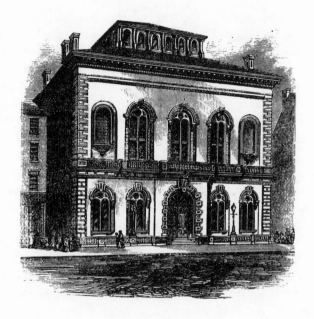

Boston Public Library.

down and promised to stay a long time yet; and between her and Mama I was comforted and went to bed with Phebe.

March 15

Friday. It came, after nearly six months waiting. I don't care much for what happened in the first part of the day; C. B. sat by me for drawing, and I read *Estelle Russel[l]*, and Annie and John got up a fight; that was all, I believe. Mama and Papa came, bringing me one letter. I looked at it once; it was a foreign letter; I looked twice; not from Kitty. I knew then. I took it very quietly into the front room and opened it. I pulled out a photograph. Her's! Then I threw myself down on the floor and lay there. Then, of course, I got up and read it. She is in Brussels, with her Mother, her sisters, and Mary Kirk. Florence and Miss Kirk have turned Catholics, to Alice's disgust. I read it to Mama and Papa, and they talked about Alice.[14]

March 16ᵗʰ

Saturday. Spelling and snowballs. Went into Boston with Mama from Neponset, to choose my mantlepiece. I got *Austin Elliot*, one of Henry Kings-

14. The letter is from Alice's old friend Alice Earle; Florence is her older sister.

---

ley's, which I like, and *Real Folks* at the Atheneum. *Real Folks* is a good name for Mrs. Whitney's[15] last; her people <u>are</u> real; I have seen several of them, and I am one myself. I like Luclarion Grabb best, I think. After waiting some time in the office I was taken to the marble store and told to choose. I chose; and Papa and Mama chose; and we went home. The mantels are arranged [in the store] so as to make passages, through which you walk, looking at your leisure. I got a cinder in my eye, but it came out. We brought home an *Illustrated London News*, sent me by Kitty, and a beautiful tea rose bud. Mama lectured me about having made Annie promise to stay that I felt very uncomfortable, and offered to excuse her from her promise, but she does not seem to want to go. Papa went down to confab with that detestable old Gosse,[16] who wants to cheat him about the horse, and I read *Austin Elliot* in the evening.

March 17ᵗʰ

Sunday. Wrote to Kitty, and made molasses candy, the smell of which sickened me so that I took ginger. Got in that old tablecloth that has been out frozen so long. *Mutual Friend* and *Antiquary*.

March 18ᵗʰ

Monday. Wrote a long, but unsatisfactory letter to Alice Earle, ironed handkerchiefs, and read, and made my bed, and sewed a little bit on my chemise. Mary and I tease Annie nearly to death about Bochda Hagel.[17] Papa and Mama got home late and very tired. Hattie Burditt got a note from Sadie at recess from one of her little sisters and says she is getting on pretty well.

March 19ᵗʰ

Tuesday. Drawing. M[ary] Scholonbach was very rough, ferocious and lively, and led me a lively time of it at recess. A girl from the lower rooms told me Mary Fifield had bidden her tell me she would fix me the next time she saw me. C. Bradley spoke to me for the second time, and not so very uncivilly this time. He looked round at me when he came to see what time it was, and said "Six." Annie left for her two weeks in Boston, amid howls from me and lamentations

---

15. Adeline Dutton Train Whitney (1824–1906), a writer of popular sentimental fiction and prose, took no part in public affairs and disapproved of woman's suffrage. Her best-selling book *Real Folks* urged her "girls" to be satisfied with the "dear fireside places," the "true" center of a woman's world (NAW).

16. Abel Goss kept a livery stable at Harrison Square.

17. "Bocha Hagel" or, in Gaelic, "Bocha H'oigeil" means "her youthful happiness" and is a reference to Annie's beau, Ronald Campbell.

from Mary. Mama has heard from Mrs. Spofford asking her if she can find Harry a place in the country, and I have hopes of getting him with us.[18] Papa left for Santo Domingo. I kissed and hugged his dear 'ceanglas' and he is gone.[19] Went over to Mrs. Buckley's, to go with her for milk, taking the high places and the glory of the Lord on the way. There was a splendid wind which I enjoyed going, but we had to wait a good while in a cold barn and I got thoughroughly chilled before the boy came and said he could not spare any extra milk. I reproved some uproarious little boys for tormenting the cows, and went home by way of the moon and the wind and the elms, and what had been the glory of the Lord. Began to set the library right, and read a little in *Real Folks*.

March 20th

Wednesday. A strange and wonderful day; a mixture of clouds, sunshine, cold, and a wind that made the elms bend and crack, roared around the schoolhouse, made us all wild at recess, and blew me home after school in a wild whirl of skirts, coat, cloud, hair, hat and dust. Made tart crusts. Emma arrived under convoy of Mama, and was fed and seen to. She immediately set to work clipping slips for the *Journal* like a born editor.[20]

March 21st

Thursday. Ran at recess in the wind and cold, and in the afternoon made apple pies, Emma and I being alone in the house. I spilt one on the floor, had to pull up the crusts to put in the water and sugar, and got rather more than double the amount of crust I needed; but Emma came to the rescue, and we made the surplus into tart crusts and dumplings. Did up the supper dishes with Mary,

18. Harry Spofford was the teen-aged son of Ainsworth Spofford (1825–1908), then librarian of the Library of Congress and longtime friend of Henry's (*DAB*). The Spofford and Stone Blackwell families often enjoyed summers together at Martha's Vineyard; Alice was therefore acquainted with Harry.

19. This would be the second time Henry visited Santo Domingo. He had gone to the island in 1871 as part of a presidential committee exploring the possibility of its annexation to the U.S. When annexation failed, he worked to promote a model commercial base in the country so that such products as cocoa, sugar, and coffee could be imported more cheaply. "Ceanglas" is Gaelic for "gray head."

20. Emma Lawrence (1851–1920), Alice's twenty-one-year-old cousin, often visited the Stone Blackwells for extended periods, assisting in the *WJ* office, occasionally writing book and play reviews, and helping out in the household. The relationship between Emma and Lucy was an especially close one; Alice observed some years later that "Emma was Mamma's baby—her first, I believe; and slept with her the first night of her life" (ASB to KBB: 21 Dec. 1897, *SL*).

and horrified her greatly by accounts of my toe paring exploits, and other matters.

March 22nd

Friday. Drawing, and a long lecture from Mr. Horne on the framework of compositions on "Kindness to Animals." Went up to the house with Emma and inspected it, and then went over with her across Neponset Bridge. I am worried as to what piece I shall speak. I like "Mary, call the cattle home," but it hardly seems the thing to speak another drowning piece so soon. Comboose it all! Made oceans of ginger snaps. Mama brought home Mrs. Campbell,[21] and I ate a second supper with them, and did up the two sets of dishes with Mary.

March 23d

Saturday. Studying spelling with Fanny Benedict. C[harley] B[radley] and [Etty] Sharpe made such a noise that I asked them to be quieter, but they didn't. As we had Geography instead of Grammar I could not recite. At noon when I came down to my place, Sadie stood talking with Charley Bradley. I felt almost as if the times of Eldorado were come again. She went upstairs and said as she passed me "I'm quite a stranger here, I suppose?" and smiled down at me again as she past up. Truly the times of Eldorado are come again! Sadie, whom I thought sick in bed, up and out! Her little sister with roses in her bonnet drives up of a morning in solitary state, with the big carriage and 'fiery steed' and a pretty little spotted dog. The snow came down thick and fast, while I read *Zaidee*, and wrote a little more on that idiotic story of mine. Mama and Emma came home snowy, and Mary and I did the dishes, of course.

March 24th

Sunday. Wrote to Florence and Miss Andrews,[22] and did several little jobs. As I sat by the stove reading *Our Mutual Friend* Mary moved the kettle and some of the water was dashed upon my foot. I hopped up squealing, and pulled off my stocking. My foot was pretty well scalded where the water touched it,

21. Margaret West Norton Campbell (1827–1908) was a close suffrage associate and friend of Lucy's. Active in the AWSA, MWSA, and NEWSA, she served as an officer, lecturer, and agent for them and also for the WJ. At this time she was lecturing and organizing local suffrage associations throughout New England (see her autobiography in WJ: 21 and 28 July 1894).

22. Jane Andrews (1833–87), educator and writer for children, operated and taught the primary school in Newburyport, Mass., that Alice had attended in 1869–71. Ahead of her time as an educator, Andrews minimized textbook learning, believing children learned best by direct experience and observation. The publication of *Seven Little*

and gave me discomfort, though I kept on cold water, and hopped around like 'my son John' with one shoe off and one shoe on, sympathizing most heartily with the devil, being in his predicament of not having both feet alike. Mama put on Arnica[23] at last, which about stopped it, though it hurt in bed. Took the honey from the box, and did sundry chores. Washed.

March 25th

Monday. The names of the prize scholars were read by Mr. H., that is the numbers were; and while he kept us on broken bottles during his preliminary remarks, I could hear my heart throbbing in my head. My number was among the rest. He said he did not know which had got the $5.00 but was told it lay between two, and that six of the Committe had been unable to choose between them. Several scholars expressed their feeling that it was unfair to have so much difference between those two prizes. I saw Sadie, who had come up with the fiery steed for her little sister and Hattie Burditt, and told her I had got a prize, and she answered that she knew it. I came in the afternoon, was examined in Grammar, and saw Sadie again. She called to me and asked what prize I thought I had got; and I called back that I was sure I didn't know. And I proceeded home adoring her.

March 26th

Tuesday. Had the usual school in the morning, but stayed away in the afternoon, as I don't take History any more. Went into Boston and renewed *Zaidee*, changed *Estelle Russel[l]* for *Phantastes* and got *Condensed Novels*[24] from the Atheneum.

March 27th

Wednesday. I am in a very happy frame of mind. I have had a compliment. But I shall keep it till I come to it. I woke up and found it snowing hard, so I went to school all done up, and found to my horror that we were to be examined in spelling. While the others corrected their History I had time for study, so did

---

Sisters Who Lived on the Round Ball That Floats in the Air (1861) established her as an author. This, as well as several subsequent books, was widely used in American elementary schools and translated into many languages (NAW). As a mentor and longtime friend, Jane Andrews influenced Alice's keen interest in nature study as well as her love of literature and writing.

23. Arnica is a plant with bright yellow rayed flowers, the heads of which were frequently dried and used in a tincture to treat burns and bruises.

24. Alice checked out Bret Harte's *Condensed Novels, and Other Papers.*

---

not fail. Managed with much manouvering to get my leggings on after school, by making two trips behind the stairs, one to pull up and one to pin.

After dinner all was excitement to get me dressed.[25] Emma was executioner, and torments I underwent are indescribable; but the effect was universally pronounced extremely elegant. I was dreadfully hurried by the announcement that the carriage, which Mama had ordered to be sent for us, was at the door. Down we hurried, and were driven to the Neponset, Emma putting the finishing touches to my costume in the coach. It had cleared up, but was very muddy. In the depot Emma kept me with my back to the fire to dry the places where she had sponged my sack, but the train came before it was done. At H[arrison] S[quare] Miss T[olman] and the girls saw me through the window, and came in, expressing great delight at finding me, as they had feared I was not coming. Fanny Benedict sat by me, Carrie Horne behind me, and Miss Tolman on the seat in front. Emma discreetly sat on another seat, and we had a fine time chattering and talking. Miss T. seeing how splendiferously I was got up said she guessed I knew how to train, only I kept my training for proper times; said she liked to see me train with Mary Fifield, and wished she was with us, that she might see us train. Under the influence of friendship and dissipation I shamelessly confessed my note passing performances, and then said I was sorry I had told, for now she would keep more of an eye on me; but she said Oh, no she wouldn't! that wouldn't be fair you know; but I mustn't send them, in a by no means severe tone. C. B. and Etty Sharp were in another car, but walked up to the Music Hall a little before us, and Mr. H[orne] superintended.

The hall was packed and we had to wait some time before we got a bad seat in the prize girls gallery. There were not nearly so many prize boys, and they had plenty of room. Some stupid speeches were made during which I noticed, when I attended at all; that whenever any one addressed the boys he was sure to look at and gesticulate at the girls. I saw Mama in the audience, but could not make her look at me, and also Mr. Garrison. Robert Collyer spoke, and two compositions were read. The Governor was on the platform, too.[26] We strained our ears, being far from the platform, for the name of our school, and at last it was read, and ours after it, and down we went, I leading the procession. I waited

25. Alice was preparing to join her classmates and other Boston school children at the Music Hall where prizes for the best essays on "Kindness to Animals" would be awarded.

26. William Lloyd Garrison (1805–79), leading American abolitionist, editor, and lecturer, was a longtime associate of Lucy's in both the American Anti-Slavery Society and the American Woman Suffrage Assocation (*DAB*). Robert Collyer (1823–1912) was a popular Unitarian minister from Chicago (see Introduction). Also on the platform was Massachusetts Governor William B. Washburn.

behind some girls whose turn I thought came before ours, till I heard him say "Any more of the Harris School?" and I presented myself as the Harris School, gave my name, and got a small roll, distinguished from those of the second prize by being tied with blue instead of red ribbon. It contained a couple of papers, one entitling me to the paper for a year, and other stating that I had got the first prize, but no money.[27]

I then left, as did all of us, and leaving Fanny Benedict with her mother went out home with Carrie Horne. On the platform we were met by a plump, very pleasant looking lady who spoke to me as knowing my name, and said she had been quite anxious to see me, she had heard so much about me from "her Charley," and as I stared, said "her Charley Bradley," so I found it was his mother. But the idea of his having talked about me! I never supposed he took any notice of me at all. But she went on to tell how he had not wanted to try for the prize against me, as I always had the best compositions in school, and it was no use, but when he found how nearly he had got it, having tried to please her, he wished he had tried a little harder. She also said something nice about talent running in the family, and told how when some of the little boys had been saying it was no use for them to try, as I had such a clever mother to do my composition for me, or to that effect Charley had come down upon them, I don't remember exactly in what words, and told them "I wasn't that kind of a girl." I said I was very much obliged to him, and we talked a little, and she said she was keeping us in the cold, and I went home with Carrie in a state of utter bliss, changed my dress and set the table. It was pleasant to be considered as "not that sort of girl," and nice also to have him stand up for me. I always thought he was less bad than the other wretches.

March 28th

Thursday. Went to school and took the Arithmetic examination perfectly. Was sent into Boston by Mama to take the inside of the *Journal* to Mr. Upham, which I did, finding my way with much nervousness up the seven flights of stairs.[28] I went in with Carrie Littlefield, who went with me to the Public, where I got *Salem Chapel*, and to the head of Bromfield St. Afterward I got *Leighton Court* and *Christie Johnstone* at the Atheneum, and went up and looked at the pictures. There is one of Fanny Kemble, a pretty young girl in old

27. Alice received Harris School's first prize and eventually received five dollars, along with her subscription. Second prizes went to Fannie Benedict, Charles Bradley, Everett Sharp, and Carrie Thorne (*BDET*: 27 Mar. 1872).

28. Mr. Hervey Upham was the printer for the *WJ*; his office was located on Bromfield St.

fashed white dress and hair done up queerly, standing by her Aunt Mrs. Siddons, who sits with a book, looking before her, but Fanny has such a look of pettishness, vexation, amusement, appeal, and withal seems just ready to laugh.[29] Mary met me with the announcement that Charley Bradley is Judge Ames'[30] nephew, which astounding fact she had just discovered that day. I then proceeded up to the house, where Mama and Emma were, in a towering rage, for I had just read a letter from my Betrothed, in which she expresses most outrageous and traitorous sentiments against the U.S.A. shamelessly array-ing herself on the side of England, at which my feelings were naturally greatly outraged. Emma said she had something to show me, and told me to look through a certain door. I did, and saw nothing but a tall man whom I took for a workman till looking at his face I saw it was Charley Blair.[31] Of course I did an unfinished swoon and hysterics, and then we escorted him to the little house. I spent the spare part of the evening in filling a large letter sheet with re-proaches to Kitty. I made it worse than anything I ever sent to Mary Fifield, and altered ferocious quotations from Whittier[32] for her benefit.

March 29th

Friday. Being Good Friday, was holiday, of which pleasing fact I assured myself by going down Mill St., catching Mr. H[orne] coming out, and asking. Emma left, escorting Charley Blair to show him the sights of Boston, and I did the slops and rubbed through the day somehow. Mama stayed in Boston over night to take a Turkish Bath, and we three unprotected females were left alone. When we went to bed (after an evening of sparring two against one) our preparations against burglars were many and various, at least mine were. I took up the tongs, put them with the dust brush by my bed, and kept a large pin and cologne bottle on the mantle. Emma and Mary slept in Mama's room, and I believe their preparations consisted of a bay rum bottle and a tooth-brush, the former to break over the intruder's head, and the latter to fling through the register as a signal to me. I meant to come into their room in my nightgown to explain my preparations and have a friendly chat; but their guilty conscinces had made them suspicious even of me, for I found the door locked,

---

29. The painting, part of the Athenaeum collection, was *Mrs. Siddons and Fanny Kemble* by British painter Henry Perronet Briggs (1791/93–1844). Sarah Kemble Sid-dons (1755–1831) was a popular British Shakespearean actress (*DNB*). Her niece, Fanny Kemble (1809–93), also briefly an actress, carved out a career in the U.S. as a popular reader and writer (*NAW*).

30. Judge Ames was Boston jurist Isaac Ames.

31. Charley Blaire had once worked at Pope's Hill.

32. John Greenleaf Whittier (1807–92), American poet and abolitionist (*DAB*).

and Emma harangued me at endless length while I stood out in the cold, trying to make me promise not to injure those within, which of course I disdained to do, till I folded my tent like an arab, and as silently stole away, leaving her haranguing the empty air, and got into bed in wrath. When she discovered my departure she proceeded with her harangue through the register, but after a few short and sharp explosions and a biting sarcasm or two I subsided into sulks, silence and bed clothes.

March 30ᵗʰ

Saturday. My head felt as though I had been hung up by the heels and all the blood had run into it, filling it almost to bursting, but did not ache. Emma prescribed a walk, and we found our way to the chocolate factory.[33] We inspected the works, and everyone was very polite to us and showed us and explained to us the whole process. The chocolate beans—cocoa-nuts as they are called—are put through a mill and broken fine, and warmed by steam so that they melt and run down little troughs into great kettles, where the stuff is boiled; then run into tin moulds and cooled, taken out and put through what seemed to me the oddest process of all; a brushing over with molasses and water to make them shiny; dried, and put up in various sorts of packages. One girl, looking just like Bell Rodgers, stencilled the names on boxes; another put up broma in silver paper packages; one tied up packages, one pasted labels on them. Among other things we saw what I took to be the pet of the factory, a white Spitzbergen dog with large dark round eyes and a sharp slender nose. He was put through his various tricks for our benefit, and every one seemed fond of him. A polite Irishman with a black beard showed us the downstair processes, and gave us a lot of small thin cakes of sweet chocolate, and some pieces of chocolate or cocoa butter, said to be good for burns and sores of all sorts; (I put some onto my foot when I got home) and we then departed. Hardly read at all, but made the greater part of a chemise, and felt my head stuffed after each meal. I meant to go minus my supper, but Mama who got home very late, advised me to have some, and I did. Mama had had a Turkish bath, and been rubbed down with shavings.

March 31ˢᵗ

Sunday. A dreary storm, and the trees all sheathed in ice. My stomach-ached, as it has done more or less for a fortnight. Wrote to Florence and Kitty, the latter an affectionate letter to be sent by one mail, while the thunderbolt of war woes by the next. Washed.

33. The Baker Chocolate Company had been in business in Lower Mills since its establishment in 1780 by James Baker.

APRIL

April 1st

Monday. Miserable with my stomach. Made applesauce on my own hook, read, and was given a spoonful of nasty, nasty rheubarb. Mrs. Moore and Nina called in the evening while Mama and I were making out a list of the flowers we want from Vick.[1]

April 2nd

Tuesday. A bright warm spring day. Went up to the house with Mama, and made apple jelly. Annie got home, not well, and set to work upon the washing. Emma says she is not so beautiful as she expected from my description; I think she will change her mind. Mary and Emma went to hear a lady named Rosa D'Erina sing last night, and are full of it.[2] Mary goes tomorrow, for which I am very sorry.

April 3[d]

Wednesday. I have seen her through the window again. Annie and I went down for a cabbage in the evening; and went round that way on purpose. We saw her both going and coming, and it was the only successful part of the performances, for the cabbage was not to be had, and the basket Mama had left was lent by the storekeeper; but those glimpses made up for it all. She stood by the table with the lamp on it—my beautiful Sadie—and we passed and re-passed several times. On the way home I astounded Annie by my proceedings on the way home, which were truly vossa, I being intoxicated with love, and doing all sorts of idiotic things without rhyme or reason, such as tumbling against trees, telegraph poles and fences, and glaring at the sky, which was overclouding blackly from the west. In the afternoon I actually called on Carrie Littlefield; she seemed glad to see me, but was sleepy, having been up till one at night cutting up. I only stayed about 5 minutes and went on down to Parks, where I bought bread, and then home, feeling acutely that my garters showed.

1. Alice had taken drawing lessons from Mrs. Moore the year before; her daughter, Nina, was currently Alice's piano teacher (ASB to KBB: 15 Oct. 1871, LC). Alice and her mother ordered their flower seeds from "Vicks Floral Guide," a popular and profusely illustrated seed catalog published quarterly in Rochester, N.Y., by James Vick (1818–82) (DAB).
2. Irish performer Rosa D'Erina appeared at Tremont Temple every evening during this week. Her two-hour program included a "novel melange" of reading, singing, and performing on the piano, organ, and melodeon; one reviewer claimed that "certainly no person has appeared in Boston who accomplished so much in the same space of time" (BDET: 2 Apr. 1872).

Ironed a little, and sustained various sharp tongue skirmishes with Mary and Emma. They wrote in my album.

April 4th

Thursday. Mary's last day here. I had made mince pies under Emma's super-intendence, which turned out very well, and read *Zaidee*, and then Annie and I went down to the station to see Mary off. She was to have gone from Neponset, but that idiotic ticket master said the trunk could only be checked from Boston, so she bade us goodbye, and went in on the next train, to start on the regular steamboat train. We saw her through the window as the car went off, and that was the last of our English violet. Mama was greatly disgusted when she heard of the train performance, [several words crossed out] People called all evening, and Mr. Blanchard[3] sta-a-a-a-a-a-a-a-a-a-a-a-a-a-a-a-ayed. Tried again to fix "The Rhyme of Duchess May," got it down to 25 verses, and read it to Emma.[4]

April 5th

Friday. Made a little more apple jelly, and wrote some poetry to Annie, to her great edification. I have behaved foolishly; I wont say made an absolute fool of myself this time; but I ought not to have lost my temper. Yet he did rile me so, I couldn't help answering back. It always does rile me to have people talk about Mama that way. I went up the hill with Annie to put the litter in the back chamber into the closet. The house is being plastered, and a man was at work at it in the room, and he seemed disposed to talk. He began by asking if we were either of us in the fire, and Annie said we both were; which assertion I corrected. She said I was Mr. Blackwell's daughter. He said we must have been frightened, and I said it was enough to frighten us. Then he asked what the name of the woman who owned that property was; Miss Jones, he thought. Annie said "Mrs. Stone," and he said "Oh! yes, he saw her in Boston and thought he knew her; she advocated Woman's Rights, he believed," in a sneering—no, not exactly a sneering, a slighting, a Podsnappian[5] sort of way that rather aggravated me, and I answered "Yes, she does," in a loftily decided manner meant to stop impudence; and that was the end of the conversation for a few minutes. When we had got all the papers and pamphlets into the closet I lifted one of a bunch of iron weights and asked Annie if it belonged to us and

3. Hiram Blanchard lived nearby on Ashmont St. ·

4: Alice was trying to condense Elizabeth Barrett Browning's 112-verse poem "Rhyme of the Duchess May" for a school exhibition reading. By June she gave up the idea, admitting her "courage failed her" (ASB to KBB: 8 June 1872, LC).

5. Alice is recalling John Podsnap, a self-satisfied character in Charles Dickens's book *Our Mutual Friend*.

ought to go in, and he spoke up and said we could leave them there; nobody would trouble themselves to steal them; that if everything that was there was offered him as a gift he wouldn't take it. I said something about it's being worth selling for waste paper but he went on without heeding me, saying "There's not a thing I've seen there yet that's fit for a man to read, much less for a woman." That riled me worse, and I said that what was fit for a man to read was fit for a woman. He said "Oh, well, there were some little bits a man might read which a woman wouldn't like to," or to that effect. I was thoroughly riled by that time, what with his abuse of Mama's books and all, and only repeated my first remark; for a man ought to be ashamed to read things that a woman would be to[o]. Then, our work being done, we left, but I couldn't help saying as a parting shot they weren't meant for him to read anyway; which was the only really rude thing I said, though Annie gave it to me coming down the hill. Afterwards Emma gave it to me in a milder manner, and between them, I got down into the valley of humiliation. And then Emma undressed in my room, we having but one light between us, and as we sat before the register gave me a lecture on phisiology and anatomy, illustrating her remarks on my corporeal frame and trying to warm her cold hands on me. To which I very naturally objected. Whereby she kept me from my natural rest, and I was very sleepy the next morning.

April 6ᵗʰ

Saturday. Emma and I were sent into Boston soon after dinner. I went to the Public and got *Jane Eyre*, and then joined Emma at the office. Then I went to the Atheneum, but could not get anything I wanted, so took *David Elginbrod* (in 3 vols. to my huge disgust) and *Magdalen Hepburn*. Stayed in the office while Emma went out, and kept an eye on an old gentleman to see that he did not steal. Got *Hereward [the Wake]* from the Public, and came out home. Mrs. Mudie called in the evening.

April 7ᵗʰ

Sunday. Went into Boston with Emma to church. We tried one church, and it was too full. We then tried the steepleless building on Tremont St. from which they tore down the pigeon's nests.[6] It proved to be an Episcopal church and we witnessed a lot of confirmations by a Bishop, who warned his protegés against progressive ideas in religion. Why do the Episcopalians make their ministers

6. This was St. Paul's Episcopal Church on Tremont St. across from the Boston Common. Completed in 1820, it was unlike the many steepled churches of Boston and was built in Greek Revival style.

St. Paul's Church (left) and the United States
Courthouse.

look so absurd by putting them into nightgowns with huge frills and flapping
white wings, I wonder? I joined in the ceremonies, I flatter myself, with great
propriety and devoutness, especially the 'miserable sinner' part. After that we
went to the Journal Office and ate the lunch that had been brought in my
satchel. We then went to the horsecar station and out home. The cars were
soon crowded and the air very bad, but the end of our journey was reached at
length;—the end of our journey but not of our troubles. For as we walked up
Emma and I were conversing about a man whose teeth stuck out; and as we
were in the thick of description he passed us! He must have heard; and to make
matters worse, I much against my will exploded in laughter, and Emma herself felt upset. Chicken for supper, and an awful headache after it, so that the
evening was spent in attempts at relieving by Emma and Mama, which par-
tially succeeded.

April 8th

Monday. Wrote in trembling and tribulation my note to Charley Bradley, and
took it, with the money pinned inside it, to school with me. He came into the
dressing room as I combed my hair out, and gave it to him, telling him that
there was something belonging to him. He received it with a bow, a smile, and a

'thank you,' and took it into the schoolroom with him. Just before school, as I chatted with Hattie Mann, carefully abstaining from looking toward him, he came along, red and grinning, put it on my desk, and scooted away, again saying "Oh, he couldn't! He couldn't!"[7]

I was No. 4, whereby sundry noses were put out of joint, the owners thereof being lower; among said no[s]es was the Serpent's, who openly told me she thought it unfair. It seems queer to be out of the seat I have had for 5 months, but happily there are no boys near me. At noon as I passed C. B. I said "I wish you would, Charley," but he said "Oh, he couldn't; It wouldn't be fair." Went to N. Quincy, looked at the dark water ebbing through the piles and came back. Emma and I went over to see the puppies, which were very readily shown to us by a rosy faced girl who soothed the mother dog when she wanted to fly at us, and gave us each one to hold. They were pretty and silky, but they squealed distressingly, and the place smelt so utterly horrible that I was glad to come away. Darned stockings.

April 9th

Tuesday. School. One session. Left at 12.5. Dampness, mist and slush. Went down for meat with Annie, came across Emma, and all went home together, I carrying the baggage, a heavy satchel, and refusing to surrender it. Emma started on the run, and I thinking she wanted to make me repent carrying the bag, though it afterward came out that she was in fear of pokes from my umbrella, gave chase, and reached home nearly dead, my underclothes splashed with mud nearly to my waist.

April 10th

Wednesday. At recess Sadie and the rest of us played catch, and she and Hattie Burdett planned a base ball party, which Sadie asked me to join, saying she was sure I should make a good player. Of course I said yes. Finally copied the Molly thing, had it inspected by Emma, and gave it in charge to her to hand in to *Our Young Folks*.[8] Started for Soda and Letters, but as I passed Carrie Littlefield's, an angel flew out upon me and secured me for base ball. Of course I couldn't resist, even after I got into mud over my ankles, while we waited for the other girls, and Sadie was very impatient. We went to the school yard, and it being found that I was absolutely and utterly ignorant of the game, I stood on one side and watched Sadie. Oh, so beautiful and graceful as she was, with

7. Alice wanted Charley Bradley to accept her prize money from the "Kindness to Animals" essay contest.

8. Alice was submitting her poem to the monthly magazine *Our Young Folks*, published by James Osgood on Tremont St. near the *WJ* office.

James Osgood & Co.

her cheeks flushed and her hair wild in the wind! She seemed to me the North Wind herself, and I stood there absurdly catching cold and feasting my eyes on her every motion. At last I tore myself away and came home.

April 11ᵗʰ

Thursday. Hostilities with M[ary] F[ifield] in the morning. As we stood by the waste basket I shamelessly observed that I was sorry she sat so far off, as I could pass her no more notes; she pretended to be shocked and said "Why Miss Tolman, this morning she called me an insane lobster!" "Well, you called me a rhinosceros," said I; and we fell to it under the very nose of Miss T. who stood by and laughed. In the afternoon Emma and I had our pictures taken. We went into Boston together and selected a gallery after several experiments. I didn't like the place; saw something dreadful on the stairs, and every one had a villainous countenance except the redhaired girl behind the counter; but we got our pictures in a hurry, as the man said the plates were drying; and such pictures! Emma was simpering and idiotic; I stern, gloomy, defiant and ferocious; decidedly bulldog like, and oh so savage and piratical! We took the whole lot and and came out home. A half letter from Kitty, minus the beginning, and a very nice whole one from Aunt Elizabeth. *Pamela* and stockings in the evening.[9]

April 12th

Friday. Walked over to Milton Lower Mills, Emma accompanying me as far as the horsecar track, and then going back. I stood on the bridge and watched the graceful undulating slides of the mighty sweeps of brown water going smoothly over hummock after hummock and then breaking up into roaring foam; and I listened to the deep voice of the water, and enjoyed it, and went home. Was tired, had a swelled throat and was dosed with various preparations. Showed a most atrocious note of M. F.'s to Miss T. who laughed herself nearly to death over it.

April 13th

Saturday. Such a time with a spelling match! I was given "exchequer," and spelled it right, but scholars would keep popping up and spelling it wrong by way of correction. As I went upon my winding way home, through the school yard Sadie flew after me, overtook and grabbed me, and walked with me as far as our ways lay together, and making me the more blissful as she has had very little to do with me for some time, and sits in quite another part of the room. Walked up to Milton Lower Mills.

April 14th

Sunday. Alone in the house with Mama. Tied up papers for Mama, and felt miserably unwell. Went up to the house with Mama, and tried to decide on my room, but couldn't and can't. The big upstairs room is <u>beautiful</u>, but right under the roof, else I should surely take it. Mr. and Mrs. Carter[10] came up the hill in their carriage, and said our front door was open, and I rushed down the hill and shut it. Read a little in *Jane Eyre*. Charlotte Bronte certainly has the knack of inventing the most disagreeable male characters I ever knew of. Both Mr. Rochester and Mr. St. John are detestable; but of the two I greatly prefer St. John. He twisted his feelings to agree with his religion, and Mr. Rochester twisted his Religion to agree with his feelings; and both of them overdid it.

April 15th

Monday. I am getting demoralized fast. It's all that villainous Mary Fifield's fault; she is making me disgrace myself and destroying my reputation. Today

9. Alice often darned stockings while listening to her father read *Pamela*.
10. The Josiah Carters, friends and neighbors of the Stone Blackwells, lived at the bottom of Pope's Hill on Neponset Ave.

we exchanged epithets during the singing of the Festival Music, and fell to fisticufs in the hall in plain view of C. B. Went into Boston to be vaccinated. Got Rosetti's poems at Boston, but it was Christine R.'s, not Dante Gabriel's.[11] However, they are nice. Mama took me to Dr. Lucy Sewall,[12] with whom I fell in love at first sight. She is something like Mama; even softer and rosier and chubbier, and vaccinated me so gently that it was really quite pleasant. We took out the housekeeper, Miss Tucker, and the choreboy, Frank Fellows. He is quite young, she quite old, and both very ugly. His front teeth are broken and she has a great scar on her chin, and seems timid and talkative.[13] Mama went away again to lecture, and I read most of [the] time.

April 16th

Tuesday. Suffered untold miseries from the presence of a strange lady and boy.[14] Snapped when my dress was tried on. Blacked my satchel and washed my hair brush. Annie cross and glum. A sunbeam at school. Sadie spoke to me in the hall, when I was going out alone, there being one session. She cu[r]tseyed, and said "The Dame made a curtsey, the dog made a bow," and assigned me the part of dog. I wish almost that I were the little dog of the Wilson family.

April 17th

Wednesday. Sent M. Fifield my first good note, addressed "Stuffing for the fatted calf, Mary Fifield." I also gave her some uncomplimentary verses which she threatened to show Miss T. and I asked her to lend me them for a minute and promised to give them back; and I did—the pieces. She called me bad names and left. Made some apple sauce and read *Hereward the Wake*. Miss Tucker knew the Wilsons, and has told me of them to my great edification. Had a sore spot in my chest all day, and when Mama came home at night she put on a mustard poultice and a wet cloth. Took Miss Tucker up to the house and showed her over it.

---

11. Christina Rossetti (1830–94), English poet, and her brother Dante Gabriel Rossetti (1828–82), poet and painter.

12. Lucy Ellen Sewall (1837–90), early woman physican, was resident physician at the New England Hospital for Women (1863–69). At the time of this entry she was devoting more time to her growing private practice. A staunch feminist, she was one of a group of eight women physicians (including Emily Blackwell) who unsuccessfully offered Harvard University $50,000 in 1881 to provide medical study for women (*NAW*).

13. Lucy described Frank Fellows as a "nice boy . . . son of a clergyman from Maine." He replaced "John" as choreboy (LS to Margaret Campbell: 20 May 1872, LC).

14. Alice is referring to Miss Tucker and Frank Fellows.

April 18ᵗʰ

Thursday. Challenged Mary Fifield to a duel, which challenge she accepted. Much tossing of heads and turning up of noses. Notes all given through third parties, as it is considered the thing to send "a friend" with your cartels. Divers[e] skirmishes. Went up to the house with Miss Tucker and showed her the garden. Mama away.

April 19

Friday. More letters relative to our duel and a mutual showing of them to Miss T. In the afternoon went into Boston. On the way to the station met Charley Bradley and another boy. C. B. nodded and smiled, and I nodded and tried to grin amiably. Got *Constance Lyndsay* and *Lucy's Two Lives* from the Public, and *Midsummer Eve* from the Atheneum. Looked at the Arundel Saints in the picture gallery.[15] I dont like them at all.

April 20

Saturday. The day fixed for my duel with Mary Fifield. I am awaiting her arrival. We had a time at school. We exchanged several abusive notes, but at recess she gave me one such outrageous one that I bolted upstairs to answer it, and when Miss T. came in showed it to her, and protested I would have Mary's blood. She laughed and read it, settling her face now and then, to scold some entering boy. Near the end of school I twitched my nose at M. F. and before I could get it smoothed out Miss T. looked and saw me. Of course she understood it, and she and I both had quite a time to keep down her laughter.

I waited in state with my weapons around me, but Mary Fifield did not come.

April 21

Sunday. Papa got back from San Domingo and brought with him a large pineapple, some guavas, and an enormous bunch of bananas, besides two pods of cocoa nut beans. Of course he was rapturously received by Mama and me, fed and washed, and then taken up and showed the house. He brought home a crop of boils, which make him quite lame. Wrote to Mary Hooper and made some apple jelly. *Antiquary* in the evening. Washed.

---

15. The Athenaeum was exhibiting its collection of fifty chromolithographs depicting the lives and deaths of saints. Published by a group of British artists calling themselves the Arundle Society, they provided viewers an opportunity to see splendid color reproductions of works by such artists as Fra Angelico, Fra Bartolommeo, and the Van Eyck brothers.

April 22

Monday. Took to school a pod of the cocoa bean to exhibit and an ivory paper knife to slay Mary Fifield for not keeping her appointment. The pod was duly shown to Addie Callendar, by her to C. Bradley and by Me to Miss T. and some of the other girls. The knife I broke against Mary Fifield's bony ribs in vengeance for her having basely filled my ink bottle with blotting paper and stuck my best pencils into it during singing time, while she had my seat; a revenge alike unworthy of a Christian and a gentleman; as I told her. Our duel is definitely determined upon for tomorrow afternoon. Papa continued the *Antiquary*.

April 23ᵈ

Tuesday. The duel came off. I was kept in 5ᵐ[inutes] for sums, so did not see Mary after school. Went home and prepared my weapons, which were as follows; the horsewhip, the tongs, the carving knife, and a pail of water containing a syringe, which last was my chief reliance. Also I provided a winding sheet for her and a waterproof to serve as Martial Cloak and armor. She rang the bell soon after 4, and greeted me with laughter and bad names. I brought her in, and showed her to Mama and showed her the array of weapons which almost sent her into convulsions. I offered her a waterproof, but she declined it, not having seen the contents of the pail, and we went up the hill loaded with weapons, and probably looking like a pair of cheerful lunatics. She was charmed with the house and it was some time before I could bring her back to the duel. She pretended to have forgotten her pitchfork, so I lent her the carving knife, measured 12 paces, and squirted water at her till she cried for Quarter, though she did not seemed to mind the wet much except when it endangered her hat. I wrapped her winding sheet around her, was stabbed to the heart with the handle of the carving knife, and proceeded to show her over the house and describe the fire. She was greatly pleased by a large mass of soft powdered and wet plaster and kneaded it with the carving knife till I made her leave. We came down and presented ourselves, as spooks, ate maple sugar, discussed book[s], recounted scrapes, and enjoyed ourselves. I showed her the bananas, lent her *Mopsa* and walked home with her. She tried to get me in to tea, but of course I wouldnt.

April 24ᵗʰ

Wednesday. My "Sister Spirit" greeted me with a shake, and has been calling me spiritual names ever since. In the afternoon took a long walk over beyond the Old Quincy Place, and brought home a lot of willow catkins and birch tassels. Got a letter from Kitty, and several from the Hooper lot.

April 25th

Thursday. Went in to the city in the afternoon, had a hat bought, and went out loaded with books.

April 26th

Friday. Awfully and outrageously hot. I could have Oh'ed for a lodge in a garden of cucumbers, for the first time this year. I went up with Miss Tucker to the house, did a wee bit of gardening and dug up part of the patch for my beans. There was a big wind toward evening, whirling weird white clouds of dust along the road, and Annie and I went out and got blown.

April 27th

Saturday. School of course. Got there very early, and had to wait for the door to be opened. As I was in the room alone Sadie came in, came over and spoke to me, and stood over me and gave me my definitions, making me supremely blest. Ball at recess, and Sadie walked as far home with me as our ways lay together. Dug and planted beans with Miss Tucker, and absurdly put all the speckled beans to soak.

April 28th

Sunday. Wrote to Florence and Aunt Nettie,[16] and washed just before supper. Went up with Miss Tucker to plant the beans I so assininely put to soak; such of them, that is, as were much swelled. But we found that the way of transgressors is hard. Mrs. Mansfield came, and people passed, and we had to keep hiding the shovel as best we could, and smiling innocently; but at last we got it done. Went up to watch the Milton woods burn.

April 29

Monday. A long singing lesson and short arithmetic. Eddy Jenkins is really getting troublesome; speaks to me in the yard, tries to monopolize my attention before school, and will talk to me, and screw himself round and watch my proceedings with an idiotic grin on his smooth pink face, till I long to wring his neck. I detest that boy! Planted beans and potatoes. The notice of declamations was given out. My chickens are hatching.

16. Alice's "Aunt Nettie," Antoinette Brown Blackwell (1825–1921), had been Lucy's closest friend when they were students at Oberlin College in the 1840s. In 1853 she became the first woman ordained in the U.S. Protestant ministry. Now married to Henry's brother Sam and raising five daughters, she was beginning to find time to investigate religious and scientific issues from a feminist perspective—an exploration that would result in many articles and a number of books (*NAW*).

April 30th

Tuesday. My first instalment of chickens—7—were cooped by the kitchen door, and Toby was duly boxed and scolded to make him keep away from them. Sadie and I were on the same side in base ball at recess, so I had the advantage of her cries, admonitions and warnings. She always gets animated and excited over the game. Went down to Fields Corner with Miss Tucker and did some errands. I charged Papa yesterday with the buying of *Real Folks*, and he brought it home. Went up to the house.

MAY

May 1st

Wednesday. The 17th anniversary of Papa's and Mama's wedding day. Two years ago today that I began to keep a diary. Well! I skipped down stairs in my night gown, got *Real Folks*, and presented it with the proper congratulations. I heard them laughing over the inscription (To my Revered Parents) followed by an apology for my lack of reverence. We were examined in Arithmetic, and mine was 100. Read *Real Folks*. Desire Ledwith seems to me like myself, something like. I have got into a very bad habit of trying to sift myself out, and find what there is of me; and it is unpleasantly plain that there is a great deal of selfishness; an awful deal; also laziness. It's got to be punched out of me; and I've got to punch it!

Mary Fifield called, by appointment. We ate 4 bananas, and drank two bottles of cider. I walked with her to Emma Adams', where I left her. On the way she unfolded to me her views of 'the pearly car,' and awful views they were. Mama told me a *Ledger* had come; that she had left it behind, and never meant to let another come into the house. I said I should get it the next day when I went in; she said it had gone to be cut into wrappers. Papa said that was adding insult to injury, as indeed it was; why need she have told me? She could have kept t[w]o back and said nothing. To stop me off right in the midst of "Mark Heber's Luck"![1] I straightway went off to bed mad, with tears in my eyes.

May 2nd

Thursday. Rainy. Grammar examination. 100 much to my surprise. Had calculated to have 88, reckoning up my uncertainties. Went in the afternoon, got my spelling, and left before school began. Crochetted, and tried to select a piece.

1. "Mark Heber's Luck, or Life on the Plains" by Leon Lewis began appearing in the *New York Ledger* on March 30.

May 3ᵈ

Friday. Am excused from school for the whole day, as it is Geography examination. Went into Boston, dined at Marston's,[2] and changed books. Climbed
up the 7 flights to the printing office twice, and went home and to bed with a
headache. Got an awful scare going over the bridge. A train was coming; I only
took every other sleeper, but it roared, shook the rails, and scared me. Ugh!

May 4ᵗʰ

Saturday. Spelling. Mine all right. At recess as they chose sides Sadie wanted
Mary Scholonbach to choose me on their side, but she didn't till the very last
one. A spelling match. I was a chooser, and chose first Sadie, then Mary
Fifield. Sadie whispered me who to choose, and I followed her advice im-
plicitly. She went to and fro at least half a dozen times, for whichever side had a
choice chose her. My side was beaten by one; a nearer match, Mr. Horne said,
than there had ever been before. Mary F. brought me *Tanglewood Tales*,
which I read during the pauses of study. Harry Spofford is to be here soon, and
I am very glad. Dug up some horse radish from up by the rainwater tub, taking
the tops, with a small bit of root to each; dug up a small patch of ground by the
apple trees near the foot of the hill, and planted between 50 and 60 roots in
rows of six roots apiece. Ironed out my sash, and finished the red and black
letter holder.

May 5ᵗʰ

Sunday. There were 9 chickens at first; yesterday there were 8; now there are
7. Those wretched cats! What shall I do with them? Washed when I got up.
  Am feeling unhappy; I don't know exactly what the matter is; I think—I
want—God. Not the "Spiritual Consciousness" or "Pervading Power," that
one supposes about; I want George Macdonal[d]'s; one to love, to really believe
in and trust to utterly. Mama believes in a Guiding Influence, and gets along
somehow; but I shouldn't wonder if her blues came somewhat from the want
of—something in that direction. As for Papa, I dont know what he does believe; I think he supposes that creation is a sort of machine, set going once for
all; and Mary Hooper says that the little wrongs—trials of young chickens and
such—are for the good of the whole. But—the God I should like to believe in
wouldn't squash individuals for the good of the whole if it wasn't for their good
as well. And being a Blackwell, I keep all the worry to myself; there really

---

2. Marston House, located at 17 Brattle St., was a hotel with forty guest rooms and a
long-established dining room. Lucy especially enjoyed eating there and carried its advertising in the *WJ*.

seems no one to tell—who I could tell. Miss Andrews is almost too good and perfect; but I fancy if Alice Earle were here, I could put my head down in her lap, and sob out the whole of it to her. After writing that last occurred a special Providence. Mr. Blanchard called, and told us that Robert Collyer was to speak in the little church by the schoolhouse;[3] so I hurried up the dishes and went with my parents. We got a seat near the pulpit. The pew behind us was filled with our girls; The serpent, Nettie Wharne, Carrie Thayer, Hattie and Lulu Mann and my enemy Mary Fifield, with whom I instantly began to cut up. She passed me an oyster cracker on her fan, and I ate it; we talked, laughed and called one another names till Mama stopped it. At last Mr. Collyer began, and I didn't attend to anything else. It was wonderfully strange that he should have taken just that subject. I think God must have put it into his head; at any rate it went right home to my sore place and did me good. It was the long prayer, and if he could have seen right into my mind he would have said just what he did. I actually cried a little, but it being in prayer time, wasn't seen. I think what comforted me as much as anything were his emphatic shalls. "The dumb shall speak, and the deaf ears shall hear," and so on. I had got what I needed before the end of the prayer. Then came the sermon; a very good one, but not especially applying to me; about the Unitarian church. The best of that part to me was the looking at him; he has such a pleasant, hearty, cheery, ruddy, jolly, good face, strong and pleasant at once, that it is a comfort to look at him. But his gestures were very funny. He kept suddenly lifting up his head as if he had heard or smelled something, or had been spoken to while woolgathering, and he swayed from side to side, and flung his great self around in the pulpit, and was so incessantly moving that it almost made me dizzy to look at him. He seemed to have found out the secret of perpetual motion. There were 3 hyms sung by the whole congregation, and I sang too, though I could only find the words of one.

When it was over, and the blessing said, the girls behind me rose en masse, with exclamations of rapture. "Wasn't it splendid? Did I ever hear such a sermon? Wouldn't I like to hear him every Sunday, and three times a day?" And so on. I saw he had come down and was talking to Papa and Mama, so I went back, and was introduced. He shook hands with me, and put his head down and said "Kiss me." I was taken by surprise, but gave him a real smack in the face of 600 people—who weren't looking at us, though. He said "Oh you little darling!" and went on talking to my folks, and I listened, till Mama began to take him up on the subject of Woman's Rights, and then I cleared after the

3. Robert Collyer spoke at the Third Unitarian Society Church on the corner of Neponset and Mill.

girls. At least, cleared hardly expresses it, for you could hardly stir in the crowd; but I overtook them at the door, and let out about the kissing to Hattie Mann. She said "Ohhh! He didn't! Might she tell?" I threatened not to leave her a hair on her head if she did, and waited for my parients. Mr. Collyer had been smoking; that I am sure of; but I could just have hugged him. I love him! Mr. Carter said I had got more than my share; and I told him he was envious. Home we went, and I to bed.

May 6th

Monday. Had no peace of my life at school, for Hattie Mann—the perfidious creature!—let out to Mary Fifield about last night's performamances before my face and eyes. I stopped her for a minute when she had got as far as "she kissed—" and Mary instantly flew into a state of the wildest excitement, screaming "Who? Who?" "Mr. Collyer," gasped Hattie between my hands; and "They set up a yell!" Mary, of course, let out to half the school; the viper! and they were alternately crying "Oh for shame!" to me, and lamenting and abusing him because he had not kissed them too. And I was reported to Miss T. as having "Upped and kissed the minister." Went up to the house with the great shears, and mowed part of the border with them. It began to rain, and I was driven into the Summerhouse. Papa left for N.Y.

May 7th

Tuesday. Waited impatiently for Harry Spofford, till Mama reported that a boy was going up the hill, and she thought it was Harry. So, according to orders, I put on my hat and started up the hill after him. He was coming down again, called out to me "Is that you?" Shook hands and kissed me, and we proceeded down the hill. He is thin, pale, black, rather ugly, astoundingly tall, and the picture of his mother. We fed him, and I went to school; played ball at recess, and came home again. After dinner Harry and I went to the station. We had to wait there a long time, as the 1.54 did not run, and we had to wait for the 2.14. He left me in Boston, and I changed books and went up to the printing office, and carried out a fearfully heavy satchel, containing 4 books, 40 papers, more or less, a bottle of yeast, and various smaller articles. I forgot to say that I showed Mr. Horne my piece, and stand committed for five pages of the "Rhyme of Duchess May." Harry came home after supper, and was fed with Frank.

May 8th

Wednesday. Stewing hot, but played base ball at recess. Went up to the house and carried with me shears and seeds. Harry and I dug up the bed (I ought to put his name first as he did most of it) and I planted the seeds and finished trimming the border on one side. Stewed almost to a jelly. And I here record a shocking fact. Harry, who I always have quoted as the one exception to the rule of total boy-ine depravity, is as bad as the rest; as great a tease as Charley Blair. Annie was scared nearly out of her senses. As I was looking out of my window I heard her shrieking to me to come down; I went, and found a little green snake that Toby had brought in sprawling on the floor, and Annie holding up her skirts in the furthest corner of the kitchen watching Toby poke it about. I got the broom and swept it out, refusing to kill it, to her great wrath. Afterward I was scared by thinking Toby had swallowed it alive. Before school I was writing to Florence, and was interrupted in the middle of my letter to chase the yellow cat over to Mr. Putnam's with a young chicken (the 5th of mine he has eaten) in his mouth. I saw him disappear under a shed with it, and proceeded to ring Mr. Putnam's bell, and tell him that if he did not keep the cat shut up we should have to kill it.

May 9th

Thursday. <u>Awfully</u> hot. Was in a state of violent perspiration nearly all day. By Hattie Man[n]'s invitation went over to her house to play croquet, meeting her at school at 4 oclock. We played 6 games; I beat in 3 and she in 3. She showed me her maltese kitten; as pretty a little creature as I ever saw, with a red ribbon around it's neck. Then she said she would walk part way home with me, instead of which she seduced me into going over to the P.O. with her. As we neared that goal of our desires Ruth Swan passed us in a carriage, and flung me a paper of gingersnaps, saying there was something to feed my wrath upon; and I fed Hattie on them. There were no letters, but we got ourselves weighed; Hattie weighed 104 and I a little over 109. It was 106 last time I was weighed. As I came home Mary Fifield passed me in a carriage, poked her head out of the door and cried "Sail! Sail on!" Read one of Robert Collyer's sermons in the evening. I like them, and some times can fancy I hear him thundering away in the pulpit. I would walk six miles and back again every Sunday to hear that man preach! A *Ledger* was charitably sent out by Mrs. Hinckley, but I heroically refrained from reading anything but "Mark Heber's Luck."

May 10th

Friday. Still very hot. No news. Grated horseradish. Tied my garter about Toby's neck as a collar, and he disappeared with it, to my dismay, but brought it back. No letters. Great wrath of Harry, Annie and myself on that account. Harry slandered my Betrothed, thereby mortally insulting me. Young Villain!

May 11th

Saturday. A vigorous fight at recess. Hattie Mann enlisted Mary Fifield, and both set upon me at once, telling me my hour was come. I was aggravated by their coming two at once, and also by Hattie's having boxed my ears from behind, and got really angry when my hair was violently pulled. So I gave Mary a kick on the shin, which made her roar, and put her 'hors du combat'[4] for a while, and scratched Hattie's wrists viciously. Having had a violent struggle, the fight at last ceased. I was ashamed of myself for losing my temper, though it was very aggravating. I thought Mary was not sufficiently paid for her share in the aforesaid assault and battery by the kick, so I invited her over for the afternoon, and prepared a salted banana for her. She not being here by half past three, I decided that she was not coming, so put on my old dress and went up the hill, to help Mama and the boys prune and fix up. I cleared out the dead part of the yellow rose bush, and cut out a lot also from the prairie rose, getting along pretty well, in spite of my fears of a large black and yellow snake which Harry says he saw, and only getting one thorn into my thumb. As I was getting chilly and thinking I might as well go down, I heard someone calling "Alice! Alice!" and saw Mary Fifield near the foot of the hill. Down the road I rushed, brandishing the pruning knife in the air; and we went in. I presented her with the salt banana, which she began eating, and contrary to my expectations did not spit it out, but said "Why, what makes this banana so salt?" "Salt?" said I, opening my eyes innocently. "Yes," said she "awfully salt; just taste there," and I took a very dainty nip, and spit out that little. "How queer," said I. "Mine isn't so." I suggested that it might only be the flavor of the rotten part, and that she should try farther down; and as I had only salted the end, this arrangement was satisfactory, and she selected a book. Mama afterwards came in and let the cat out of the bag. Mary vowed vengance, which vow I fear she will keep only too well. I walked home with her, and we had some fun and chases on the way. Bought bread at Parks, and saw Charley Bradley parading up and down on horseback.

May 12th

Sunday. Read and got along as best I could. Went up to the house and worked some; weeded a little and trimmed a considerable part of an althea. Afterwards went up again with Papa, went into the house and sat under the trees. Picked some very young cones to show Mama. Harry had a bad headache, and lay around in chairs with his eyes shut, looking white and miserable, which distressed me. I made him a cup of sage tea, which he drank with unexpected

---

4. Spelled correctly, *hors de combat* is French for disabled.

---

meekness, soaked his feet and bayrum-ed his head. While he was undergoing that last process he said "How Mary Fifield would laugh if she saw what you are doing!" and I said "She's quite welcome." Soon after the lamps were lighted he betook himself to bed. Bathed. Read one of Mr. Collyer's sermons in *Nature and Life*, and liked it. Cut something concerning him out of a paper.

May 13ᵗʰ

Monday. I accused Mama of scratching out something in my diary, and she confessed to having done so.[5] We had a conversation which nearly resulted in my giving up keeping a diary and burning the old ones, but the affair ended satisfactorily. Took Pirus Japonica[6] and fruit blossoms to Mary Fifield.

May 14ᵗʰ

Tuesday. Harry aggravated me by saying he should get a divorce from his wife unless she took his name, which seemed to me both a skit[7] at Mama and an assertion that he had any right to decide for her in the matter. Transplanted a row of violets to the side of the Summerhouse, and pruned rose bushes. Am feeling very unhappy because I cant love God. No letters.

May 15ᵗʰ

Wednesday. Gathered some half blown lilies of the valley, the first of the season, and took them to school. Encountered Sadie, who perceived them with rapture, seized and smelt them, and thanked me when I gave her them. Said they had a bed, but it being under the trees did not blossom so soon. Lent me her definitions to copy. Mary abused me for not giving them to her, and on the strength of it filled my inkstand with peanut shells, and knocked me on the head with my own History. After school as we came out Sadie said her mother was sick of rheumatic fever, and the flowers were just the thing to give her. Said she would pay me back in rosetime; I told her we had lots of roses; she mentioned cherries, apples, pears etc. but we had them all, and I told her if she wished to pay me to come and see me sometime; to which she made no answer. Josie Jones tried to make me promise her some. Passed two notes to Mary Fifield and balled at recess. Went into Boston with Josie, who made the conductor let me pass free, much to my disgust. Her father has something to do with the road. I charitably let her inflict her company on me from the station to the Public Library and Hamilton Place. Went carpethunting with Mama. We

5. Lucy had scratched out several words from Alice's entry on April 4th.

6. *Pieris japonica*, sometimes called "Valley Valentine," is a broad-leaved evergreen with deep rose pink flowers.

7. A "skit," in this context, means a satirical reflection or "a hit upon."

saw some beautiful ones, and I dont know which to choose. Decided on a dress at Hoveys, and came out home. Got books.

May 16ᵗʰ

Thursday. Took 3 bunches of Lilies to school; gave one to Josie, one to Hattie Mann, and the other to Mary Fifield. Went in a second time to look at carpets with Papa and Mama, but did not decide on any. We went into one large store where we were taken up and down in an elevator.[8] My eyes were sore, and hurt me. Finally worried about that idea Mr. Collyer put into my head, as to whether I had just to try my best to 'do my duty in that station of life unto which I am called' or whether it is no use unless I love God; which I dont. I decided for the first. I wish I could love him. Maybe if I try my best to do right he will help me about the loving; certainly I dont see that I can help myself. Papa and I jumped upon a moving train, which Mama missed, and we afterward drove about with a trial horse; that is Papa did; I sat shivering behind.

May 17ᵗʰ

Friday. Hattie Mann gave me some violets. Played base ball before school and at recess. Cut a picture of a queer creature out of *Harper[s]*, and pasted it on white paper; wrote under it "This is the animal that fills people's inkstands with rubbish. Scat you brute!" and gave it to Mary Fifield. Went in for the third time with Mama to look at carpets, and finally decided on a dark crimson. Still no letter! Heard Mrs. Livermore in the office detailing her woes and vexation to Mrs. Hinckley, and enjoyed it. I always like to hear Mrs. Livermore talk.[9] Came out alone, and walked up with Mr. Horne and Sarah Glass. Harry had a headache.

May 18ᵗʰ

Saturday. Ball at recess, and a good deal of Sadie's notice. Took two great bouquets of lilies of the valley to her and Hattie. I hid them under my cloak, but Josie smelled them out, and of course I was surrounded; and if the rightful owners had not opportunely arrived they might have missed their flowers, though I did my best to save them. Went into Boston again, kept office a while,

8. They probably shopped at Goldthwait's, a carpet store on Washington St., that featured in its ads a "passenger elevator to all parts of the building." Most elevators at this time were drum and rope elevators.

9. Mary Livermore (1829–1905), temperance and suffrage leader, and lecturer, was a close associate of Alice's parents. In January 1872, she resigned as editor of the WJ and began a lecturing circuit that would last for the next twenty-three years, averaging 120 lectures a year (NAW).

and came out bringing flowers with Mama. After supper went up the hill to dig a place on the mound for the verbenas we brought out, leaving Mama, who was coming after, to bring the plants. She didn't, so I went back for them; when I got them up I found she had changed her mind and did not want them planted till next day. After some wandering about the house came down, leaving Mama to go back with Papa, Mr. Carter and the Hinkleys, who were driving up the hill.

May 19th

Sunday. Made some cookies all myself. They were very good, only not quite sweet enough. Then I tried a thin cake made the same way, only with apple and pear blossoms which I put in to flavor it (but they didn't.) Washed my chimese, made my bed, read *Nature and Life* a little, and fed my chickens. A very dreary, rainy disagreeable day, followed by a very rainy, misty, dreary, disagreeable evening. After supper we all took a ride with our new horse, whom I want to call Du Guesclin, but we had some trouble with the harness. At last we started, and rode over to Mr. Haines', getting back at about half past eight. He is a splendid goer, and does what Papa calls ambling. Papa paid $400. for him; a frightful price, and is beginning to repent, so tries to see all the beauty in the horse he can; and it really is a splendid creature. Bathed.

May 20th

Monday. Ball. Carried a huge lot of valley lilies to school, and distributed them. Of course there was a rush for them. Got Kitty's answer to my renunciation at last. I copy it word for word.

"Madam:
I accept my dismissal. I fling all your charges in your teeth! Base slanderer of a gallant sailor, I defy you to prove me a traitor! I have never hitherto believed, but am now forced to do so, that *"All* Women are faithless."
Beware! My anger is excited, and I hereby vow vengeance.
Defiance till death to slanders! Protection to the oppressed!
R. Kidd.
Captain R.N.
H.M.B.S.S. Vanguard
H.B.M.D.A.C."

I dont understand all those titles, but I have no doubt they mean treason. Now I suspect Kitty means to follow up her vow of vengance in person. The letter is not dated, and I think she left it behind for Aunt Elizabeth to post. I think

Uncle George is escorting her home.[10] If there wasn't something up would she have waited 17 days before answering my letter, and sent <u>such</u> an answer, just about the time she must have received my conciliatory letter. Now to the winds, all my vain dreams! The persons name shall never defile my diary again—till next time. I perpetrated some dismal poetry, and planted two hills of musk melons secretly. Got a *Young Folks*, and to console me for The Person's villainy, find that the Molly thing is accepted.[11] But I haven't told. Went down to the Square for some bread and to call on Mary and show her The Person's letter. She was out, but I met her, showed her, and she said it served me right, and wanted me to finish my unsuccessful call; but Sadie appearing and poking me with an umbrella bade me walk home with her, and of course I followed my Leige Lady. I went with her to Fields Corner, and she said her mother bade her thank me for the lilies. I left her and went home. At recess the leader of the other side of the base bawlers said that such a girl was hers. "Well, Alice is mine; aren't you, Alice?" said my sovereign; and I said "I am." She said "I am proud to own you, Alice." I said, "I am proud to belong to you." Then the girls laughed and we played.

May 21st

Tuesday. Went into Boston in the afternoon, renewed two books and changed the rest, left a message at Goldthwait's, and lugged out the heaviest load I ever took yet. Gathered a bunch of lupines between here and Neponset, fed my chickens and helped Miss Tucker do up the supper dishes. Read in the evening. M.P. No. 2.[12]

May 22nd

Wednesday. Gave Carrie Horne her lilies . . . and Miss Tolman what was left of the ch[r]ysanthemum things, after the assault in the yard. Sadie chose me at recess, and when I batted the ball away said "Good! I stand up for Alice!" A row between Annie and Miss Tucker. Finished the maple sugar. Worked at the house. Planted seeds under Mr. Murphy's directions, and got Frank to roll out the stump, on which I planted various things. Dug up part of a bed by the

10. George Blackwell (1832–1912), Henry's younger, unmarried brother, was a successful businessman who lived in New York City. He had been visiting his sisters Elizabeth (in London) and Anna (in Paris), as well as other relatives in Scotland and Wales. Kitty frequently accompanied him on short trips outside of London; in this case it is unclear where the two of them had been.

11. Notice of the acceptance of Alice's poem "Molly and the Brook" appeared in the May issue of *Our Young Folks*.

12. This is Alice's notation for her second menstrual period.

Summer house. Got a letter from Kitty, which has entirely reinstated her in my affections.

M.P. Continued.

May 23ᵈ

Thursday. Lent M. Fifield *Ungava*, and got a mis-spelled note in return, full of protestations of hopeless adoration, accompanied by threats of suicide. Had good luck at baseball. Our side got in and stayed in till the end of recess, and made the rounds safely twice. Rainy. In the afternoon made three lemon and one orange pie, also a lot of tarts and some bad lemonade.

May 24ᵗʰ

Friday. Took flowers to school, and played base ball. Sadie almost always chooses me, to my bliss. Worked in the garden, planting, weeding, etc. and dug a pailful of greens, for which I am to receive $.15. Nearly broke my back doing it. Began a letter to Kitty.

May 25ᵗʰ

Saturday. Rainy. Thunder and Lightening. We had one of Mrs. Caudle's "curtain lectures" for the reading lesson, and such a time as we had over it![13] A universal chuckling and tittering filled the room; Hattie Mann was as red as a boiled lobster, and Josie Jones had her face down on her desk in hysterics. We were almost all of us shaking like jellies, and my voice shook in spite of me when I read. We got worked up to a high pitch of nervous excitement, and were kept 10ᵐ after 12, because Willie Elder and Etty Sharpe were too much overcome to read, and had to be waited for. They would get up, begin, stop short and shake all over. Went to Boston through a furiously heavy rain, kept office and got *Mrs. Caudle's Curtain Lectures*. Came home, gathered lupins and saw a snake.

May 26ᵗʰ

Sunday. Worked in the garden and got catnip for Toby. Wrote to Kitty. Took a ride in the afternoon over to Mr. Jackson's greenhouse, where we saw some beautiful plants, though he was away. I didn't enjoy the ride much, being cold, and squeezed onto the front seat with Papa and Mr. Carter, who talked horses and politics.

13. The class was reading from *Mrs. Caudle's Curtain Lectures* by the British humorist Douglas William Jerrold, known by his pseudonym, "Punch." The "lectures" were a series of diatribes delivered by Mrs. Caudle to her long-suffering husband, Job, on the joys, duties, and vicissitudes of their married life.

May 27th

Monday. Took flowers and hid them in the long grass on the bank till the owners appeared, yet had to stand a violent siege. I had given Hattie Burdett some lilies, and Sadie, who had none, accused her of having got uncommonly fond of me lately; but seeing one of the calicanthus buds, she begged it of me, and having received it said she had always considered me an angel. I instantly underwent a storm of reproaches from the other girls, who had tried in vain to get the said bud. School is not to stop the week after the fourth; a prospect most horrible, and at which we scholars are justly indignant. Trimmed 5 or 6 altheas, and trie[d] to doctor the rose bushes for bugs according to the receipt in *Scribners Monthly*, but did not succeed very well. A letter from Florence. She has seen that thing in the *Young Folks*, and I must write and shut her up, or my plot will be prematurely exploded.

May 28th

Tuesday. Miss Tolman and half the school were absent at parade drill, whatever that may be, and half the rest stayed away on that account. Mr. Horne gave us a long and stupid general examination. In the afternoon hurried down to school, and got permission from Miss Tolman, who arrived just as school began, to spend the afternoon playing truant. The rain escorted me from the schoolhouse to Tremont Temple and cleared up when I got under cover. Spent a very stupid afternoon, as neither Mr. Garrison nor Mr. Collyer spoke, though Mr. G. was there.[14] I sat in a dark pew and made my eyes ache trying to read the Caudle lectures. There was a sharp faced young lady on the same seat who reminded me of Desire Ledwith.[15] Mr. Garrison shook hands with me at the end of the meeting though, which was something. Dried my feet at Mrs. Larissey's fire,[16] took supper at Marston's, and then went to the evening session. Mrs. Campbell spoke, Mrs. Livermore splurged, and I dozed through it in the gallery. Two young puppies on the bench behind me disturbed me by talking, sneering at the speakers, and kicking the bench, and when they went away one of them patted me on the back and said "Goodbye, dear." Horrid little scoundrel! When the Editress of the *New North West*,[17] a lady I dont like at all, began to speak, I retreated to the dressing room, and waited, sleepy and

14. Alice was attending the afternoon and evening sessions of NEWSA held at Tremont Temple (*BDET*: 28 May 1872).

15. Desire Ledwith is a character in *The Daisy Chain* by Charlotte Yonge.

16. Mrs. Larrisey either assisted in the *WJ* office or lived in an apartment in the same building.

17. The "Editress" of the *New Northwest* was Abigail Duniway (1834–1915), Oregon suffrage leader and lecturer (*NAW*).

Tremont Temple.

thirsty, till the meeting was over, and we drove home with Du Guesclin, who had been left at a livery stable. Posted my letter to Florence.

May 29th

Wednesday. Made my head ache over the arithmetic examination, and was invited by Hattie Mann to play croquet with her in the afternoon; which I did. Hattie and Lulu and I played first several games, in all of which I was beaten; then a Miss Whitton, whom they called Esther,[18] joined us, and we played two more games, in the second of which Hattie and I won; and I left with the glory of victory upon me. The apple trees were full of canker worms which swung in the air about our heads; and the girls were constantly shrieking to have them pulled off their necks. Mrs. Campbell slept with me.

May 30th

Thursday. Decoration day and a holiday. Worked in the garden trimming currant bushes and weeding the strawberry bed. In the afternoon went into

18. Esther Whitton was probably related to Alice's Harris School chum Maggie Whitton.

Boston with Miss Tucker, got the letters from the P.O. and returned 3 books at the Atheneum. The Public was closed. Came out in the rain, got wet, and washed.

May 31ˢᵗ

Friday. Miserably rainy, as I did not wear any water proof to school. Grammar examination. Made a lemon pie and some burnt tart crusts. Miss Tucker nagged me till I was ready to burst with rage, and privately exploded to Harry, who reciprocated. Had a long rainy dreary disagreeable dreary ride, during which I lost one of my garters.

JUNE

June 1ˢᵗ

Saturday. Spelling examination. Weeded the strawberry bed, planted the marigolds and put wood ashes on my melons. Annie left, looking, O so pretty, and left me feeling O so miserable. Robert Collyer—not the Laird animal—is going to preach in Boston Tomorrow and I am going to hear him.

June 2ⁿᵈ

Sunday. Drove over to the South End with Papa to hear Robert Collyer.[1] We got a seat under the desk in the front row, where we heard every word, though when he stood up I could not see more than the top of his head without stretching my neck. Of course it was a good sermon; very good; the text was "Let your light shine" and I came home with a vision of sparks dancing before my eyes, and a determination to snuff my candle. He acted very much as he did in Harrison Square, rolling about in the pulpit and gesticulating violently; and once he amused me very much by leaning over the desk and shaking his fist at the congregation, to add force to his remarks. During the hyms I sang when I had the words, and Papa, who did not have them at all, stood up and howled melodiously. I like to see Mr. Collyer get excited, and red and shiny, and he is so much in earnest that you must respect him if you dont agree with him, though I do. After the sermon Papa wanted me to go up and speak to him, but I was afraid he would think I wanted another kiss, so I didn't. We drove home through the beautiful weather, with every horse chestnut a mass of bloom, and Papa seeming much happier than usual, and I feeling extremely good. Hadn't I been to church, and taken my testament with me? Drove to Squantum in the afternoon and got white violets. A fight with Papa and *Antiquary*.

1. Collyer preached at the Church of the Unity on Newton St.

June 3ᵈ

Monday. Went to school, and found there was none, so went into Boston and decided on a grey and rose carpet, the expensiveness of which rather rubbed my conscience, dined at Marston's, looked at papers, and changed my Public Library books. Selected 4 at the Atheneum and found none could be taken out. Rode home with Mama and bought a lot of things at Field's Corner.

June 4ᵗʰ

Tuesday. School. Drawing. Base ball. Hattie monitor. I No. 6, and next Eddy Jenkins. Weeded the strawberry bed with Harry. I told him what Annie said about his having a fine voice, and he said he hadn't, for it was changing; but I saw him lying among the strawberries grinning and he sang and whistled all the rest of the time. Mrs. Campbell came.

June 5ᵗʰ

Wednesday. A great storm. Went over to Squantum in the afternoon on account of the storm, and got soaked above the knees, so that I had to change everything. Went around Moswetusket hill and picked some seaweed. Mrs. Campbell scared me by hinting that I was going to die, and I had an imaginary lung fever on the spot. But I am alive, though Mama lectured me and was disgusted with Mrs. C. and Miss Tucker for letting me go.

June 6ᵗʰ

Thursday. Read *Woman in White* to Mrs. Campbell in the afternoon. A *Ledger* came, and was duly devoured.

June 7ᵗʰ

Friday. Went in to Boston and chose my wall paper. A Grammar ex.—in afternoon. Mine all right but that detestable "sons' in law"—horrid creatures! Tried to make up my mind to bear my expected deafness and was pleasantly reassured by Mrs. Campbell's proving it was my heart I heard beating.[2]

June 8ᵗʰ

Saturday. Was interrupted in the thick of *The Cameron Pride* by Mama's suggesting with a sweet smile that I should empty the slops; I did it, barely

2. In letters to Kitty at this time, Alice details her problems with plural possessives. She also complains about the beating in her left ear, concluding that she believes she has every disease she can think of, from heart disease to insanity, and "tuberculosis on the brain" (ASB to KBB: 2 June and 8 June 1872, LC).

refraining from an explosion. I hate—oh how I do hate that amused pity and grinning 'poor little mouse' that one's elders sometimes inflict on one! I understand now how Kitty hated the "Poor little foal of an oppresse'd race." Went over to Hattie Mann's by invitation, to darn stocking. Annie Phips came, and after she left I had some fun with Hattie. We fainted and tried gymnastics, then took a walk, stopping at the P.O. and Hattie treated me to a pickled lime, which I ate and enjoyed. Papa and Aunt Marian came, the latter looking sweet and Quakery with her white hair like silver. And Capt. Kidd's diary came!! I squealed like a steam whistle, and hugged it to my bosom.[3] Had the nightmare, possibly because I kept cloves in my mouth all night in fear of toothache.

June 9th

Sunday. Mince pies, and made up a bundle to Kitty. Bathed. Annie [McLeod] came in the P.M. according to promise, and was hugged. Went up to the house with Papa and Aunt M. Washed.

June 10th

Monday. A shindy[4] at school with Mary F. In the afternoon went into Boston to see the dentist and get my picture taken, as Aunt M. wants one to match Florence's, (a very good one which I covet). The D. was out; the pictures universally pronounced the best I have had taken for years.

June 11th

Tuesday. Harry moved to his room in the upper house. We bought a cow. Had a dreadful time getting up in the morning and going into Boston in the P.M. but am much much too hot, mosquitoey, and aggravated by Miss Tucker's presence to write about it now. I went to Neponset, and got upon the train without a ticket; got off at H[arrison] S[quare] and came back for it. Got some pennies from Miss Tucker and scurried to Neponset. Got there barely in time, found to my horror when the conductor came round that the fare was 22c[ents] and I had but 15. Was allowed to go at half price. Dentist out. Changed books, waited for Papa at office, went with him to choose gas fixtures, and drove home with the duke.

---

3. Marian Blackwell (1818–97), Henry's one sister without a strong professional interest, was ready to leave the U.S. for Europe, where, for the rest of her life, she would divide her time living with or near her sisters, Anna (in Paris and Nice) and Elizabeth (in London and Hastings, England). Kitty had sent her diary first to Emily Blackwell with directions that it should next be sent to Florence, and then to Alice (ASB to KBB: 12 Oct. 1872, LC).

4. A "shindy" is also a shindig, meaning an uproar or commotion.

June 12ᵗʰ

Wednesday. School in the morning. Washed windows and swept up at the new house, and didn't enjoy it. Thermometer 78 in the shade. Stewed in my summer things. Am worried dreadfully by the bellowing of our cow, who roars at intervals of from half a second to five minutes. It's really unbearable! Have been stimulated by *Stretton* to a wish for the particulars of the Indian Mutiny or Sepoy Rebellion, or whatever is the correct and historical name of that disturbance in India 14 years ago. ⁵

June 13ᵗʰ

Thursday. Another stewing day. No ball. Washed a window at the upper house. Found an account of the India mutiny in my history, but short and not very satisfactory. Sufficient unto the day was the heat thereof,—and more so.

June 14ᵗʰ

Friday. The anniversary of my great villainy. One year ago today I did the meanest and wickedest thing I ever did in all my life; and learnt a lesson against curiosity which I hope will last me one while.⁶ It is a stewing day, the hottest yet; and oh so mosquitoey! The house is in a most uncomfortable state, as we are just in the betwixt and between of moving, and have no rest for the soles of our feet, except on bare boards. Nothing particular has happened. Those villainous carpet men have broken their appointment again. A thunder shower in the afternoon with lightning that scared me onto the bed.

I have been reading over the account of that vile performance in my other diary; and I think I feel in a small way as Peter must have done after he swore at Jesus; only I was totally without excuse. I am ready to bite myself when I think of it. Read *Stretton*.

June 15ᵗʰ

Saturday. The boys declaimed. We are just at that stage of the moving during which we live in neither the one house nor the other, and have no rest for the soles of our feet. When I came back from Boston where I had gone to the dentist I found they had moved most of the things to the upper house. Then

5. Alice's interest in India was not only prompted by Henry Kingsley's book *Stretton*, but also by the fact that her late uncle, Howard Blackwell (1831–66), had been caught up in the 1858 mutiny when he worked there on behalf of the East India Company. Physically debilitated, he never recovered from the ordeal.
6. Alice is again referring to her reading of Alice Earle's diary.

the beds went up, and I slept in my old room for the first time since the fire. My room seems pleasant, cool and nice, but my furniture hasn't come.[7]

June 16th

Sunday. I am just ready to swear! That detestable woman, Miss Tucker, rushed upon poor Toby to put him out of the dining room; I seized her; she shoo'd; he fled; I threatened to make her run (when she boasted of having made him run), by popping out upon her from behind a door, all of course in fun, when Papa and Mama came down upon me and shut me up, as if I had been swearing; and I forthwith drew into my shell and maintained a stony silence during dinner, while I inwardly boiled with wrath. So Miss Tucker is to insult me and my cat at pleasure, is she, and I not to say a word, even in fun? I hate her—I hate her; the nasty provoking stuck up insolent thing! And Mama likes her so much that I am afraid she will stay, as she stays now, holding her threat of leaving over our heads as if it was not the thing I should be gladdest of, and making the house unbearable to me as she did to poor Annie, so that she left, which I cant, worse luck. But if she continues her insolence and perpetual nagging, I'll beg borrow or steal money enough to pay my passage to England, and be off by the next Cunarder; for I wont stay here and be insulted by that conceited old mischief maker—I wont, that's flat! Drove over to Mr. Weld's, and was talked to some by him. He asked me how I was and if I lived according to the laws of nature; and [I] didn't know what to say, so said I was afraid not; he asked if I took plenty of exercise in the open air, and I said I didn't; and he said "Be thyself, child; don't be anybody else!" and I said I couldn't be two people at the same time, and I guess looked very much puzzled as I certainly felt, for he twisted his face all up, and laughed, and as we got into the carriage to go bade me again most emphatically to "be myself." He is so queer! And as we drove home I thought of how I felt the last time we came back from there, nearly a year ago, after a little bit of retribution.[8]

---

7. Alice chose a dark red carpet for her room, dark furnitiure and white curtains (ASB to KBB: "n.d." and "1871" added incorrectly in another hand; internal evidence, however, indicates the letter was written sometime in June. LC).

8. Theodore Dwight Weld (1803–95), fiery abolitionist orator and educational reformer, was living with his wife, Angelina (1805–79), and her sister, Sarah Grimké (1792–1873), in the Dorchester area known as Hyde Park. The Grimké sisters' determination to lecture on antislavery in the 1830s (when it was considered unwomanly to speak in public) catapulted them onto center stage of the earliest woman's rights controversies. After 1840, the three turned their energies into less public reform activity and also operated or taught in progressive schools in New Jersey, New York, and Massachusetts. In 1871, Alice appeared in a school dramatic production that Weld directed. The family,

June 17ᵗʰ

Monday. No school, on account of the battle of Bunker hill, 96 years ago. Bells and guns before I was up, after dreaming of *Stretton*; one of those queer dreams I sometimes have, which I am really sorry to wake from; not that they are specially pleasant, but absorbing and intensely interesting.

June 18ᵗʰ

Tuesday. Hot. Went to Boston to look at furniture with Mama. The set I liked best cost $300, and of course was out of the question, so I chose one cheaper but still expensive. Then we looked at chairs. I am to have one big easy one, and I want one of two Turkish chairs we saw—and sat in. Harry went to the Jubilee.[9]

June 19ᵗʰ

Wednesday. Fanny Benedict sent me a note asking for the moss rosebud on my desk; I gave it [to] her and asked her to come and see me; she is to ask her mother. Went over to Hattie Mann's to play croquet. We played 19 games; I beat 12, she 7, and I whitewashed her once; but she beat the last game in a very provoking manner, so I left with demonstrations of wrath and vengeance, and threats of poison. A *Ledger* came, and was read. Harry left.

June 20ᵗʰ

Thursday. I am cross! I have had to undergo a severe trial of my feelings; I have had Fanny Benedict and Minnie Knapp carry on a violent flirtation in my presence, and been a witness to that idiotic spectacle. I was going to cultivate the "social virtues" and had invited Fanny over for the afternoon and gone down to the school house to meet her at 4 oclock, when the afternoon school was let out. She was engaged with Minnie, and proposed we should go the long

---

by then in semiretirement, but still with vigorous opinions, enjoyed a close circle of longtime reform friends, among them the Stone Blackwells, who apparently also shared with them an interest in Alice Earle and her family. Alice's reference to retribution suggests some connection between her reading of Alice's Earle's diary with a visit to the Weld's the year before (*DAB*, *NAW*, and ASB to KBB: 19 Mar. 1871, LC).

9. The anniversary of the Battle of Bunker Hill, the first major battle of the American Revolution, coincided with the opening of a two-week International World Peace Jubilee and International Musical Festival, crowding Boston with visitors and dignitaries from all over the world. Features included parades with British and German bands, flag-decorated buildings, special exhibits, concerts, and receptions. Many activities centered around a vast Coliseum ("temporarily" built for a similar Jubilee in 1869), located on newly developing Copley Square.

way, so she could walk part way home with Minnie, and M. gave me her books to carry, being too fat and lazy to do it herself. She recommended me to read them, and I took her at her word and dove into a piece book, as they sauntered along at the rate of a mile a day. Presently "There they go, and we aren't going their way nor they ours." Then Fanny caught up with me, and proposed that we should cut across lots. I supposed the attraction was some young men lying under a tree, but found it was two of the high school boys going up our hill. By cutting across we got onto the same road with them, and then began the horrors. Fanny and Minnie began talking very loud, and wishing they could find a 4 leaved clover, and trying to attract the attention of the young men before us, also talking of my Betrothed very loudly, and making me very uncomfortable. We overtook them just by our gate, so I slipped through, and quickly put a hedge and two bushes between me and the creatures, with whom those girls had stopped. So the 4 chattered outside the gate for some quarter of an hour, defacing our hedge meantime. I stood in the yard and remembered the third commandment.[10] At last Fanny and Minnie parted from the entra[n]ceing youths, and Fanny rushed in and commanded me to get two rosebuds; I did so; the boys were going down the hill; she flung the buds over the hedge, but the boys did not see them. She then flew to the Summer house, sat in the window and waved her hand kerchief at them. When they were gone, I remarked to the air that I was going to write to Kitty and tell him that if he came home to dangle at my apron string and make me do all the courting I would break the engagement.[11] As I will. Which remark greatly edified them. The boys reappeared, and produced more excitement. At last I got them onto the housetop. They didn't look at the view; they looked for the boys, and made mysterious signs at them with handkerchiefs. At last they left. I walked a little way with them, but seeing those males waiting in the road, abruptly took my leave and came home, with a comparitively low opinion of my fellow creatures. I descended to the cellar, groped my way to the milkroom, and soothed my irritated feelings by drinking an enormous quantity of milk.

In the morning Mary and Lottie Bathgate called. Mama being out, I took them to the top of the house, where the[y] drove me nearly frantic by inquiring about localities, of the which I am profoundly ignorant. Among other things they asked me if Beacon St. was at Savin Hill! [12]

---

10. "Thou shalt not take the name of the Lord . . . in vain."

11. Alice deliberately used male pronouns here to perpetuate the myth of her engagement.

12. Savin Hill is in Dorchester. Alice's guests confused it with Beacon Hill.

June 21st

Friday. The longest day in the year, and certainly the hottest we have had yet. Stewing, boiling, frying, baking, roasting, fricaseeing. School in the morning, with the first class absent and also half the second. Weeded the strawberry bed in the afternoon. Drove down to the station to get Emma [Lawrence], as Frank does not know her. I wanted to go alone, but Mama was afraid to have me drive Du Guesclin (whom they will persist in calling Billy.) Accordingly, when we were fairly under way, I got Frank to give me the reins, and drove both ways.

June 22nd

Saturday. Another stewing day. Only about 12 scholars present, out of the 50. At dinner Papa said he was liable to fits of insanity, especially after drinking cider, which remark would have scared me dreadfully had I not known that he is given to making extravagant speeches. Also a counter-irritation was produced by Mama's expressing her belief that we are coming to poverty. However I know how to empty slops, and if worst comes to worst can probably get a situation as chambermaid.

June 23d

Sunday. A heavy sea fog. Garden work, and wrote to Kitty.

June 24th

Monday. Promotion, ex. in Arithmatic. Went in with Emma to the Public. Emma got a letter calling her home at once, so I went with Mr. Campbell.[13] Books at Public, and home.

June 25th

Tuesday. For several days there has been a heavy sea fog, which still lasts. A day of disasters. We just missed our train, so were late. A number of smaller aggravations arising from Miss Tucker, and a standing ride to the Coliseum, where I arrived in a very savage state of mind. We had tickets, but every seat was full, as were aisles and sides, and we had to stand up. The music was fine, but the anvil chorus was not so loud as I expected, maybe because it lacked the

---

13. John Campbell, Margaret's husband, an artist specializing in crayon drawings, also worked with his wife on behalf of the suffrage cause. When the couple were in Boston, they lived in the same building that housed the offices of the *WJ*, and where he also kept a studio.

cannon accompaniment.[14] We left, and walked over to the South Boston depot, and at last got home. From the time I left Hsn Squ. to the time I got back, I had not sat 5ᵐ· I haven't been so tired for an age. My carpet smelt so, I had to sleep in the upper room. At the office I found a check for $3. in payment of the Molly thing. Papa had opened the letter, and he and Mrs. Campbell teased me; which didn't increase my amiability.

June 26th

Wednesday. A heavy sea fog still. Went into Boston with Mamma in the after-noon; got *[Glenmahra; or] the Western Highlands,*[15] also a *Ledger.* "Mark Heber's Luck" is finished up.

June 27th

Thursday. Promotion examination in Grammar. Mr. Horne took me up into the hall and made me read him Mrs. Caudle's curtain lecture. He wants me to do it at exhibition. Soon after dinner I drove Mama down to the station and left her there, she warning me to be careful of the corners coming home, which warnings I somewhat laughed at. Coming round the corner into our yard, the carriage upset, and I found myself being bumped about and then lying on the ground while the Duke tore on to the barn with the carriage bouncing about behind him. Finding that none of my bones were broken I picked myself up and went into the house, feeling somewhat bewildered. Miss Tucker, when she found me alive went out with Frank and me to see if the Duke was hurt. His hind legs are scratched, but that is all. I did up my bruises with arnica, and went down to meet Mama, who I knew would expect the carriage. Meeting Sadie and Addie Calender, I gave them an account of the performances, and repeated it to Mama when I met her. Mama became very blue and lamented that horse and carriage had not both been knocked to bits. My damages consist of 5 bruises and a bump. The scare had the effect of tansy tea, and brought on M.P. number 3.

14. Alice attended the Peace Jubilee festivities at the Coliseum the same day President Grant was in the audience. One newspaper account headlined, "Four Acres and a Half of People in the Coliseum" and claimed that between ten and fifteen thousand people packed the building, so vast a crowd that many were unaware that the president was there. The gargantuan concert featured Johann Strauss conducting an orchestra of one thousand members, a "vast" chorus, and one hundred firemen who hammered on anvils (imported from Birmingham, England) during the performance of the "Anvil Chorus" (*BDET*: 17 and 26 June 1872; *WJ*: 29 June 1872 [story by Emma Lawrence]).

15. Alice wrote this as *Tales of the Western Highlands.*

June 28ᵗʰ

Friday. Could hardly stand on my feet in the morning, and couldn't go to school. Mama put me to bed with hot flat irons and gin, and when I felt better I got up and spent the day reading, dawdling and practicing on our recovered piano.

June 29ᵗʰ

Saturday. A tiresome rehearsal for exhibition[16] and a visit from the Swedish minister, in honor of whom school kept till a quarter past 12, to the wrath of Charley Bradley. He remonstrated, and Miss Tolman came down upon him. Said the Merman piece at last. Awfully hot.

June 30ᵗʰ

Sunday. Papa arrived, and the first effect of the news of the accident on him was to make him scold. The hottest day I have ever known, or at least one of them. We all stewed. Wrote to Florence. Drove out to Squantum in the evening. Picked up Mrs. Butterfield and took her along.

JULY

July 1ˢᵗ

Monday. The last day of school, and the hottest of the year. Stupid rehearsals in the morning. Went in white through a stewing sun, leaving my music books, and had to race home for them, getting back barely in time. The hall was fearfully hot, and Mr. Adams in his speech "welcomed the audience to this oven" and said as they were probably half done they would be glad to know that the performances were nearly done too, and begged their pardon for baking them a little longer. He said that Harris was the highest among the Dorchester schools, and [Charley] Bradley had the highest % of the Harris [students] and so was the 1ˢᵗ scholar in Dorchester; and Mr. Horne corrected him by saying that Mary Fifield had just the same %. There was singing and recitations etc. Sadie Wilson spoke "Ivry" and she <u>can</u> speak.[1]

---

16. Alice and her classmates were rehearsing for the Harris School exhibition to be held on 1 July at Lyceum Hall.

---

1. Sadie was reciting the ballad "Ivry, A Song of the Huguenots," by English statesman and historian Thomas Macauley (1800–59).

First Parish Church and Lyceum Hall—Meeting House Hill.

July 2ⁿᵈ

Tuesday. A Mrs. Dennet[2] and two men came to dinner. Mrs. D. is going to stay over night. She kissed me when I was presented, and I slipped away to the pump and washed my face. Cherries were picked by me, with the help of Collins and another little Irish boy sent down to me by Mama. Made a table for my den out of a box and towels.

July 3ᵈ

Wednesday. Sick at my stomach, and went minus my dinner. Rode into Boston with Papa, Mama and Mrs. Dennet. Sent off *The Boy in Grey* to Miss Andrews, and got *The Cruise of the Midge* from the Atheneum.

July 4ᵗʰ

Thursday. Overslept myself and was late for breakfast. Guns. Transplanted my squash last night. Rained and blew. A sore throat. Drove down to the

2. Probably Mrs. Oliver Dennet from Portland, Maine, who, that fall, helped Margaret Campbell set up local woman suffrage organizations in that state.

dressmakers with Papa, and had a bad fright coming home on account of the lightning and our horse getting scared. Fireworks were flashing all round the horizon when I went to bed.

July 5th

Friday. Weeded, and tried to fix a bower under the altheas. Shelled peas, and read and practiced. Mrs. Dennet is still here. Picked a basket of cherries for Mrs. Campbell. Florence, Edith and Grace are invited here.[3]

July 6th

Saturday. Had a beautiful sail with Mr. and Mrs. Campbell. They were to hoist a black flag, and I was put upon the watch for it, and wished it had been my pirate lover. When it appeared Papa, Mama, Mrs. Dennet and I drove down to the shore in the carriage, and found Mrs. C. sitting in the boat, her husband having gone up to the house to call us. When he came back we had a beautiful sail, lunching on cake and crackers, and landed on Moon island,[4] where we stayed just long enough for me to take a delightful bath. Moon Isl. reminds me of M[artha's] V[ineyard] only the cliffs are not high enough, and are grass grown. We landed at Squantum, where the carriage awaited us, and drove home with Mrs. Campbell.

July 7th

Sunday. Reading, ripping, practicing, etc. Sent a vituperative note to Mary Fifield, Papa being going there to see about a man.

July 8th

Monday. Drove into Boston with my parents. Dined at Marston's and changed my books. Waited 2-1/2 hours in the Public Library, and then Papa came for me and we drove home.

July 9th

Tuesday. Mama sick in bed all day with diarhoerra, and I did the nursing. Tried cherry jelly and failed.

July 10th

Wednesday. No *Ledger* nor letters. Papa brought a gentleman home. Walked down to Mary Fifield's to see about bathing houses, but she was out. I saw Sadie's little sister. There is a hammock in their yard.

---

3. Florence, Edith (1860–1906), and Grace (1863–1941) were Alice's cousins, daughters of Samuel and Antoinette Brown Blackwell.

4. Moon Island is now a peninsular extension of Squantum.

Savin Hill, from Old Colony Railroad.

July 11ᵗʰ

Thursday. Played a game of croquet and made a lot of lemonade. Mr. Oberlin Smith left.⁵ Got a letter from Kitty. We drove over to Savin Hill to see Mrs. Moore, and on the way saw Sadie, slender, dark haired and lovelier than ever.

July 12ᵗʰ

Friday. Papa and I made current jelly and wine in the morning. In the afternoon went into Boston and got the letters and *Ledger*. I had to race both ways, and dared not wait for my soda.

July 13ᵗʰ

Saturday. As I sat in the station waiting for the train to Boston, Mary Fifield appeared at the window, came in after shaking her fist at me, and we had a palaver. She knows where the bathman is, and agreed to go with me in the P.M. Had dinner and soda at Boston, and when I came out went to Mary's. She took me to her room, rightly called Barnum's museum, and showed me my letters, and some poetry Sadie had made on the death of a puppy. We bought and devoured some candy, and went to Mr. Cotter's, where we rang and knocked without effect, so we went down to the beach and found Mrs. C. who gave me the key of our old bath house. Mary could not go in, but lent me her bath house, dress and life preserver, and I had a delightful bath; in company with Sadie and sisters. Mary's bath house has all the modern improvements.

5. Oberlin Smith (b. 1840) was a mechanical engineer from New Jersey (*NCAB*, v. 12, 461).

July 14th

Sunday. Made two pincushions, footstool and wall case for our bath house. Took a ride in the evening.

July 15th

Monday. Perspired all day, and did not do much of anything else, except anticipate my evening bath, which Mama at last forbid. Nervous and miserable.

July 16th

Tuesday. Cherry jelly, which wont jell. A cold bath just after breakfast. Felt queer and nervous in the evening.

July 17th

Wednesday. Sick. In bed the first part of the day. Mary Fifield and Maggie Whitton called in the afternoon, and Mary and I after much mutual abuse made an appointment to drown one another tomorrow morning at 9. No *Ledger*!

July 18th

Thursday. Too damp and foggy to bathe. Drove to Mr. Garrison's and into Boston. Changed my books and inquired for my *Ledger*. Mrs. Hinckly said it came Wednesday. It was not among the papers in the office, and most certainly Papa has not brought it out. Got my August *Young Folks*. Molly has not yet appeared. Started to drive home with my parents, but they loaded the carriage so full of things that I couldn't stand it and came by the cars. Papa read ~~Waverly in~~ the *Antiquary* in the evening.

July 19th

Friday. Hot. I was not allowed to go in bathing, my feelings upon which had best not be recorded. Went down in the evening to call on Mary Fifield, who was with Lulu Mann. We disported ourselves in the streets in a decidedly disreputable manner, till it got so dark that I had to go home. Before I did so I kicked them both upon the shins and made them limp. As a general thing kicking is not fair, but they set upon me both at once, and I had to defend myself as best I could.

July 20th

Saturday. Went down to Mary Fifield's and found she was out. I underwent the severe trial to my feelings of speaking to the ferocious parent, who mistook me for a patient, as I went into the parlor during his hours, to wait for Mary. I got tired before she came, and started for the bathing house. Maggie Whitton saw my red sack disappearing around the corner, and came flying after me. We went in together, and had a good bath. I went out beyond my depth 3 times, twice with the life preserver and once without. I ducked Maggie Whitton's head under and she did the same to me. I lent the life preserver to Sadie's little sisters, and came out, after staying in rather too long. *The Antiquary* was read upon the roof, and I chased Papa about to tickle his toes. Florence is coming tomorrow. When I heard the news I screeched and flew off with two big bags.

July 21st

Sunday. Moved down to the lower room, with much regret.[6] Picked berries and then dressed. I heard carriage wheels and flew out. Papa, Uncle George, Florence and Edie. Florence has had her hair cut, and looks queer. Edie has become a real little beauty.[7] Florence and I played croquet and confabbed. Edie made straight for the book case. I put her to bed. We were all up on the roof, and Florence and myself, having got there first, were much vexed at the advent of the seniors and junior, and wrote brief but emphatic maledictions upon bits of slate, which we passed to and fro. Edie horrified us by reading aloud one which she had made out upside down.

July 22nd

Monday. We had counted upon a bath, but it was rainy and cold till afternoon. Read, practiced, wrestled with Edie and confabbed with Florence. Edie is so soft and plump and supple and warm and rosy and vigorous that I confess to being most unchristianly envious. Florence and I took a promenade in the evening, and read an account of the horrible murder of Mary Belle Secor, and the lynching of her murderers by the enraged populace.[8]

---

6. Alice had abandoned her regular room for a little southwest corner room on the third floor where she stayed during warmer weather, since it was "quite out of the temperate zone of furnace heat." She admitted that her mother preferred having her downstairs so that "she might feel me under her wing," but Alice found she took "more comfort up there than in my lower room. . . . There is the view and the airiness, and then my lower room is beautifully furnished and I don't feel at ease in it—I am always afraid of soiling or spoiling something" (ASB to KBB: 17 Jan. 1873, SL).

7. Edie was then eleven.

8. These grisly events took place in Mercer County, Ohio (sixty miles north of Dayton, on the Indiana border). Secor was on her way home from Sunday school on June 23, when she was "outraged," then murdered, and her body "thrown aside" to be partly consumed by hogs before it was discovered. Three men were arrested and jailed in Celina, where three thousand enraged people later gathered and forced the prisioners from their cells, marched them to a farm twelve miles away—the site of the crime—and hung two of them. The youngest prisoner was returned to jail (*Toledo Blade*: 9 and 10 July, 1872).

July 23ᵈ

Tuesday. Florence, Edie and I went down to bathe soon after dinner. Florence being unwell did not go in, but sat on the shore and timed us. The water was cold, and I did not hear Florence's call, and stayed in rather too long. As for Edie, she had been in a great state of eagerness and excitement until she reached the water, when she got scared and kept near the shore. Potted some geraniums and ivy. Upset my nerves with *Thief in Night* on the roof.

July 24ᵗʰ

Wednesday. Florence, Edie and I went into Boston. Missed the train, went by the horsecars, dined at Marston's, changed books, looked at pictures and pottery at the Atheneum, and had soda, and went home. Florence was quite ill, and I got her some tansy, which she refused.

July 25ᵗʰ

Thursday. Bright and hot. I took Edie down to bathe and watched her while she did it. Saw Charley Bradley in a boat. A blue shirt is by no means becoming to him. Aunt Sarah and Anna arrived, and we have a housefull. Walked with F. in the evening.

July 26ᵗʰ

Friday. Blew great guns and rained cats and dogs. So cold and damp that Papa made up a fire in the library, and it was a real comfort. Read and ached. Anna and Edith were afraid to go upstairs in the dark, so I put them to bed. When they tried to tickle me I turned the gas out and fled. F. and I talked villainously all the first part of the night, and kicked and shivered through the rest.

July 27ᵗʰ

Saturday. Having missed my nights rest was miserable for a while, but it was a splendid day, and I played croquet with F. beating her every time. Florence and I helped ourselves to a couple of pickled limes, and fled from the wrath to come, with F's bathing dress. We got to the shore and her courage failed her to my great disgust, because of the men on the shore. When we got part way home I exploded with wrath, upon which she altered her mind, and we went back and bathed. Came home and found the supper cleared away, so we supped on plum bread and milk in the washroom.

July 28ᵗʰ

Sunday. Chiefly devoted to croquet. I am the best player and can do about what I please with the game, so I beat till they get savage, and then let them win. Rode out with Papa, Uncle G. and F. and endured much agony of mind, but reached home safely. Went upon the roof. Cold and windy up there.

July 29th

Monday. Croquet and cider making. Agnes Reed[9] came up in the afternoon, bringing a girl for trial. Dishes and chickens.

July 30th

Tuesday. Florence and I bathed, Edie arriving from Squantum for her's while we were dressing. The waves were like Mrs. Browning's; 'bright and bleak' but any waves were a pleasant change. Dear little Anna left, after I had kissed her well. Poor little thing! She is slipping through our fingers I am afraid. Croquet. F. and Edie squabble continually. Edie takes the most unreasonable occasions but F. pitches into her without any occasion at all. Edie cannot speak or even grunt without exasperating her, though it must be owned Edie's speeches are not generally conciliatory. Florence and I went up onto the roof, and Edie came and bumped the door, and once lifted it a little way, so that we applied the avoirdupois.

July 31st

Wednesday. Went into Boston, changed my books and got out in time for dinner. Croquet. I was repeatedly beaten and whitewashed and betook myself to singing hymning. I have got a very good set of books this time, though I have read them all before. We have got a nice new English girl who looks like Aunt Elizabeth and is called Agnes Winny.

AUGUST

August 1st

Thursday. We went down and bathed. Some one had got in and used my bathing clothes, for the window was open and the clothes were not hung on the nails where I left them. Left a note for Mary F. and afterward found her on the beach. We exchanged defiances and I came home. I have been playing croquet, and have enraged Edie because she thought I played out of turn; but I didn't. She is very hot and hasty, and will fling herself upon the grass and howl at a moments notice. We dodged her and got upon the roof where we had a duel because she was aggravated at my sentimentalizing over Capt. Kidd.

9. Agnes Reid was a classmate of Alice's at Harris School. Her mother helped place several young women as domestics in the Stone Blackwell household.

August 2nd

Friday. Croquet and roof. Florence and Edie bathed, but I did not feel like it and stayed out, for which I afterward repented. Put Edie to bed, visited F. and went myself.

Aug. 3d

Saturday. I write under difficulties, as my small cousin Edie is trying to read it upside down and now and then threatening me with her fist. I must stop and drive her away. Gray and gloomy. Croquet under difficulties. Swept my room. Practiced. Florence reads *Ravenshoe* and likes it.

Aug. 4th

Sunday. Arranged the big room into a den for myself and F. Edie has the corner room by the pine. Croquet. Florence and I went onto the roof as usual, and stayed till it got cold and late, and Edie was sent up to say there was a fire in the sitting room. When she had gone down and we tried to follow, we found to our wrath and indignation that the door was fastened. Of course we laid it to Edie's charge, as she had several times threatened to do it if we would not let her up. Instantly on finding that we couldn't get down we became twice as chilly as before, and debated what we should do. We didn't call for help, as I was loth to give Edie the triumph; and also, as Florence suggested, we might have howled blue murder and no one would have heard us. So we waited, with an occasional tug at the door for exercise, for Edie to come and release us; but she did not come, and I began to have serious thoughts of climbing down the lightning rod. At last we heard Edie's voice in the depths, and Florence called her to come up. When we heard her beneath us we burst out. "If you have done this," said I, "you had better undo it." "Open the door, Ede," cried F. We heard her undo the catch, and pulling up the door, found her whimpering on the top step. She protested her innocence, and being under the impression that a ghost had done it, begged me to sleep with her. After she was put to bed I went down to the Library, where Papa and Mama denied having had a finger in the pie; so it is decided that it caught accidentally.

Aug. 5th

Monday. Hot. Croquet. Florence and I wanted a bath, and were beset by Edie, who was determined to go to[o]. After chases and sieges we escaped, but our bath was not a very good one, as the tide was too low. F. and I were weighed.

Aug. 6ᵗʰ

Tuesday. Croquet. Florence and Edie took a bath; I went part way with them, but was seized with stomach ache and came home. I gave a dinner party in my den to Florence, Mama and Edie. Walked with Florence in the evening.

Aug. 7ᵗʰ

Wednesday. Aunt Emily came,[1] was welcomed and fed. Picked beans and cut up apples. Hot. Florence and I stole away to bathe. It was stewingly hot, and Florence and I broiled. I went through fire to my fate. For I was hailed while in the water, and saw Her—Sadie—on the shore. She rushed into the water and I swam toward her. I could hardly bear to go out of the water while she was in it, and so stayed too long. Walked home with her, talking to her. She is sallow just now, and F. is not struck by her beauty. A wild windy time on the roof.

Aug. 8ᵗʰ

Thursday. Broiled into Boston with books and F. and out again. At the present minute am stewing in my nightgown in the den. Supper, roof and bed.

Aug. 9ᵗʰ

Friday. Mortally hot. Stole away to bathe with F. and saw the Light of my Eyes. Croquet, and wrath of Edie. Promenades—no roof.

Aug. 10ᵗʰ

Saturday. Hot but windy. Sorted apples and played croquet. Bathed with F. and saw the light of my eyes with her two small sisters. Also Charley Bradley. He is often down there with the King creature.[2] All the way home F. tantalized me by hinting at some wonderful discovery she had made which concerned me, but which she refused to tell me the nature of. Provoking toad! Promenades and roof.

Aug. 11ᵗʰ

Sunday. Made some very successful jelly which quite eclipses Papa's. Croquet with F. and Edie. Wrote stories and promenaded. Papa and Aunt Emily talked old times.

1. Henry's sister Emily (1826–1910), a pioneering woman physican, was then in full charge of the New York Infirmary for Women and Children, the hospital she cofounded with her sister Elizabeth in 1856. After Elizabeth's move to England in 1869, Emily also served as director of the new medical school recently connected to the Infirmary (NAW).
2. Sam King had just graduated from Harris School.

Aug. 12th

Monday. Croquet. Dodging Edith for croquet. Maria Barlow and Grace Greenwood came,[3] and Flo slept with me.

Aug. 13th

Tuesday. Papa did not bring the basket till late, but it was presented. Our visitors left. I was sent into Boston by Mama, with letters. Changed two books.

Aug. 14th

Wednesday. Eloped. Being bound to have my *Ledger* and Library books, and having tickets, I started out, but was met by Papa, who asked where I was going and if Mama knew. I said I was going to Boston, but when he mentioned Mama, I took to my heels and fled, leaving him calling behind me. Sadie and her parents were waiting for the train. When it came she sat by me, talked about Plymouth, where we were going next day, looked over my library books, and put me into a state of bliss by arranging to give me rowing lessons. My state of mind was indescribable, therefore shall not be described. Got my *Ledger* and changed my books. Told Mrs. Campbell and Mr. Livermore[4] about the elopement, and he looked at her and said I "was wild today," upon which I told him that I generally was, and left. A storm came up in the afternoon, and F. and I were up in the den, where we had a squabble over her poetry book. She had been reading one to me and stopped half way, and we struggled for the book. As we lay in a heap on the floor, we made some remarks to each other, and finally she said she should think I had enough of reading other folks things, and added something [that] made me certain she had read my diary. I let her go; she left; and I went down on my knees in a heap. I don't remember what I said, but I was shaking with rage, and hardly spoke to her during the evening. When she was going to bed I put my head in at the door and begged her pardon for what I did about her book—and waited [for] a fitter time to make remarks about my diary. She said "All Right"—but it wasn't. A dreadful thunder-shower in the night, louder thunder than I ever heard and more of it. I got

---

3. Maria Barlow was most likely the daughter of Lucy's brother-in-law, Ira Barlow, from Ware, Mass. He had remarried after his first wife (Lucy's sister, Eliza) died in 1838. Grace Greenwood was the pseudonym and, later, personal name adopted by Sara Clarke Lippincott (1823–1904), a popular writer of articles and books for both adults and children, as well as an active lyceum lecturer (*NAW*).

4. Daniel Parker Livermore (1818–99), husband of Mary Livermore, was a Universalist minister in Hingham, Mass.

Old Colony Railroad Station.

scared a little after midnight, and stood on a pillow in the middle of the floor, and from there ran to Mama's bed with grunts of terror. Went and comforted Edie afterwards.

Aug. 15ᵗʰ

Thursday. We went off to Plymouth in a great hurry. It was a disagreeable excursion to me, for what with hot sun, an uncomfortable dress, numerous waterproofs and bundles which Mama would insist upon making us carry with us, headache and worry of mind, I was decidedly miserable. We saw Pilgrim hall,[5] wherein were displayed pots, pans, spoons, chairs, bibles, sofas, a wig, etc. That belonged to the May flowerists; the sword of Miles Standish, which he doubtless flourished at John Alden, also a sampler worked by Lor[n]a Standish, his daughter, and one of Priscilla's slippers, which is nearly as absurd as those they wear now a days. We sat in the governor's chair, and saw a tall and venerable clock, aged 172 years, which goes still. There were more things than I can describe, very odd and curious. We had hired a carriage, and drove th[r]ough some pleasant woods to a pond, where we lunched and waded

5. Pilgrim Hall had been built in 1824.

in the warm clear shallow water. We then took a long hot ride to the beach where Edie & I had a bath. The water was almost like that at Kennebunk.[6] I stayed under long enough to duck my head and give a howl, and then scurried out. We had no bathing clothes. We then drove to the station and went home. I don't like Plymouth much; it's smelly and dirty, and the Fathers had very bad taste to land in such a place. A dreadful headache. Mama mustard plastered my neck before I went to bed, and it did a great deal of good. P.S. I forgot to say that in front of Pilgrim Hall there was a bit of the rock, surrounded by a railing with the names of the settlers on it. Over the real rock is a three cornered granite monument which contrasts very queerly with wharves and coal yards.

Aug. 16th

Friday. Reconciled myself to F. who swore by the river Styx that she had not read my diary, but had merely put that and that together. We bathed but the water was oily and the weather disagreeable. We played croquet between the showers. Edie had diarrhoearr, and F. and I fought Aunt Emily, who wished to go up and attend to her. She was obliged to cry "Enough" but we were hoarse and bruised.

Aug. 17th

Saturday. Rainy. Wrote on our stories and played croquet and read.

Aug. 18th

Sunday. A bright clear hot day. Such a pity we couldn't bathe! Lounged. Went upon the roof and scribbled poetry.

Aug. 19th

Monday. Escaped Edie, and bathed. My angel appeared after I was out of the water, to my aggravation. F. lent the preserver to small boys, from whom it was rescued by Sadie's interference, and F. and I went over to Mrs. Colter's and paid the $5. for the bath-house. While by the water Sadie promised to come up for me next morning, and I called her an angel, at which she laughed. Promenaded with Florence after supper, and was teased half to death about Charley Bradley and George Cook, whom she calls Monsieur Dirty-nails. Judging others by herself she doubtless thinks I am spoony—that's vulgar—goosey over both. Ugh! I assaulted and battered her finally.

6. Kennebunk is in Maine.

Aug. 20th

Tuesday. Was on thorns till Sadie came in her carriage for me. Mama and Aunt Emily left to spend a few weeks at Gloucester. Sadie and I drove to her house, she took the oars and I the oarlocks, and we went to a pretty little white boat.[7] She took the oars first, and rowed to a shady place where she said she sometimes came to read; we each ate an apple and then the rowing lesson began. I learned to row with one hand, and she praised me and said I took to it splendidly. We rowed to Mill street and I ran up home and got some towels and the bath house key, and we rowed to the landing and went from it to her house. She invited me in and I sat down in that parlor which I had seen through the windows when oonyacking, and she brought me a glass of icewater. We then went down to the shore and bathed and she got dressed first and went home. My state of mind being indescribable is not described.

Aug. 21st

Wednesday. I had a diarhoea, but said nothing, being bound to go to Boston, but privately took rheubarb. Papa and I missed our train, and he went by the horse cars. I called on Mary Fifield while waiting for the next train. Went on it, got my *Ledger* and books and came home. Edie acted like a little fury at croquet.

Aug. 22nd

Thursday. Bad diarhoea. Took ginger, and lay on the lounge most of the day. Edie nursed me. Was much struck by the obstinacy of that child. Florence having locked her out she waited several hours rather than go round to another door, and finally had to be let in, as it rained and F. feared she would catch cold.

Aug. 23rd

Friday. Diarhoea and misery. Mama brought Aunt Emily home from Gloucester. M. found I had dysentery, and announced that shocking fact.

Aug. 24th

Saturday. Dysentery. Prone upon my back in bed, with books to read. Papa read some of *The Antiquary* in the evening.

Aug. 25th

Sunday. Ditto.

7. Alice and Sadie Wilson were rowing on the Mill Pond; access to it was only a short distance behind the Wilson house.

Aug. 26th

Monday. Ditto, only no *Antiquary*. Florence, Edith and Aunt Emily left. Each came up and bid me goodbye. Aunt E. kissed me twice, F. once, and Edith numerous times. I jumped out of bed and went to the window as the carriage drove off. I shouted, they shouted, and Mike shouted; the last made me remember how I was dressed, and dodge back. A letter from Kitty, with an inclosure for Flo arrived some quarter of an hour after she had left. Agnes [Winny] amused me in the evening by showing me her friends pictures, and telling me of them. The musquitoes tormented me so that I betook myself to Flo's bed in despair. Religious talk with Mama. Set spinning and let go is her theory. I'd rather be blue Orthodox and believe in Hell than believe what she does. She'll have a pleasant surprise when she dies.

Aug. 27th

Tuesday. Up at last, but decidedly shaky, and kept on a very strict diet. Quite miserable at times. Made some very successful cake and was not allowed to eat any. Pottered about the garden, read and practiced. Drove to depot and Glovers[8] with M.

Aug. 28th

Wednesday. Pottered about the garden, read, and practiced. Papa came home in the evening and said the Republicans had endorsed W.S. [woman's suffrage] upon which we hugged him.[9]

Aug. 29

Thursday. Pottered about the garden, and in the afternoon went to West Brookfield with Mama. We had a new *Ledger* to read on the way, and after a long ride caught sight of Coy's hill.[10] We rode up on the stage, got out at the

8. Glovers or Glovers Corners was just north of Harrison Square.

9. Henry had worked for the strong wording of a resolution supporting woman suffrage by the Massachusetts Republican party, meeting in Springfield. The final resolution read that the party was "in favor of extending Suffrage on equal terms to all American citizens, irrespective of sex " (*WJ*: 31 Aug. 1872). This was in sharp contrast to the National Republican platform put together in Philadephia in June, where Henry also worked valiantly on behalf of woman's suffrage. Its wording went only so far as to say that "the Republican party is mindful of its obligation to the loyal women of America" and "the honest demands of any class of citizens for additional rights should be treated with respectful consideration" (*WJ*: 7 Sept. 1872).

10. The Stone family farm was named for its location on Coy's Hill in West Brookfield, Mass.

foot of the hill, and cut across lots, coming in at the back door of the barn, where the cows were being milked. I had a headache, but was glad to see and be welcomed by every one. Tip is a great dog now, and is shaped much like Bravo. It began to rain soon after we got there. Had supper and slept with Phebe.

Aug. 30th

Friday. It rained all the morning. I was shown how to make a tapioca pudding, and practiced a little. I found a book of songs and ballads set to music and containing Capt. Kidd. Copied music and ate cheeserinds. It cleared up in the afternoon, and I ran down to Mrs. Vans—the first time I have felt like running for ever so long; but this air would make any one feel strong. I don't wonder Mama is brave, having grown up in this glorious hill country. Even I, if I stayed there long, might get to be less of a coward. Mrs. Van was very glad to see me, and showed me a cunning little brown girl baby, born since I left—the dearest little thing I ever saw. I had some new milk from the cow, Uncle B[owman] milking into my cup, and we got ready for the glories. We were rather late, and I walked on ahead, thinking as I came up higher and higher, past the woods and the Gleason house, of that negro song in What Answer;

> "The Glory of the Lord, it am comin' it am coming
> The Glory of the Lord, let it come;
> The Glory of de Lord, it ar comin, it are coming
> The Glory of the Lord, it ar come!"

I was barely in time to see the sun, and when Mama and Phebe overtook me at the top, the Glory was about gone, but we rode along the top of the hill before going down. Found I had lost my pin.

Aug. 31st

Saturday. Went up the hill to look for my lost breastpin, and was overtaken by Mama. We went along the top of the hill, selected the crown thereof, and laid a plot to buy and build on it unbeknownst to Papa. We wandered about all those lovely hills and fields, Hemlock wood etc. and I went down after dinner for a farewell call on Mrs. Van. While I was there the carriage came by with P[hebe] and Mama, took me in and went to the station, where we took the cars and went home.

SEPTEMBER

Sept. 1ˢᵗ

Sunday. Aunt Ellen[1] arrived. We showed her over the house and garden and enjoyed her raptures. Covered my school books and got them ready.

Sept. 2ⁿᵈ

Monday. Aunt E. is enthusiastic to give me music lessons. I took one, and read and pottered over an unsuccessful attempt at pear jelly. Aunty and I started to go to Field's corner for yeast, but were overtaken by rain before we turned the first corner. Aunty has made some very pretty sketches of views from the uper windows. A little gardening. Sang and musiced and Antiquaried in the evening.

Sept. 3ᵈ

Tuesday. Cold. Pottered in the morning, made some rich fruit cake in the afternoon, and in the evening Papa read the *Antiquary* by a nice woodfire in the library.

Sept. 4ᵗʰ

Wednesday. Rode into Boston with Papa and Aunt Ellen. Suffered agonies on the way. Showed Aunt E. the Public Library, the deer[2] and the Atheneum. She did not want to leave the pictures, so I gave her directions how to find the office, and went to it for my *Ledger*. Papa had gone, taking the newspapers with him, to my wrath and disgust. I felt that to wait till night for my *Ledger* meant insanity, so went to the printing office, where I found his satchel and extracted the precious document. Came out to H[arrison] S[quare] and nursed Mama, who has a sick headache. Aunt Ellen got home late, having been carried on to Wollaston Heights.[3] Papa did not get hom[e] till 12 p.m.

---

1. Ellen Blackwell (1828–1901) was then living in New York with her sister Dr. Emily Blackwell and serving as her housekeeper. Although Ellen had studied art in Boston, New York, Paris, and London (under John Ruskin), family demands seemed to preclude her serious work as an artist, with the exception of a period in the 1860s when she opened a studio in New York and gave drawing lessons to young women.

2. A small number of deer grazed under high wire grating on the Common, near the Boylston St. mall. Known as Deer Park, it remained as part of the Common from 1863 to 1882.

3. Wollaston Heights was two stops beyond the Neponset station on the Old Colony and Newport Railway.

Deer Park (3) and scenes from Boston Common.

Sept. 5th

Thursday. Went down to call on the Manns, but they were out; ditto Mary Fifield. Reading of *Antiquary* and potting off plants.

Sept. 6th

Friday. As I was digging up earth to fill a box Hattie and Lulu Mann came bouncing upon me. They made a call, were shown my den, etc. and then left. Nursing of a sick ~~picture~~ chicken (Agnes is responsible for that blur—the wretch!) and pottering. *Antiquary.*

Sept. 7th

Saturday. Music, and a cupful of canary pudding[4] of my own manufacture. Retribution; another taste. I laughingly bade Agnes not read my diary, and she mentioned various cases of readings and expressed her opinion of the readers. She told me how her sister promised to thrash the others for something of that nature. I almost wish Alice had thrashed me when I confessed. Oh dear! Oh what a tangled web we weave When first we practice to deceive!

Sept. 8th

Sunday. Read, practiced, and ate. Pottered and went for a long drive after supper, much against my will. The Duke misbehaved going down the hill and scared me horribly.

Sept. 9th

Monday. I made some hanging baskets out of beets, and hung them on the apple tree, where they astonished my parents when they drove up. Gardening, music and reading. *Antiquary.*

Sept. 10th

Tuesday. Was sent into Boston with Mama's Editorial, and changed two books. Papa brought out a Colonel Fabin,[5] a gentleman with an aquiline nose, gray curly hair, and a very pleasant smile. He is about the first man I ever saw who knows how to talk. His conversation actually wiled me from the charms of *A Brave Lady* just from the library. He told about his camels and I shut up the

---

4. Canary pudding is a boiled yellow pudding, usually made from eggs, lemon rind, butter, and sugar.
5. Joseph W. Fabens (1821–75) was a Boston-born adventurer involved in various schemes to develop Santo Domingo and secure American political control over the island (*DAB*).

book and listened till he and papa got upon the subject of Consuls and politics; confound both! I wanted to hear more about the camels.

Sept. 11ᵗʰ

Wednesday. Went into Boston, changed my books, had lunch and did various errands with Aunt Ellen, but did get my *Ledger*.

Sept. 12ᵗʰ

Thursday. First day of school. I went, became 1ˢᵗ class,⁶ and gave myself a headache over sums.

Sept. 13ᵗʰ

Friday. School. Less headache. They brought home various mysterious parcels at night. Sentimentalized over the last night of my 14ᵗʰ year, and went to bed.

Sept. 14ᵗʰ

Saturday. Before I was up in the morning Papa and Mama entered in nightgowns, made me get up, and each taking me by one arm, marched me into my den, which I found matted.⁷ Then I was left to dress, and came down to breakfast. Mama there presented me with a work basket, a quantity of various colored paper and envelopes, a dish for flowers, a ball of scented soap, an ice cream freezer, two neck-ribbons, a blotting paper, an ink stand and glue bottle, and a cornelian breastpin. Aunt Ellen had given me another pin much like it, not knowing of Mama's; and best of all, I had a beautiful upright writing desk. Fanny Benedict and her cousin came over in the P.M. and stayed to supper. I had made some ice cream in my freezer and we had it for supper. They borrowed some books and took some fruit home. There was a splendid sunset, but I was worried in my conscience because I was to have a rooster killed, and did not go up to see it.

Sept. 15ᵗʰ

Sunday. Rainy and blowy. Was scooping some beets under the pines, and Mama came out and gave it to me for soiling my waterproof. *Antiquary*.

Sept. 16ᵗʰ

Monday. Vile weather, cold and rainy. Wore my fall dress. We expected one session, but didn't get it. Folks away in the afternoon.

6. Alice was now in her final year at Harris Grammar School.
7. For her birthday, Alice's parents had carpeted her den with straw matting.

Sept. 17

Tuesday. A mutiny in the army. It was wet, but not raining, and the bells rang, but were not listened for and therefore unheard, and we left at 12. When I got back at 2, I found the girls in wrath and commotion; every one at home had heard the bells, and they were "in great alarm and discontent" as the History says. For myself, I felt like the division stationed a[t] Newburg. No explosions however.[8] Finished *The Antiquary*.

Sept. 18th

Wednesday. Went into Boston, and got into the Public Library. Before I got out a pouring rain came on, which pretty well soaked me below the knees before I reached the office, for I had an umbrella but no rubbers. I got my *Ledger*, and read it as I dried by Mrs. Larrisey's fire. When I was ready to go to the Atheneum the rain had stopped. Went out loaded with books and bundles. Mama drove me up home. Sadie and Hattie Burdett were on the cars. Papa got home after I had gone up to bed, and came up to kiss me.

Sept. 19

Thursday. One session. A note from Mrs. Messinger, asking about a meeting, and I had to answer it as best I could.

Sept. 20th

Friday. Clouds wind and sunshine. After school walked over to some beautiful woods in the direction of Milton, and got a lot of moss, partridge vines and sweet acorns.

Sept. 21st

Saturday. Fanny Benedict and her cousin called late in the afternoon, while Mama and I were potting the great ivy. It was a few inches high last fall, and we bought it for five or ten cents; now it had trailed all over the bed. There were bushels of it. The girls did not stay to supper, but took books and apples and went home. Mama hid a library book and made me feel cross. Mr. Spalding[9] put our cow in the pound, and she had to go after it, which made her so.

---

8. The meaning of this entry is unclear. It appears that some kind of alarm bell had rung, alerting parents that school children would be returning home early. Children at the Harris School did not hear it and returned home at the usual time at noon. There are no reports of this incident in Boston newspapers.

9. Mahlon D. Spaulding lived on Train St., a block west of the Stone Blackwells.

Sept. 22nd

Sunday. Hot. Potted some ivy sprigs, and read. Got myself into a scrape by making pretences. Gave Papa to understand that I had found "Jesus I my cross have taken"[10] on a loose slip of paper, when I had really picked it out myself and he came in soon after to hear it; and I couldn't show him the paper or he would have known; and I hid lost it, and had quite a time managing to dodge him without fibs. We rode out to a wild beautiful place among the quarries. I really enjoyed it. *Nicholas Nickleby* read aloud.

Sept. 23rd

Monday. Hot. School. Saw Mary Fifield at recess, and Sadie after school just for one moment.[11] Rained a little. Practiced. *Nicholas Nickleby* aloud in the evening. Musquitoes—hang-found them!

Sept. 24th

Tuesday. Mr. Horne read from the bible, "Oh praise the Lord, for his mercy endureth forever!" Not only while you are good, or only till death, nor only to the elect; at least it doesn't say so; and—how dare they twist God's truth about so as to make it mean so?

Practiced and potted ivy.

Sept. 25th

Wednesday. Went into Boston with Hattie Mann. Got my books and *Ledger* and came out again. I got *Two College Friends*, and some of Harriet Prescott Spofford's. Now and then I like to excite myself.[12] Papa and Mama stayed in to a meeting. As I came home from the station Sadie called me, and came flying down the path with her oars, and took me out rowing, and said she had to row every evening for exercise, and put me on shore, and I saw the last of her through Addie Calendar's trees as I walked up home. Eddy Benedict brought home the basket. *Christian's Mistake.*

Sept. 26th

Thursday. Agnes Winney has got back. She is to be married in 5 weeks, and I am to be bridesmaid. At last. Hurrah! A grey day. Have begun a letter to

10. This hymn, by Henry Lyte, began appearing in American hymnals in 1831.

11. Both Mary Fifield and Sadie Wilson had graduated from Harris School in June, and Alice was no longer seeing them on a daily basis.

12. Harriet Prescott Spofford (1835–1921) was popular and prolific American author, whose books and short stories were often characterized by a blend of romanticism and realism (*NAW*).

Kitty, but not finished it. Sang with Papa in the evening. I have confessed the "I my cross" imposition. He tried to instruct me in the mysteries of singing a third below, giving me the note with long, melodious howls, and making such queer faces while he sang that I could not help laughing. *Nicholas Nickleby* aloud.

Sept. 27*th*

Friday. Studied for the examination, and took it. But it's really abominable to give us things we haven't had this year. We had the Niemen river, which belongs with Western Europe; and I missed it, and what's worse, Hattie didn't. Ugh! you selfish little brute! You <u>deserve</u> to have your front tooth go, you do!

Sept. 28*th*

Saturday. Arithmetic and Grammar examination. Went into Boston and heard Mrs. Stowe read.[13] She is a pleasant looking elderly lady, but her voice is hardly strong enough to be heard in a large hall. I changed a couple of books and went home.

Sept. 29*th*

Sunday. Mr. and Mrs. Campbell were here. Papa and they and I sat round the library table fixing circulars, and talking politics like sixty five while I wrote and listened, with an unpleasant consciousness that Papa's conscience was tough as Sam Lawson's.[14] Mr. Campbell proclaimed himself a spiritualist to my amazement. I asked him if he had ever seen a ghost, and he said he had, and I begging to know what it looked like he said like an ordinary human being, and told me various wonderful stories, some of which I believed and some of which I looked upon as dreams and fancies. Mama was wrathy at his telling me such things, but I liked to hear. They left at night.

13. Harriet Beecher Stowe (1811–96), American author, best known for her enormously popular antislavery novel *Uncle Tom's Cabin*, also wrote a number of other novels, essays, children's stories, and biographies. Alice had heard about Stowe from her father, for he and his family had been her neighbors in Cincinnati during the 1830s and 1840s. Alice attended this reading at Tremont Temple, where Stowe was introduced to the large audience by William Lloyd Garrison (*NAW*; *WJ*: 5 Oct. 1872).

14. The MWSA was sending out circulars advertising lecturers who would speak on behalf of Republican candidates who supported woman suffrage. Sam Lawson was a droll character in Harriet Beecher Stowe's *Old Town Fireside Stories*. Alice had just heard Stowe depict Lawson during her reading at Tremont Temple the day before.

Sept. 30th

Monday. School. HURRAH!! I am hed of the 1st class and of the school! It seems very queer to have her place, at the outer door.[15] While we were at supper Mr. Campbell appeared.

OCTOBER

Oct. 1

Tuesday. Unspeakably aggravated by Eddy Jenkins, who has Bradley's place. He a monitor! A suit of clothes stuffed with staw would be exactly as much use. The boys race and clatter down, and he stands looking at them without a word, with an expression of amiable idiocy, or talks to me. And I am very polite to him. Fixed t[w]o shells at the sides of the bow window in my den. *Nicholas Nickleby.*

Oct. 2

Wednesday. Went into Boston with Hattie Mann and Mama's editorial. Changed my books and got my *Ledger,* and came home. My books are very satisfactory this time.

Oct. 3d

Thursday. Made a cake, fought Agnes and read Mrs. Leonowens' book.[1] *Nicholas Nickleby.* I had meant to go to Milton Lower Mills, but it was wet.

Oct. 4th

Friday. Had the fullest intention of going Miltonward, but Emma Adams asked me to go out rowing, and I accepted with pleasure of course. Hattie went with us, and we all three raced to Commercial point. The boat was launched with some trouble, and we started out. It was delightful to be on blue water once more, and be able to dip my hand in the blessed brine. We had to come back at last, and I had leave to row one oar, which I liked. Hattie and Emma gave me contradictory orders, but I obeyed the Skipper of course. As we made for the pier, we ran aground in the mud. I pushed the boat off once, but it stuck again—fast. And the tide was still falling. And rowing, and pushing, and

15. Alice had replaced Sadie Wilson as monitor and head of the first class.

1. Anna Leonowen's new and much publicized book *The Romance of the Harem* was an account of her experiences as governess to the royal children of Siam. It had been serialized earlier in the *Atlantic.*

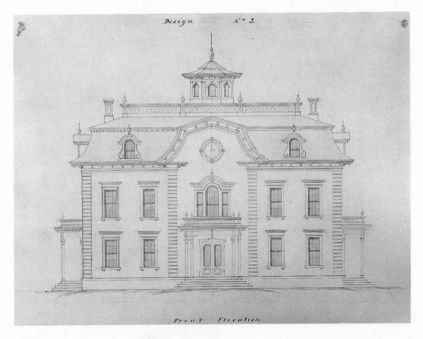

Harris Grammar School, from a drawing by the architect, Luther Briggs, Jr.
(Dorchester Historical Society)

Harrison Square Train Depot. (Dorchester Historical Society)

Meeting House Hill with First Parish Church and Lyceum Hall on the right.
(Dorchester Historical Society)

The Boston Athenaeum (center right) in 1895. At the time of Alice's journal the
surrounding buildings were much the same as in this photograph, with the offices of
the *Woman's Journal* out of view but located on a short street just around the upper
right corner. (Boston Athenaeum)

Feb. 20th (29)

Tuesday. Saw Sadie go into the yard, but came up later. Was a few minutes before her in the afternoon. The girls have got up what they call "Mystic Album" in which you are to write, fold and seal the leaf down, and write on the outside your name, and when it is to be opened. Read in the afternoon, and darned stockings at night. Went out to the stable and held the lantern while Papa fed and watered Billy.

Feb. 21st

Wednesday. There was a sort of a celebration which I had hardly known of, in honor of Washington's birthday being tomorrow; singing, playing, declamations and a reading by Charley Bradley of Wm's address. A villainous lot of horrid little boys from the lower rooms sat on settees ranged round behind us on purpose, and aggravated me beyond endurance. When they sang America I sang "God Save the Queen", through the two first verses, which are really idiotic. I dont think any one found me out, though. I got there before Sadie, and called to her from the window, but she did not hear, and Mr. Horne came down upon me, asking me to think how it would look to the people outside. A battle royal took place at recess between us girls, each having taken the name of some English or American General of the Revolution. Those who had muffs used them as weapons; Sadie had none; she was Burgoyne; Hattie Burditt was Howe; I was Clinton, to be on their side; Maggie Whitton was Washington. The fight ended with a general stampede at the end of recess. Mary Fifield and I prac-

The reading room of the Boston Public Library as it looked when Alice visited it in the 1870s. (Boston Public Library)

Crowds outside the Coliseum during the Peace Jubilee celebrations. This lithograph pictures President Ulysses Grant tipping his hat in the center carriage as he arrives for the concert of June 25, 1872, the same concert that Alice attended and described in her journal. (Boston Athenaeum)

The interior of the Coliseum during one of the Peace Jubilee concerts of 1872. The immense chorus (estimated at over two thousand members) is standing on risers that run across the entire back of the hall. (Boston Public Library)

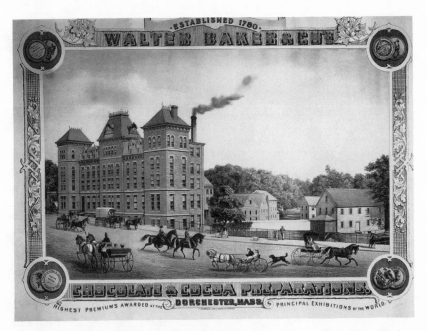

The Walter Baker Chocolate Factory at Lower Mills, pictured in a chromolithograph, c. 1872. (Boston Athenaeum)

William Lloyd Garrison, c. 1872. This photograph was taken when he was in semiretirement, after a long career as an abolitionist leader and woman's rights activist. (Boston Athenaeum)

Unitarian minister Robert Collyer as he appeared in an engraving done at the time of Alice's journal. (*Harper's Magazine*, 1874, vol. 48)

Mary Jane Safford as pictured in an engraving done shortly before she began her training as a physician. (L. P. Brockett and Mary C. Vaughn, *Woman's Work in the Civil War*, (Philadelphia, 1867)

British author George MacDonald a year before Alice heard him in Boston. (*Scribner's*, 1871, vol. 2)

Ruins from the Boston fire. This panoramic photograph was taken from Chauncy St. on November 22, 1872. (Boston Public Library)

Chauncy Hall School, c. 1880, when it was located on Boylston St. at Copley Square (1874–96). (Chapel Hill–Chauncy Hall School. Reproduction copyright © Alice Solorow)

laughter and vexation, were of no use; we couldn't stir her a hair's breadth. A little crowd of men and boys collected on the wharf and watched us with great amusement. A man hailed us from one of the little vessels at anchor, and bawled to us to push off and row so and so. He might as well have told us to go to the moon; we <u>couldn't</u> push off; that was just it. Finally he came to our assistance in a wherry, took Hattie and me into his boat, and towing and pushing and tugging and grunting hauled our boat into the channel; paddled after an oar we had left stuck in the mud, received our thanks and paddled away. We only ran aground once more, and were triumphantly hauled up to the pier by a rope we flung to the men and boys thereon collected. We then retreated to a boathouse and exploded.

Oct. 5th

Saturday. Read the *Shield* and got so wrathy I could hardly hold in;[2] and I raced down the hill and went to work picking pears with such vigor that Mike afterward told Mama I "stripped all one tree and half another in 5 minutes." That wasn't strictly true though.

Oct. 6th

Sunday. Read and practiced etc. and walked over to Milton. Mrs. Moore and Lowell called in the evening, and Lowell ate supper with me. Will Morris came to see Agnes. I don't like the looks of him at all. Wrote to Kitty.

Oct. 7th

Monday. Papa drove me down to the bath house before school to get the clothes. The blue trousers and the towels and one pincushion had been stolen. Mama is sick with erysipelas rash. A headache. Picked two dishpansfull of grapes. *Nicholas Nickleby* aloud. A toothache violently disposed of by means of cloves.

Oct. 8th

Tuesday. Made some grape jelly in the afternoon.

Oct. 9th

Wednesday. Went in on the 1.16; got my books and *Ledger*, did my errands and came out home. At 4 PM the lot on the corner was sold; it is feared for a

2. The British publication *Shield* was similar to the *Home Guardian* in that it dealt with issues such as female prostitution and moral reform. Alice strongly objected to the double standard existing for men and women on moral (especially sexual) issues.

smallpox hospital. Was met by this sweet news on coming home from Boston. Am divided in my mind between suicide and elopement. Mr. Horne overtook me on the track and arranged to have me remind him of the exercises by raising my hand at 3 P.M.

Oct. 10

Thursday. Raised my hand and reminded Mr. Horne. Violent excitement about the smallpox hospital. In the evening Mr. Roads came over and informed us that it was all a swindle and a sell, he having made inquiry about it. The idea of those people setting up such a story to make us all combine to buy the land at an enormous price! Glorification and *Nickleby*.

Oct. 11ᵗʰ

Friday. School of course. Miss Lucy Chadbourn, a young lady from Eastport who is to fill the place of Miss Tucker and Agnes when they leave. At first she startled me; she was so <u>very</u> tall—half an inch taller than Alice, as I afterward found; but I think I shall like her.[3]

Oct. 12ᵗʰ

Saturday. We are to choose our declamations this week. Went in to Boston, got *The Great Rebellion* (and was afterward disgusted by Mama's informing me that its author, Headley, was pleasant but quite unreliable.)[4] Heard Miss Charlotte Cushman read in the music hall. We had, without exaggeration, nearly the worst seat in the house, and could not see her well at all, but we afterward went down and stood up close to her. I was struck by the likeness of her "Macbeth" witches to Mr. Weld's. I did not like her reading of Macbeth very well, and in "Massachusetts to Virginia" I thought she thumped the table rather too much; but last she read "Betsey and I are out," which was just about perfect. The people stamped and applauded at intervals through it, and Mama fairly shrieked out with laughter. Take it all in all, I never heard anything like it. Mrs. Kemble was different, but I wont say better.[5] Came out with Mary

3. Lucy Chadbourne, from Eastport, Maine, was a printer by trade, a skill she put to better use in 1874 when she began working at the Riverside Press (ASB to KBB: 22 Mar. 1874, SL).

4. Joel Tyler Headley (1813–97) wrote over thirty biographies, histories, and travel books (*DAB*).

5. Charlotte Cushman (1816–76), an American actress who achieved acclaim in this country and England, retired from the stage in 1852 to live in London and Rome. She returned to the U.S. in 1870 and toured for several seasons with a popular series of dramatic readings. Stately and commanding, with strong features and a remarkably

Fifield, Hattie, Addie Calendar and Emma Adams. I noticed how very pretty Emma looked with her dainty little pearl-gloved hands and gold bracelets and striped grey lace edged sleeves. Little Monkey! There certainly is a liking for that kind of thing in me, though it doesn't appear. Mr. Horne and lady walked along with me from the station, and we got talking about the declamations. He asked if I had heard Sadie Wilson rehearse "Ivry." I had heard it at exhibition of course, but the room was hot and close and though she did very well she didn't half do herself justice. At that rehearsal it was only fair to say that without exaggeration it would not be too strong to say it was Splendid. As if I could have doubted it! Of course she was splendid and always will be. I quite took to Mr. Horne: and whatever else I do forget, I'll remember to raise my hand at three.

Miss Chadburn came out to stay for good.

Oct. 13th

Oct. 13th

Sunday. Enjoyed the morning extremely. Spend it sitting by the fire roasting my feet, munching apples and reading *The Last of the Mortimers*. That is a very pleasant story indeed, like most of Mrs. Oliphant's.[6] A stormy day, and a wild wailing wind. My chest worried, and was mustarded at night. Papa and I took Miss Chadbourne to the house top, where we were all blown crystal clear by freedom's northern wind. *Nicholas Nickleby.* I saw two notices of George Macdonald's speech in Cambridge. I am bound to hear him; for, as the little Quaker lady in *The Waterbabies* said "It is borne upon my mind that that is a good man." I liked the notice of some things he said about Burns, (the subject of the Lecture.)

Oct. 14th

Monday. What sort of a wild beast from the Maine woods have we got here? This 5 feet 8 Miss Chadbourne, who sings, runs, flies about, and talks sense and nonsense by turns—in short seems to me an exaggerated copy of myself. I wonder whether I shall hate or like her? Thank goodness, poor Miss Tucker

---

deep and versatile voice, she was at the time of these readings suffering from cancer but continuing to make public appearances in order to distract herself from the pain of her illness (*NAW*). The reading "Massachusetts to Virginia" was by John Greenleaf Whittier, and "Betsy and I Are Out" by Will Carleton (1845–1912), a poet and author of ballads evoking the simple life (*BDG*: 12 Oct. 1872).

6. Margaret Oliphant (1828–97), a popular Scottish writer who specialized in historic and domestic novels, was Alice's favorite female author at this time. Widowed early in her life, she supported herself and her family by writing over one hundred books and numerous articles (*DNB*).

---

will go soon. A cold day. Fought Annie Phips at recess, and collapsed. Sat up till half past nine talking books and Woman's Rights and religion with Miss Lucy. All the world was cold moonlight when I went up to bed.

Oct. 15th

Tuesday. School. A letter from Florence. Am going—all by myself—to hear George Macdonald tomorrow night.

Oct. 16th

Wednesday. Went in on the 1.54, changed my books, and was left in the office when it was shut up. I went down to Marston's, got my supper and came back to the office, where I read and nibbled at what I had brought in my satchel till it was time to start for the lecture. I got there a few minutes before the door was opened, and following my directions made for the gallery and got the best seat I could; right over the stage, a little behind the speaker. Read *Alec Forbes* till he appeared, when I was notified of the fact by an outbreak of applause, and he began. He is neither bald nor gray, and by no means so old looking as I had—I dont know why—expected. He spoke very queerly—the Scotch accent, I suppose; and got many outbreaks of applause. Once the cheering was really ferocious—that was when he proposed reading Tam O'Shanter, and would have to speak over his time if he did so. Such a noise! And one cried out "More!" There was something about him that suggested—not whited-sepulcralness exactly, but—might have suggested it if I hadn't known to the contrary. On the whole I approve of him. They had the English and American flags, with "Welcome" between them, in front of the stage.[7] After it was over I went back to the office and tried to sleep on the sofa. I never knew how hard that sofa was till then—till they came for me, and we drove home by moonlight. I forgot to say that the *Young Folks*, with "Molly and the Brook," appeared at last, and I had the pleasure of aggravating Mr. Campbell by refusing to let him see it.[8] Miss Tucker has left, for which O be joyful!

Oct. 17th

Thursday. Mama away all night. School. There has been a mysterious murder of a harmless gentleman down at the square, followed by an assault and rob-

7. George MacDonald spoke on Robert Burns to a packed audience at the Boston Music Hall (*BDG*: 17 Oct. 1872). Alice's misspelled notice of his "sepulchralness" anticipates the fact that soon after this talk, MacDonald became seriously ill, the apparent result of his overambitious U.S. tour.

8. Alice's poem "Molly and the Brook" appeared in the November issue of *Our Young Folks* (see Appendix 2).

bery at the old Colony depot. It was all the talk at school, and I feeling myself in danger of being burglared, took the bread knife up to bed with me.

Oct. 18ᵗʰ

Friday. A precious time. Every one late, and I not down till 8 because no bell was rung. Much amazement concerning the disappearance of the breadknife, till I produced it from under my bed. Mama away all night again. Papa read me some of *Alec Forbes* in the evening.

Oct. 19ᵗʰ

Saturday. Went over to Hattie Mann's, by her invitation, and spent the afternoon in playing two games of chess, in the mysteries of which she instructed me. I beat the first game, she the second. Posted two letters at Field's corner, and took the key of the bath house to Mrs. Colter's and gave it to a woman in charge of the house apparently. Drove in with Mamma and Lucy to hear a lecture. While we waited to be let into the hall I watched a lady opposite me, who reminded me of an imaginary heroine of mine, Marion Ellersleigh. Dark hair and eyes, rather small, erect, and with a very—inexpressible face. I could have imagined her doing almost anything very brave or [good?] or very wicked either. It was a very stupid lecture, illustrated by some very pretty experi-

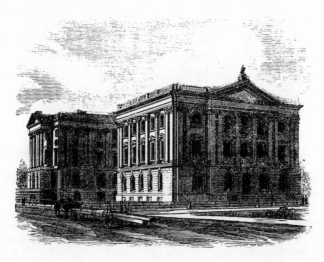

Massachusetts Institute of Technology (left) and Society of
Natural History.

ments, which latter were applauded.[9] We sat on the steps, Lucy and I, the hall being full. Drove out home with Papa.

Oct. 20th

Sunday. Read, fixed the pots on the stand in the upper hall, and rode over to Mr. Garrison's with Papa. The tree[s] were splendid—the great maples expecially were a pure golden glory. Papa told Mr. G. that I was always ready to go riding when we went to his house, and he laughed and said he should take it as a compliment. I asked Papa afterward why he told, and he said because he knew it would please Mr. G.; and to be sure, he took more notice of me than ever before, and asked me to come and see him myself when I could. He had a nice motherly little grey cat which I straightway made friends with; Mr. G. likes cats.[10] *Nicholas Nickleby.*

Oct. 21st

Monday. Went home with Fanny Benedict after school. While I was there her little cousin was run over in the street, and instantly a flock of relatives rushed out and brought him in with his face bloody, howling at a rate which showed that his lungs at least were not hurt. I left, and came home. At dinner Agnes and Miss Chadbourne both went at me on the Sunday question and it would have been great fun, their hammering away at me, if they had not had a tendency to lose their temper. *Nicholas Nickleby.*

Oct. 22nd

Tuesday. Went out rowing with Emma Adams and Hattie, and witnessed a new sight—flirtation at sea. Their attention during most of the time was taken up by the manoevers of a little 2 sailed boat which it seemed contained a couple of their ganders. C[harley] B[radley] must be pretty well over his dislocated shoulder for they said he was in one of the boats. Got home after dusk, meeting Mamma driving down the hill as I walked up.

9. John Tyndall (1820–93), British physicist and professor of natural philosophy at the Royal Institution in London, was delivering a popular course of Lowell Institute lectures at the Massachusetts Institute of Technology (MIT). The proceeds from his book *Six Lectures on Light, Delivered in America in 1872–73*, were devoted to the encouragement of science in the U.S. (*DNB; BDG:* 18 Oct. 1872).

10. Garrison was then living in semiretirement in nearby Roxbury with his invalid wife, Helen. Contributing articles from time to time to the *Independent* and giving occasional public talks, his many reform associates and friends had recently collected over thirty thousand dollars to pay off his mortage and provided him with a comfortable lifetime income.

Oct. 23ᵈ

Wednesday. Went into Boston and got two most unsatisfactory books, and NO
LEDGER!!! Had a dress fitted at Boston and looked in at Hovey's with Mamma. *Nicholas Nickleby.*

Oct. 24ᵗʰ

Thursday. Agnes's sister Sarah, a quiet, placid looking English girl, was here
to tea and I plagued Agnes within an inch of her life. Those boys have been
cutting up too violently in the dressing room, and we got a public rebuke and
warning from Mr. Horne. Rehearsed my piece up in the hall, and he said 'very
good.' Dreamed that Mr. Horne and Miss Andrews were married, and was
greatly bewildered as to how Mr. H. came to have one wife already. I believe I
finally decided that it was a case of bigamy. Oh such musquitoes.

Oct. 25ᵗʰ

Friday. Went in after school, changed 2 books and got my *Ledger*. Mama was
not at home. Lucy, Agnes and I talked so late that it struck 11 as I got into bed.

Oct. 26ᵗʰ

Saturday. Will Morris arrived in the evening and we fed him, inspected him
and joked with him a little. Lucy brought out a big wedding cake without any
frosting. *Nicholas Nickleby.*

Oct. 27ᵗʰ

Sunday. We—Agnes assisting—frosted the wedding cake. After breakfast I
put on my best dress, and officiated as brides maid in dressing Agnes, helped
at the last by Lucy. Lucy and I held a great dispute about Agnes' hair, for I
wanted her to have it down, but she didn't; she wore it in a great soft red gold
coil. She and I sat on the back seat, I holding her hand, and Will and Papa in
front. Agnes seemed in pretty good spirits, and we passed the Reeds on the
way, found the church after some difficulty, and got a front pew. There was a
dull sermon and some sweet singing, and I flatter myself I went thro' the
service with commendable propriety, especially the "miserable sinner" part.

   After the service most of the people stayed to see the marriage. Papa, who
had arrived with Sarah Winney just in time to prevent our asking Mr. Reed to
supply his place and give away the bride, took Agnes on his arm; Will took her
sister and I brought up the rear. We marched up the aisle to the altar, Agnes's
lilac silk train being gorgeous to behold, and arranged ourselves in front of the
altar. And her sister and I got transposed after all, so that they stood together,
which was better after all, though the dresses did not match. The minister in

his absurd dress stood on the other side [of] the railing, and read the service, Papa handing over Agnes at the right time. She made the responses faintly but clearly, all but the last part of 'troth,' and flushed so when she said "I will," that I feared she was going to faint; and Will looked yellow, which I suppose is his way of turning pale, and his big black eyes looked big and excited. And what with seeing Agnes and Will so excited, she heaving and throbbing visibly, and looking faint but happy, and his hands shaking, and the congregation murmuring the "Amens" behind us, I got excited too, I suppose, for I felt my legs shaking under me. Then we all knelt, and when they rose up married, and the minister shook hands with them and wished them happiness, we went into the vestry, and arranged about the marriage lines, and got into the carriage and drove home, Mr. and Mrs. Morris and Sarah on the back seat and Papa and I on the front, I with just three ideas in my head; that I had seen a wedding; the remembrance of Agnes's face as she responded, and a conviction that if I saw any flirtation tomorrow I should burst; for I could not stand it after seeing the real article.[11]

Agnes quite recovered her spirits as soon as it was all over, and ate a good dinner, with the Christmas pudding we made yesterday. All the afternoon Will and Agnes sat about together in the parlor, utterly unable to keep apart for two minutes, and a state of absurd happiness delightful to see. It quite softened my heart toward Will to see him so fond of her. We sang and played some, and had the wedding cake for supper, after which I gave Agnes in private my good opinion of her Betrothed, and we hugged each other, and I gave her my blessing, and she said she was very happy. As if a mole couldn't have seen that! We had a little *Nicholas*, and then I ran into the parlor, where Will was in an excited state, kissed Agnes goodnight, ran upstairs taking a bit of wedding cake to put under my pillow and dream of my lover on; religiously thought of Kitty before getting in; slept with the utmost stupidity and dreamed of nothing whatever, to my profound disgust.

Oct. 28

Monday. Took leave of Agnes when I went to school. She turned white as we hugged each other, and I feared she would faint; I saw my face in the hat rack glass, and I think I was pale too. So we said goodbye and I went, Lucy having promised to see to the throwing of an old shoe after the wedded pair. Dear Agnes Winney! She was gone when I got home. Examined in History and

11. Agnes Winny ("of Boston") and William Morris ("of Providence") were married at St. Mary's Episcopal Church, at the corner of Bowdoin and Topliff streets, in Dorchester. (Marriage record provided by the Episcopal Diocese of Massachusetts.)

Geography. There was an awful question about Latitude in the Geog; Hattie, Fanny and I all sat in a row glaring at the board, and exchanging demonstrations of despair. At the end of my paper I wrote "Mr. Horne, that 9ᵗʰ question will rise up against you at the day of Judgment!" and gave it in. Such O's as the girls indulged in when I told them! I went home with a pleasing fear of five checks in deportment, and with the wedding cake under my head dreamed that the whole school went elephant hunting with Mr. H. as chief hunter.

Oct. 29ᵗʰ

Tuesday. Arithmetic and Grammar examination, the latter a perfectly awful one. After school we girls flew at one another about the parsing.[12] Mr. H. when he returned our papers laid his hand on my shoulder and said "Not against me I hope," and he had written against my "P.S." "I trust not." When he came around afterward to speak to me, I, feeling very much ashamed of myself, begged his pardon, he laughed and said "Oh not at all!" I like him—I do!

Oct. 30ᵗʰ

Wednesday. Spelling examination; Emma Adams and I were the only ones perfect. When into Boston, got 2 satisfactory Atheneum books and my *Ledger*, and was dress-makered.

Oct. 31ˢᵗ

Thursday. Miss C. went into Boston and Mama and I ate together to our great content, and got supper ourselves. I have a very bad chilblain on my foot. Mamma told Miss Chadbourne about Mr. Garrison and her own early doings. I love to hear of them, and listened wide open. It was very interesting; and I resolved to take off that setting hen tomorrow. Ugh! How I do dread it!

NOVEMBER

Nov. 1ˢᵗ

Friday. School etc. Mamma took off the setting hen, so I did not have to. After school She, Sadie, stood at the door, handsomer than ever, and talked to me.

Nov. 2ⁿᵈ

Saturday. Some of the second class spoke. In our new seats Eddy Jenkins sits right before me, I am sorry to say. Went into Boston in the P.M. and heard

12. To parse is to break down a sentence into its component parts of speech with an explantion of the form, function, and syntactical relationship of each part.

Macdonald lecture on Tom Hood. Mamma and I sat on the platform within two feet of him, and Mamma liked it. Stood up both going in and coming out. Changed two books. Mrs. Stanton, a pleasant, short, excessively fat little old lady with white curls, and her daughter Hattie, who had come out in special compliment to me, and whom I was therefore expected to entertain. [1]

Nov. 3ᵈ

Sunday. Mrs. and Miss Stanton were here, and were shown over the house, and then driven into Boston. Made a little cake and wrote to Kitty and Aunt Elizabeth.

Nov. 4ᵗʰ

Monday. Took *Real Folks* to school for Fanny Benedict. We had our music lesson of course. Papa went to make a speech, and we all went to bed early.

Nov. 5ᵗʰ

Tuesday. Failed!! TWICE!!! in HISTORY!!!!!!!!!!! The first time in two years! I took Fanny Benedict out for Geography, got into the dressing room, told her not to speak to me, and just cried till I didn't dare to cry any more, for fear it would show when I went into the other room; and I'd not have it do that for anything. And I came within an inch of another failure in Geography. You see Fanny had been telling me about her father, who got his death of consumption with Sherman, when he marched to the sea;[2] and how he had been three days and nights up to his waist in water—I can't go over the whole of it; and how she came up here and all the other girls had fathers—she fairly made me cry. I longed to hug her, but I only squeezed her hand a little; and expect sympathy is bad for the brains, for I failed, as I said; and dreamed all night of

---

1. Elizabeth Cady Stanton (1815–1902), pioneer in woman's rights causes and early associate of the Stone Blackwells, broke with them in 1868 when she and Susan B. Anthony founded the NWSA (*NAW*). Stanton had been exchanging letters with Henry and Lucy for several months prior to this visit, as all three tried to move beyond their differences and rally suffrage support for Ulysses S. Grant, the Republican presidential candidate. On the previous Tuesday, Stanton had failed to find them at the WJ office and in a note, beginning "Dear Friends," had promised to call the following week. The visit of Stanton (and her sixteen-year-old daughter Harriet) to Pope's Hill indicates further healing had taken place in an otherwise strained relationship (Elizabeth Cady Stanton to "Dear Friends": 29 Oct. 1872, National American Woman Suffrage Association Papers, LC. See this collection for other letters exchanged during this period).

2. Led by General William Tecumseh Sherman, Fanny's father was one of over sixty thousand Union men who marched across Georgia in one of the most destructive and controversial episodes of the Civil War.

---

failures and marks and tardiness; and thought of that con—cerned history the first thing in the morning when I woke.

Nov. 6th

Wednesday. Felt decidedly joyful, in spite of those abominable failures yesterday, at the thought of hearing Robert Collyer. Books, *Ledger* and supper disposed of, Lucy arrived at the office, and we all went to the music hall, which was crammed of course. We had pretty good seats. The lecture was "Our Folks and Other Folks" and was GOOD. A big piece of it Woman's Rights too.[3] After it was over we went into the dressing room where he spoke to them and shook hands with us. Mamma said how good it was to have had the chance to say all that for the women and he said "Warn't it now?" and told Mama it was like summer to see her face, and we went out home in a pouring rain, and walked up through floods. But the sight of him was as good as the smell of black birch; and his very hat and coat were delightful to look upon. Lucy gave her opinion that seen near by he is as rugged as a pine fence. And I agreed. That is a grand good fellow, whatever any one may say to the contrary.

Nov. 7th

Thursday. It rained, and there was but one session. I sorted rags, did chores and practiced. Papa went to N.Y. so I read *Nicholas Nickleby* in the evening. Was good, and tried, really. Lucy and I had our feet soaked at night, and were dosed with tansy tea, tho' I for one didn't need it. I drank to the health of Roberts Kidd and Collyer. Ugh how bitter it was!

Nov. 8th

Friday. The cow, not being tied, got out of her stall during the night, ate about a barrelfull of apples, poked her nose into the corn, and everything else; so this morning the barn was in a sweet mess. A splendid day, after the atrocious rainy weather we have had. Practiced some, and was good.

Nov. 9th

Saturday. Declamations up in the hall. Sadie Wilson and Hattie Burdett, Sam King and another Creature, and all the primary schools.[4] I had to speak first, which was villainous; but I did it some how; and it wasn't specially dreadful

3. Collyer spoke "earnestly and eloquently" in favor of "granting women every right enjoyed by men" and cited many instances in which women were distinguishing themselves. This talk was given the day after the presidential election (*BDG*: 7 Nov. 1872).

4. Dorchester primary schools participated in this program held at Lyceum Hall.

after all. But Eddy Jenkins was excused (I guess because Mr. H. saw he was sure to break down) and Mary Emma Ryder, after going very well through the first part of her short piece without moving a muscle, stopped, said "Mr. Horne, I cant go on;" came back to her seat, cried, sobbed and shook, with as little noise as possible, and nearly had hysterics. They didn't all speak. Tried to be good. Emma came and was duly hugged. We all went up to the den to see a great fire in Boston, the blaze of which lit up the city steeples and state house, and the roar of which was plainly to be heard here, four miles away. After much trotting up and down stairs in dishabille, I finally went to bed.[5]

Nov. 10th

Sunday. Mike and the girls brought home from church and mass news of the fire, which still burns. We went down to Fields corner to post a letter, and smelt the smoke very strongly; and stopped at the Carters and got a paper and some particulars. The glare is not ablaz[e] tonight.

Nov. 11th

Monday. My eyes were very bad. Hattie read the History lesson to me and so I learned it. In the afternoon all the scholars in our room went to Emma Danley's[6] funeral but Perrin, Coleman and Craigin. They held high carnival in the school room, I looking on, till Mr. H. came back and came down on Coleman. There were no lessons in the P.M.

Nov. 12th

Tuesday. My eyes were very bad, and I stopped going to school. Was sorry, as I hate to lose my place in the class, and dont exactly see how I am to make up the lessons; but of course I must save my eyes at all costs. Worked in the house in the morning, and in the garden in the P.M. Went down to Neponset with Emma in the evening, and got some crochetting cotton.

---

5. This devastating Boston fire covered sixty-five acres and destroyed one thousand business firms, at an estimated loss of $100,000,000. Discovered about 7:15 Saturday evening, it began on the southeast corner of Summer and Kingston streets, quickly spread to adjoining streets, and was not brought under control until noon the next day. Accounts of the fire took over most of the space in local newspapers for the next several days. The *WJ* also printed an account of the fire, written by Lucy, in which she wrote of her own experience: "The roaring of the fire was heard miles away. . . . The awful grandeur of the sight will never be forgotten by those who saw it" (*WJ*: 17 Nov. 1872).

6. Emma Danley remains unidentified. Boston newspaper obituaries for this period were sporadic, at best, because of the amount of coverage devoted to the fire.

Nov. 13th

Wednesday. Made some apple jelly. Glanced over a *Ledger* which Mamma would not let me read. Worked. Papa got home, bringing hickory and walnuts, and apples from our dear old West Bloomfield place, making me horribly homesick.[7]

Nov. 14th

Thursday. Made pear and apple sauce, worked, longed to read, and read some of my scribblings to Lucy. Comforted myself by sitting on the floor by the upper hall window and cuddling *Nature and Life*, which I could not read, during the dusk of the evening. Emma got home from Boston very wet. Read my *Ledger* and made my eyes smart.

Nov. 15th

Friday. Emptied the two great vases and unpacked Mamma's writing desk; was pretty busy with chores, and spells of piano in between. Finished and sent my letter to Aunt Ellen. *Nicholas Nickleby*.

Nov. 16th*

Saturday. Went into Boston to Dr. Derby. He asked all sorts of questions concerning my general conduct and character; said there was no danger; that I had overstrained my eyes; that resting might or might not restore me their use, but that he would advise my being put under treatment. (Emma is writing for me on account of my eyes, but is not responsible for the grammar or sentiments; but she is accountable for the spelling and capitals.) Parents being going to St. Louis for a week nothing was to be done till they came back.[8] We, that is, Emma and myself, went in together and got several glimpses of the burnt district, but were prevented by soldiers from entering those enchanting regions. But mamma and I afterward had a fine view of it from the upper window of Hovey's store. It has a very strange dim volcanic look with piles of masonry emerging from a sea of smoke and fire engines spouting promiscuously among them. Emma (who is behaving in a very aggravating [way] and blotting this horribly) got herself vaccinated in three places, and it is to be hoped some of them will take.

---

* Entries marked with an asterisk indicate that they are written in Emma's hand.

7. Henry held onto their former home in West Bloomfield (now part of Montclair), N.J., as one of a number of real estate investments.

8. Lucy and Henry would be in St. Louis for the annual meeting of the AWSA.

Ruins from the Boston fire.

Nov. 17th*

Sunday. Passed a decidedly dull morning making jelly, and unable to read. In the afternoon went over to St. Mary's Chapel, leaving those two vagabonds Emma and Lucy at home; I did not like the looks of Dr. Mills at all.[9] The sermon I thought good, only rather too much of the sit-still-and-let-God-have-his-own-way kind. Fanny Benedict walked home with an ugly boy whom I learned from Fanny Brown (walking home with <u>her</u> young gentleman) to be great irresistible, Walter Brock. And that vicious looking puffy-faced little negro was described to me by her as "<u>handsome</u>"!! Truly there is no accounting for tastes. *Nicholas Nickleby.*

9. William A. Mills, rector of St. Mary's Episcopal Church in Dorchester, sometimes served St. Mary's Chapel, a small, newly built mission church at Lower Mills on Dorchester Ave. near Ruggles Place. Services were often held on Sunday afternoon or evening.

Nov. 18th*

Monday. Papa and Mamma started early in the morning for St. Louis. I strung the ivies, made jelly, churned; loitered dismally through a great part of the afternoon with nothing to do. Did up the supper dishes; was musical in the parlor with Emma and Lucy in the evening. Emma is the most aggravating of cousins. Oh you WRETCH!!

Nov. 19th*

Tuesday. Cleared the bushes of the dead morning-glory vines; Lucy and I made cake which was intended for jelly cake, but which became cake minus the jelly. Went down to the school-house at four o'clock with a note for Fanny Benedict, expressing my opinion of that Brock boy. Hattie was monitor, of course, and when the files had gone out dragged me upstairs into the school-room; therein I created more commotion during the ten minutes I sat there, than in all my career before in that place. I never supposed I was much liked, but changed my mind on the subject. Hattie clutched me on one side, to make me correct her composition while from the other Fanny Benedict poured male-dictions upon me for what I had said of her beloved, while Mr. Horne and Miss Tolman smiled amiably upon me from the front. Walked home with Hattie and Lulu Mann and Emma Adams, had a little fun and came home.

Nov. 20th*

Wednesday. Made cake on my own hook, and devoured my *Ledger* when it came which was worse for my eyes. Went to ride with Emma and Lucy over to Milton and was scared nearly out of my life, and was half frozen. Lucy read Nicholas aloud. Emma is an angel!

Nov. 21st

Thursday. Made some little cakes in the morning, and in the afternoon walked over to Milton by a round about way, and came back by the straight one. Emma brought home some dates. *Nicholas Nickleby.*

Nov. 22nd

Friday. Emma brought home some more dates, but did not fulfill any other of the small commissions I gave her. She thought she had brought home three lemons, but they proved three oranges, to my great disappointment.

Nov. 23d

Saturday. Went down to Hattie Mann's in the P.M. and was received with acclamations. Emma Adams and Annie Phipps were there, and we played

Honor Bright, and there was a good deal of squealing and blushing, and I got quite worked up, though of course there was nothing very dreadful to be got out of me.

Nov. 24th

Sunday. Went down early to Hattie's, after bolting my breakfast, and wearing my purple dress for the first time. We got Emma Adams and met Mary Fifield, and went to the Sunday school. It was a pleasant carpeted room with benches, and after a sermon or address from Mr. Adams, the benches were turned face to face as you turn the seats in the cars, and each class took possession of two. Our class consisting of Hattie, Emma, Annie Phips and M. Fifield and two girls I dont know, declared with one voice that they didn't know a word of their lesson, so the teacher proposed to talk about Thanksgiving. This proposal was received with favor by the class, and he stated his views of Thanksgiving and we contradicted him. I enjoyed it though I didn't like the teacher's looks at all.

*After that we went into church and sat through a stupid sermon.[10] We walked home along with Addie Calender, who asked me about "the Molly thing" and told me of a very fine compliment which had been paid me on that score by a gentleman who said I had the true poetical genius—if I wrote it. She refused to tell me his name until I gave her a copy of the piece, but said he was about fifty years old, and otherwise aggravated my curiosity by hints. Hattie told her of my sins, such as sewing on Sunday. She was horrified and incredulous and we had quite a shrieking time going home.

Nov. 25th*

Monday. Got some moss in the pasture above the school-house and made two small ferneries with it. Left a *Young Folks* at Addie Calender's and learned the name of the mysterious gentleman; Dr. Fifield. Got some honey at Field's Corner.

Nov. 26th*

Tuesday. Made a lemon pie. Lay in wait for Agnes Reed after school and went down to her house to inquire after a girl. Mrs. Reed knew of none. She did not seem half so terrific as Agnes Winney's account of her had led me to expect.

10. Alice was attending Sunday school and church at Dorchester's First Parish Church (Congregational-Unitarian) on Meeting House Hill. Nathaniel Hall had served as pastor there for thirty-seven years.

Nov. 27th*

Wednesday. Read a *Ledger* which came yesterday, and horrified Lucy by something I said in the religious way as we cleared off the dinner dishes.

Nov. 28th*

Thursday. Thanksgiving. Papa, mamma, Emma and I took a long ride, and came back to our dinner at three o'clock. Dined off my massacred roosters, besides cranberry sauce and squash pie, et cetera. Papa and I had cider and toast in the evening and Papa read *The Newcombs* aloud. The story has by this time become hopelessly complicated. Did several chores.

Nov. 29th*

Friday. A dismal day. Snoud[11] (Emma is responsible for spelling and did that out of pure cussedness) part of the day. Practiced, and did chores. Emma slept with me.

Nov. 30th

Saturday. Emma and I went into Boston and shopped a pair of gloves and shoes for me, and did some other errands.

DECEMBER

Dec. 1st

Sunday. Moved down into the lower room. Mr. Blanchard called and Papa made absurd demonstrations of wrath.

Dec. 2

Monday. Read and practiced from notes and tried my eyes and decided they were better.

Dec. 3d

Tuesday. Eyes were worse again. Went to sit through the history but only sat through the first hour of an examination by Mr. Adams.

Dec. 4th

Wednesday. Carried down the little black and white kitten to Mrs. Ross's in my arms. It was dreadfully scared by the railroad trains and struggled under

11. Emma's deliberate misspelling of "snowed" was enough to compel Alice to resume writing the rest of this entry, and several succeeding ones.

my cloak, but I placed it safely under Mrs. Reed's care, and went on to Hattie Mann's, being joined on the way by Mary Fifield. Hattie taught Mary, who had brought along some worsted, to make those starry mats, and I learned at the same time.[1]

Dec. 5th*

Thursday. The switch man at the station was killed by a train. Went into Boston with Mamma and bought two ounces of shaded green worsted for mats, found at the office a letter from Miss Andrews asking me to come Thursday. Accordingly I bolted home, bolted my dinner, packed my bag in a hurry, and went back to Boston through a snow-storm. Mamma escorted me to the Eastern depot and I was dispatched to Miss Andrews rightside up with care. Got there all safe, walked up to the house and was received with rejoicings. Indeed, as Miss Andrews said I was the Prodigal Son; or as I maintained the Prodigal Daughter.

Dec. 6th*

Friday. Miss A. kept me busy and did not let me read much. Under her guidance I began [a] parlor holder, modelled after a very striking mosaic patchwork, one which she had made as a Christmas present. We made apple-snow and chicken-stuffing. Miss A. is a regular gold mine as regards Christmas ideas. She suggested making court-plaster cases for some of my folks, and we sallied forth to buy materials.[2] We stopped at Nina Stone's[3] house and rang the bell several times, but no one came and we gave it up in despair. On the way I told Miss Andrews all about Mr. Collyer; and she made some remarks. She knows too, after her own fashion. We did our shopping, went home and set to work on the court-plaster cases. Mr. Hale met us while we were out, and I stood as stiff as a ramrod while he was with us, to his great admiration; for the first remark he made when I was out of the room was how straight I had grown. He and Miss Emily and Miss Andrews and I went to a

---

1. Alice was learning how to make heavy mats out of knotted worsted balls, sewn together to form stars. This kind of "fancy work" served as decorative additions to tables and also protected wood surfaces from the stains of kerosene lamps.

2. Parlor holders were usually made out of perforated cardboard that was then embroidered and decorated with yarn and paper. They were used as wall pockets or table top portfolios to hold newspapers, visitors cards, etc., or simply as room decorations. Court plaster cases, made from similar material, were fancy holders for bandages. Apple snow is a sweet dessert made out of cooked and mashed apples, whipped egg whites, sugar, and lemon.

3. Nina Stone had attended Jane Andrew's school with Alice.

Eastern and Fitchburg Railroad Stations.

microscopic and calcium light-exhibition. Nina was there and she and I sat together during the exhibition, which was very interesting. The lecture showed magnified bed-bugs, fleas, jellyfish and various other things, animate and inanimate. Miss A. had told me how much Nina was improved and I was rather disappointed, for during the half hour or so we sat together before the lecture began she talked of hardly anything but her numerous flirtations and an old French Professor who fell in love with her while she was abroad.

Dec. 7th*

Saturday. Sewed some more on my holder. Nina came over as I had asked her to, bringing the numbers of our old school paper. We hunted them all over for the piece I wrote about Wild Azalias as Nina and Miss A. both urged me to send it to the *Young Folks*, but one leaf was gone and the thing was minus; so I went over to Nina's and copied it from her copy. She showed me her cabinet of curiosities and likewise a beautiful picture of Aurora which made me break the 10th commandment on the spot.[4] Mr. Hale was at the station to see me off when I went, though whether Miss Andrews might not have been the chief

4. The Tenth Commandment prohibits coveting the possessions of one's neighbor.

attraction I cant say. Mamma met me at the Boston end of the line with the carriage and drove me home to Dorchester.

Dec. 8th*

Sunday. Got up early, and bolted something that stood for breakfast and departed for Hattie Mann's, and thense with her to Sunday-School. I had not meant to go to the sermon afterwards but Addie Calendar told me there was a nice preacher instead of Mr. Hall, so I did. The minister reminded me of uncle Henry Lawrence only that he had yellowish hair and beard and not so much of the latter. He preached a very good sermon from the text "What the Lord speaketh that I must do," about our consciences. Made apple snow, but it was not so good as Miss A's. Emma is a beast.

Dec. 9th

Monday. Made mince meat For Pies[5] (Emma is responsible for capitals and my only comfort is that these reflect eternal disgrace upon her). Got to reading *Man and Wife*, and forgot all about school till evening. *Newcomes*. Emma is an atrocious clod hopping tadpole, and I have taken to writing myself in sheer self defense from her atrocious alterations and misrepresentations. Posterity, if you find any thing surprisingly vile and vulgar in her writing, dont lay it to <u>my</u> charge, I beg.

Dec. 10

Tuesday. The anniversary of our house-burning. Sat through the history recitation and returned Hattie Mann's Sunday School book which I had accidentally carried home from church. Made pound cake. Emma is a traitor, a liar and a Villain. These blots be on her Chignon. I have no words bad enough for her. I mean to ink her nose. (a scuffle; partial success.)

Dec. 11

Wednesday. Went down to Hattie Mann's in the P.M. and was shown about the making of my green mats.

Dec. 12

Thursday. School. Fought Emma in her chamber, and retired to bed wounded by the wires of her bustle, which I had used as an offensive weapon. Lay awake till very late.

---

5. Alice resumed writing her entry after "Pies."

Dec. 13

Friday. School. Worked on my green starry mats. A good selfconceited person, Mrs. Fletcher,[6] who lectures, was here.

Dec. 14th

Saturday. Mrs. F. still here. Went into Boston, and enjoyed hearing George William Cu[r]tis lecture at the institute of Technology. All through the first part of the lecture I was worried to think who Mr. Curtis looked like. It is Mr. Hale, and the resemblance is very odd and extremely striking. I like the effect of an audience of ladies very much; there is a pleasant little rustle and whisper and friendliness and—indescribable sich.[7]

Dec. 15th

Sunday. Hurried off to Sunday school with only a slice and a half of bread for breakfast. ~~There was a new minister and I~~ Did not stay to church. Took a long ride with Mrs. Fletcher and my parents.

Dec. 16th

Monday. Went into Boston, and bought Christmas books with Papa. *Good Words for the Young* was not to be had, and had to be sent for. Mama took me to Dr. Safford, whose office is right opposite Mrs. Whitney's in Boylston place to be vaccinated.[8] She is a very small slim pleasant woman, and when she had vaccinated me felt of my belt to see how I was dressed and greatly approved. She thought it was due to a "strong minded mother" till I told her the contrary.

6. Mrs. Matilda Fletcher, of Council Bluffs, Iowa, had been lecturing in the West and Midwest that fall, sponsored by various Republican campaign committees (*WJ*: 21 Sept. 1872).

7. Sich may be Alice's phonetic spelling of the Old English words siche or sike, meaning sighing. George William Curtis (1824–92), author and orator, served as editor of *Harper's Weekly* from 1863 to 1892. Active in a number of reforms (including antislavery and woman's suffrage), he was a close associate of the Stone Blackwells (*DAB*). He spoke at the Institute of Technology on "Woman in the Past, Present, and Future," saying it was time women be given a choice of "spheres" if their love of learning made them wish a life, not in the nursery "but in the library, the laboratory, or the observatory" (*BDG*: 14 Dec. 1872).

8. Mary Jane Blake Safford (1834–91), Civil War nurse, physican, and advocate of dress reform, had just begun a private practice at 4 Boylston Place, after moving from Chicago. She soon joined the Boston University School of Medicine as professor of women's diseases and later also served on the staff of the Massachusetts Homeopathic Hospital. A lecturer and writer on women's dress, exercise, and hygiene, she took a

I stayed to the Ladies' Club tea and discussion and enjoyed both. I like to hear people with brains who like to think [and] discuss. Dr. Clarke was speaking of the weakness of girls.[9] I griped Dr. Safford's hand with all my might, and delighted her with my muscle. The supper was very nice, and I fraternized with a little Kitty Tolman who at the supper table addressed me and said she thought she might speak to me as I had smiled at her before supper. We were very friendly together, and she was very earnest with me to come and see her, and I kissed her goodbye. We drove out home through a snow storm, I having had a splendid time, and decided that if one smiles at people they are very apt to smile back again, and that there may be other poor little cats shying about in strange garrets who relish a friendly look as much as I do.

Dec. 17th

Tuesday. Mrs. Fletcher went away. Worked at Christmas presents.

Dec. 18th

Wednesday. Mama went away in the afternoon and I howled because I was forbidden to sew on court plaster cases, but got leave. *The Newcomes* has got exciting. Papa read about Lady Clara Pulleyn fainting at sight of Jack Belsize. I sympathized with poor Jack very much; but if I had been in his place catch me letting her marry that detestable Barnes; I would have eloped with her and married her out of hand.

Dec. 19th

Thursday. Alone all day with everybody gone. In the evening Mama drove Emma and me in a sleigh down to a literary society in Neponset. It was rather dull, assembled in two very small rooms. There was a dull essay, and then a

---

warm interest in efforts to better the condition of working women and became one of the first women to serve on the Boston School Committee (1875) (*NAW*). The *WJ* carried a long article about Safford shortly before her move to Boston, describing her homey office with its lace curtains, plants, and oil paintings, observing: "We didn't espy a solitary spitoon, not a nauseating pipe, a pair of muddy boots, or even a cigar stump, those customary sweet relics of masculine medical offices." (*WJ*: 18 May 1872).

9. Dr. E. H. Clarke, author of *Sex in Education* (1873), read his paper on "The Higher Education of Women as Influenced by Physical Conditions" at a New England Woman's Club meeting at 4:30 that afternoon; a club tea followed at 7 in the evening. Clarke's contention that college education arrested women's reproductive development and "masculinized" them sparked much debate at the gathering; later the *WJ* reported that although other prominent men, such as President Charles Eliot of Harvard, agreed with Clarke, " the ladies without exception differed from his conclusion." (*WJ*: 17 May 1873).

lady read *Virginia* and Mrs. Stowe, and candy was passed round, and Emma was unanimously elected a member by a vote of about three hands half held up, every one else being engaged chattering. They wanted me to become a member, but I excused myself with some difficulty.

Dec. 20

Friday. Stormy. Emma taught me how to make worsted balls. Worked at Christmas presents. *The Newcomes*.

Dec. 21st

Saturday. Heard Mr. Higginson lecture with Emma at the Technology, and did not <u>very</u> much admire it.[10] Bought various Christmas things with her assistance, it being my last chance before I go to N.J. and came out late.[11] Met the sleigh before we reached the Turnpike and drove out home. *Newcomes*, and worked on presents.

Dec. 22nd

Sunday. Last day of Sunday school. Papa drove me down in the sleigh. I delight in the smooth swift motion. Pilgrim day.[12] Worked hard at Christmas presents, and took a long cold ride with our folks. Oh it is <u>the</u> coldest weather!

Dec. 23d

Monday. Emma came into my room early, and presented me with a silver and green cornucopia, bidding me think of her whenever I dropped anything into it. Went into Boston thro' a snowstorm and was started by Papa for N.Y. Rode all day, the first part of the way thro' a snow storm, and got to N.Y. a good deal behind time. I saw nothing of Aunts, and it was a huge empty Coliseum of a depot, so I got into the 4th Ave. cars, which stood in the depot clamourously demanding passengers—I mean the drivers did—and demanded to be put out at Cooper Institute. As the car moved out of the station, Aunt Ellen got in, having given me up. I left her at Cooper's, sending a telegram north to say I

---

10. Thomas Wentworth Higginson (1823–1911), abolitionist, Civil War colonel, woman's rights advocate, author, and Congregational minister, had officiated at Lucy and Henry's wedding in 1855. A frequent contributor to a number of popular literary magazines, especially the *Atlantic Monthly*, he remained closely allied with the Stone Blackwells as a contributing editor to the WJ (DAB).

11. Alice was preparing to spend Christmas in Somerville, N.J., at the home of her uncle and aunt, Samuel and Antoinette Brown Blackwell.

12. Pilgrim Day commemorated the landing of the Pilgrims at Plymouth in 1620.

---

had arrived right side up, and went to the infirmary. I found Uncle George and Aunt Emily getting a private supper in the back parlor, and I partook.[13]

Dec. 24th

Tuesday. Worked a little on Christmas presents and saw Cornelia and Hannah.[14] Uncle G. had said Neelie's forehead was grown over with hair to the eyebrows, and that she formed the connecting link between man and monkey, etc; most atrocious Baron Munchausen lies, as I discovered. I believed him, and with what my parents had said, was prepared for something monstrous. I was very pleasantly surprised on being ushered into the nursery to see t[w]o pretty babies, one white, one brown, the latter being no more a monkey than Uncle G.'s self, nor as much; and having all the forehead she needs. She made friends with me at once. Nannie was shyer, but did so presently. Aunt Emily, the Nurse, the babies and I went out to Somerville. Nannie cried with terror at getting into the hack, and had to be tenderly guided and guarded all the way but Nina stared around her with large round black eyes, somewhat wondering but entirely plucky. I had charge of her part of the way, and she took my hand and trotted along stoutly where she could walk, pushing at a market basket ahead of us which impeded the way, with an energy delightful to see. When she had to be carried in the crowd she let herself be hauled along just as it happened, in a most unceremonious manner, without a howl, only an occasional kick. Uncle Sam met and drove us up. At supper, just as U. S. had begun to carve, the table began to slope down toward the middle from the ends, and crockery and lamps and all came down with a prodigious crash and a horrible mingling of milk and kerosene on the carpet. Uncle S. seized a lamp from the wreck and blew it out; all was confusion. Happily it was good kerosene and did not explode; but we had to wait some time for our supper. The accident was caused by a defective leaf. Hung up our stockings.

Dec. 25th

Wednesday. Christmas day. F[lorence] and I got our stockings and opened them in bed. We found some goodies and a slate pencil in each. About noon

13. Alice made the eight-hour trip to New York City alone, arriving at the massive Grand Central Depot, completed the year before (at Fourth Ave., between 42d and 45th streets). Apparently she thought she could find Ellen Blackwell at the Cooper Union (housed then in a brownstone building between Third and Fourth avenues just north of the Bowery), a tuition-free school that included a school of art for women. Alice spent the night at the New York Infirmary for Women and Children, a large house on Second Ave. and 8th St. that also provided living quarters for Emily and Ellen Blackwell.

14. Alice's New York aunts had recently adopted baby girls: Hannah ("Nannie") belonged to Emily Blackwell, and Cornelia (called "Neelie," "Neenie," and "Nina") belonged to Ellen Blackwell.

Aunt Ellen and Uncle G. arrived, and then we were let in to the tree. I got some note paper from F. a drawing book and some smaller things. Likewise a book called *Insects at Home*, which the grown folks read with interest and viewed with profound disgust. My taste does not lie at all in the direction of Natural History, and I was greatly disappointed, tho' I tried not to show it. After the tree came dinner, and then Aunt Emily and Uncle G. went away. We had games and snap dragon in the evening; the snap dragon was a success, the games not much. And between you and me and the post, it was not a very nice Christmas.[15] F. and I were neither grown ups nor children, but miserable mediums, and bewailed ourselves accordingly. But still, it was Christmas.

Dec. 26

Thursday. It snowed all day hard, and Aunt Ellen and the babies could not get away. Consequently the house was over-run with babies. I read and practiced, and told some story to Edie and Grace. In the evening U. S. read some fairy stories out of *Is it True?* aloud. Aunt Nettie says *Vanity Fair* is a dreadful book, dismal and horrible, without a single good person in it. I always supposed it was rather funny.

Dec. 27

Friday. Snowed up. Said to be the deepest snow for 15 years. One person got to Somerville, and brought back news that 3 trains had got through. Read and practiced and told more story. U. S. read *Isaac T. Hopper* aloud. They have a custom here I like very much; evening exercise. When the lamps are first lighted U. S. and Aunt N. percuss one another—she told me to say at home she beat U. S. every day—and occasionally she makes a dive and percusses on[e] of the young ones, who dont like it all.[16]

Dec. 28

Saturday. O <u>such</u> a quarrelsome set! Dug a snow house outside the kitchen door. U. S. read more Isaac T. in the evening.

15. Snapdragon was a Christmas game in which players snatched raisins from a bowl of burning brandy.

Alice may have been missing her parents, who stayed in Boston to work on the *WJ*. Earlier in the day she had opened the sealed note that they sent with her and learned that their Christmas gifts of "a scent bottle, note paper, and Encylopedias" would be awaiting her at home.

16. Tapping or gently striking another's back and upper shoulders was thought by many to induce beneficial circulation and muscle relaxation.

Dec. 29ᵗʰ

Sunday. Flo tried to get to Sunday School through the snow. We had church in the parlor. Read and played. More Isaac T. in the evening. U. S. got me to talking about Mr. Collyer and things, and I wished I hadn't. I generally do wish so afterward. Stiff and sore from snow digging yesterday.

Dec. 30

Monday. Ate between meals and had the stomach ache. F. and sisters fought like Kilkenny cats as usual. Talked over old times, scrapes and misdeeds with F. When Edie intruded on us we talked a chow-chow of all sorts of languages.

Dec. 31ˢᵗ

Tuesday. Rode down to the station in the sleigh with U. S., Aunt Nettie and Edie, and . . . U. S. saw me onto the Orange horsecars, and I went out to Roseville. It was so changed I should not have known it. I inquired for the Hoopers, and found them. They live in what used to be the white violet swamp beyond Bank St. Now it's all built up with French roofs. The Hoopers jubilated over me, and fed me, and Nellie and I tried to make much of one another. She is much as she used to be. Mrs. Hooper talked to me, spoke of Mr. Collyer, then in N.Y. and said some things of him for which I could have hugged her. That his life shamed people who believed as she did, etc. I had but a couple of hours to stay, and Nelly went down to the station with me. I went round by our house hoping against hope for a sight of Purr; but got none, and seeing it only made me want to cry. I got safely to Second Ave. and was only insulted once. In the evening the old folks went to hear Proff. Tyndall, and I read Keats and played blocks with Edie.[17] She and I went up to bed, but when I had lighted her gas and started for my own little room, I opened the door, heard a cough and breathing and hastily retreated. Evidently there was someone in my bed. I told E. my intention of going down and sitting up till my aunts came home; but she flatly refused to go to bed with a burglar in the next room, and began to put on her boots again. In desperation I lighted a match and went to see who it was. As I softly opened the door a head arose from the bed-clothes and a voice inquired, "Am I in the wrong spot?" I told her she was, and she said she was Miss Crane, and had mistaken the room—was on the wrong floor. She departed, and I pulled off the sheets—I was not going to sleep in them after goodness knew who—and went to sleep between the blankets. Aunt Em. told

17. Because Alice had already heard John Tyndall in Boston, she stayed home to read from the English poet John Keats (1795–1821).

me next day I need not be alarmed, as Miss Crane was a nurse and had no disease. I forgot to say that I had made Aunt Emily stethoscope me, to see if there was anything the matter with my lungs, which she did after some teasing, with great parade, Edie looking on with terror stricken and breathless interest.

THE JOURNAL FOR 1873

JANUARY

Jan. 1st

Wednesday. Rode all day on the cars with Edie going home. Dozed through a good part of the journey. Had my seat to myself most of the way, but when the rear car broke down the people from it had to be seated in the other cars, and one big man sat down by me. Papa and Uncle Stone[1] met us at the Boston depot and drove us out home in the sleigh. My head ached hard. Mamma was glad to see us. The Hoopers told us of a notice in the *Herald* that Mamma would not lecture this winter because her infant son was but 4 weeks old, and wanted to congratulate me. When I told Papa he said he wished it was true. So said all of us but Mamma. Poor little Anna is ill again, and Emma cannot come back.

Jan. 2nd

Thursday. Took Edie down to school and presented her to Mr. Horne, who asked her some questions, and will put her in Miss Boynton's room.[2] Did house-chores, and kept house with Edie, all the folks being away.

Jan. 3d

Friday. Edie and I worked under Mamma's direction in the A.M. making beds and doing various things. Read in the afternoon.

1. "Uncle Stone," Lucy's brother Bowman from West Brookfield, had just begun a one-year term as a representative from his district to the Massachusetts Legislature, where he chaired the House Committee on Woman Suffrage (*WJ*: 8 Feb. 1890, obituary).
2. Edie had just turned twelve when she began this extended stay at Pope's Hill. Her teacher at Harris School was Elizabeth Boynton.

Boston and Albany Railroad Station.

Jan. 4th

Saturday. In the morning we had our first lesson in English History, and I think I shall like it very much. Afterwards went into Boston with Edie to get her vaccinated. She was much scared and I was revaccinated before her, as the last did not take and Dr. Safford offered, as I thought it might give E. courage. But it didn't—only scared her the more I think; however, she got through it, and brought home a dreadful account of its hurting. We forgot the certificate of vaccination and had to go back for it. We lunched at Marston's on strawberry sauce and fried oysters. I got Charles Lamb's *Essays of Elia* from the Atheneum, and we came out home. It's queer how many little bits about C. Lamb I have come across since I read about him in Mr. Collyer's "Root and Flower,"[3] and then noticed.

Jan. 5th

Sunday. Read a good deal, my eyes being well, and practiced. Washed all over. Practiced.

Jan. 6th

Monday. Took Edie down to school and delivered her to Mr. Horne. Went and recited English History in the P.M. and when Edie was let out we went down to

3. "Root and Flower" appeared in *Nature and Life,* a book of sermons by Robert Collyer.

Field's Corner after some yeast and had her weighed. She weighs 92. I hope she will gain a deal before she goes back. *Newcomes.*

Jan. 7th

Tuesday. Worked nearly all the time I was at home and went after more yeast. Got some pickled limes. School.

Jan. 8th

Wednesday. School. Uncle George appeared in the morning. I have been giving Edie music lessons, and as she was eager to try a tune I let her begin on 'Mary to the Savior's tomb,' which is easy. We are going to keep it a secret from Papa, and surprise him. *Newcomes.*

Jan. 9th

Thursday. School. Walked over to North Quincy with Edie, and slept better after it than I have for some nights past; from which I opine that open air walking is good for insomnia. O what a word.

Jan. 10th

Friday. A natural philosophy lesson. I think it is going to be very interesting. Next lesson Mr. H. is actually going to "Weigh as the weight of the wind"—the air at least, and even gas. I never supposed gas had any weight, as it goes up. But I find the air buoys it up as water does a bit of wood; and without the air the gas would fall down like the wood. After school got my sled, which had gone to be mended, and when Edie was let out we went into our yard and we rode down hill. Papa and Uncle George came out and rode some and Papa was determined to start us on a trip. Now Papa preferred to go down one way, so as to cross the ice among the appletrees, and E. and I liked to go the other way; so he gave us a tremendous start in the way we did not want to go, in spite of my outcries and protestations. As neither Edie nor I could steer, that happened which might have been expected; near the end of our course we ran against an apple tree, and Edie, who sat in front, bruised her leg. But she walked up the hill, took another trip or two, and then we went in. Edie's foot hurt, and I found her crying, and Papa, trying to comfort her, doubtless feeling like a murderer. We doctored her with molasses candy internally, and hot water and arnica externally; which proved of use.

Jan. 11th

Saturday. Went into Boston to buy mittens and *The Life that Now Is*. Sadie came into the depot and talked to me, and I found I did not care for her any more. Emma [Adams] and some of the others came in. Emma said she saw me striding along swinging my arms, and waved her muff at me, but I would not look at her, and that she did not believe I would have stopped if Robert Collyer had been behind me. I said "Wouldn't I?" Got the mittens, and inquired the price of fur caps, as Mamma had ordered me, which was a severe trial to my feelings; but seeing that I ought, and that I was going to buy Mr. Collyer's book, I thought I must, and did. Then I bought it ($1.50) and brought it home, and showed Mamma and Edie. I mystified Edie at first; told her it was something good, and so it was, I'm sure.

Jan. 12th

Sunday. Down in the Slough of Despond again.[4] I did think I was through that. Mr. Collyer pretty effectually pulled me out before, and I went and read *The Life that Now Is*, and was pulled out again for the time being. But for Mr. Collyer and those two books of his, I don't know what I should do. I really felt as if I was praying that night when I said God bless him. Walked nearly to Milton with Edie.

Jan. 13th

Monday. English History, and a tiff with Edie in the evening. Still in the Slough of Despond. It appears that last nights pull out was only for the time being. I felt dreadfully; went into the parlor in the evening, and down on my knees in the dark, praying and crying for help, with a dreadful feeling that after all I might be praying and crying to nothing, and no one any where to hear me.

Jan. 14th

Tuesday. Did not have to go to school. Felt a little better, but still in trouble. Mamma at dinner told Edie and me a story about a slave woman, Margaret Gar[ner], who killed one of her little girls and tried to kill the other when she found they were to be recaptured. And Mamma went down to the court room when her case was to be tried, and a Mr. Somebody—Joliffe, I think—asked leave of the court for Mamma to speak, and she spoke. The court stood breathless, and the slave holder sweat as Mamma said she never saw a man before; and when Mamma ended and came down, he promised her Margaret Gardiner

---

4. Alice is referring to John Bunyan's *Pilgrim's Progress*, likening her despair to that of the character Christian, who fell into a bog called the Slough of Despond and could not get out because of the bundle of sins on his back. In the story, Help came along and aided Christian out of the sticky mire.

should never be sold into slavery again; but he lied, and sold her in New Orleans. The boat she was on was run into by another, and when the water rose where she sat chained, holding her baby, she let it float away and drown; but she was saved—and sold. I don't wonder that man sweat—I did as Mamma told—at least Edie says so; and I know I felt like it. She said that when they asked her if she offered the woman a knife (she had asked her if she had one) she said yes; and in her speech said "If I had the law against me, and the church against me, and the Constitution of the Country against me, and the Public Sentiment against me, etc. I would tear open my veins with my teeth and let the earth that had never injured me drink my blood, before I would be sold back into slavery!" Mamma got excited again as she went over it, and wished she could remember what she had said. I thought it at first rather dreadful to kill her children, but Mamma thought it was grand of her; and especially to kill the girls. The boys would not be so badly off as slaves. "Ah, Margaret Gar[ner]," she said, "you will be one of the tallest angels in heaven, for you were one of the bravest women here." "Mamma," said I, "I think you will be tall in heaven." And so I do.[5]

In the evening reading I brought in some codfish and vinegar, and papa shut the book and refused to read, unless it was taken out, and opened the window at the risk of freezing the geraniums, and made a great fuss. As he wouldn't go on reading, and the open window made the room cold, Mamma came out into the dining room, and told Edie and me about Mr. Collyer, some things I never heard before; and finally we went back and the reading was finished.

Jan. 15th

Wednesday. Natural Philosophy. I locked Edie into the parlor to make her do her practicing, and she wouldn't; then I went to do mine, taking a cloak and a book in case she should lock me in, which she did. Afterward she softly unlocked the door, but not being ready to come out, I stayed and finished my practicing.

Jan. 16th

Thursday. English History. Kept house in the morning, and read a good deal. It didn't hurt my eyes, and they are certainly better. During my usual evening

5. In her biography of her mother, Alice described Margaret Garner, her trial, and the events surrounding it. The trial took place in Cincinnati in 1856 and attracted newspaper attention partly because of Lucy's testimony. Even though she spoke after the court was adjourned, she did so in a courtroom and in the presence of the judge and spectators—all unprecedented privileges for a woman at that time. Many considered her action legally and morally improper, and she was dubbed a fanatical female (see Alice Stone Blackwell, *Lucy Stone*, 183–85; *Liberator*: 29 Feb. 1856).

squabble with Edie she hit me a blow on the nose which made it ache till I went to bed, and it is still tender. I have taken to rubbing Mamma's knee in the evening. It is good for her rheumatism, and she sleeps better for it. *Newcomes*. Oh, that book makes me *so* savage sometimes!

Jan. 17th

Friday. Furiously rainy. Natural Philosophy in the A.M. Worked most of the rest of the day. *Newcomes*.

Jan. 18th

Saturday. Worked. Wind, hail and rain, in spite of which Emma and Lucy Chadburne arrived. She has been to Mrs. Whitneys, but Mrs. W. was sick and could not see her. *Newcomes*. A scrubbage with E. for poetry.

Jan. 19th

Sunday. Read and practiced. Went to church and looked at the pulpit from which Robert Collyer had preached, and tried to decide which was the pew where I sat; while I waited for the service to begin; for I got there a great deal too early. I had some idea of going up and touching the bible on the pulpit He read from, but didn't quite dare. The sermon was unutterably stupid, though good, but Mr. Horne and Carrie Littlefield spoke to me, and Esther Whiton invited me to sit in her pew, and the singing was good, especially "Nearer My God to Thee."

Jan. 20

Monday. Went to Eng. History. Mr. H. apparently had a dreadful headache. I pitied him and hoped it was not small pox. But of course he has been vaccinated. Music from Emma.

Jan. 21st

Tuesday. Went to see Dr. Safford. She showed me no end of wonderful and queer things; pictures of birds, a soup tureen in the form of a turtle, white elephants, and idols of all sorts and kinds. I looked at these last with much interest, especially the Siamese, on account of Mrs. Leonowens.[6] How could they worship such hideous things! They might have made prettier ones while they were about it. I couldn't describe one ninetieth part of what I saw, so I won't try; but she likewise showed me a section of an eyelid through a micro-

---

6. Alice had recently read Anna Leonowen's book about Siam, *The Romance of the Harem*. Mary Safford collected her curiosities in the course of extensive travel abroad, partly in connection with her surgical training in Vienna and Germany (1869–72).

---

scope, and it was really very pretty. I got home late for dinner, with a bad headache. A letter from Kitty in the evening. She has been reading *Petronel Fleming*, whom she describes as one of the kind who like the men best who are able to thrash them, but refrain out of consideration for their weakness—like Doris, I suppose—and says she expects <u>ME</u> to be one of the Petronel kind when I marry her!![7] My first impulse was to pen a second thunderbolt, even fiercer than the first, and again break the engagement. I took Edie into the hall, and knocked her down seven times. I meditated, and finally decided to marry, and disappoint, her.

Jan. 22nd

Wednesday. Philosophy, with an experiment in capillary attraction. I promised Hattie Mann to go down and play chess with her in the afternoon, and forgot all about it. Went after yeast with Edie, and was florally inclined in the P.M. Dr. Safford encouraged the idea of a green house, and I studied Vick[8] and *The Three Little Spades*. Edie and I had a squabble in the third story for the key of the cedar closet, and she gave me (unintentionally) a kick on the cheeck which nearly broke my jaw. Emma read *The Newcomes*.

Jan. 23d

Thursday. Papa got home from N.Y. Hattie Mann invited me to play chess with her, and I forgot to go. Edie and I went for yeast. Emma and Edie got to plaguing me, and I, thinking of Mr. Collyer, blushed so furiously as to astonish both them and myself. Emma evidently thought there was something up, and oh how they did go at me!

Jan. 24th

Friday. A furious storm of drifting snow, through which Edie and I fought our way to school. Made piecrust for the mince meat, and completed the $5. list from Vick's with Emma's help. Newcomes.

Jan. 25th

Saturday. I sent off a Subscription to the *Household* for Miss Andrews, and much gossiping was stirred up by the mysterious letter. Emma guessed it was Fields and Osgood;[9] Mamma, Robert Collyer, which last guess much upset

---

7. Kitty was reading *Petronel* by British author Florence Church Lean.
8. "Vick's Floral Guide."
9. The Boston publishing firm of James Osgood had been preceded by Fields and Osgood.

me. I asked her afterward what on earth made her guess <u>that</u>, and she said she thought I might have read something of his (she caught me reading his sermons a few evenings ago) so good that I wanted to write and thank him for it. As if I should have <u>dared</u> to write to him! All the folks rode into Boston leaving me to keep house, and Hattie and Lulu Mann came up to see me and played and borrowed books. No *Newcomes*. Made apple sauce.

Jan. 26th

Sunday. Went to church with Emma and Edie. Worked and read.

Jan. 27th

Monday. Snow. History examination, working reading and practicing.

Jan. 28th

Tuesday. At home all day. Papa and Mamma away in the evening. Emma set Edie and me a puzzle, and we talked and told riddles. Emma spoke of the sermon she heard last Sunday, and abused Pamela. But <u>I</u> would rather be the author of ten books like *Pamela* than one poem like "Don Juan." I don't think the shockingness in *Pamela*—the calling ugly things by their own ugly names—is half so bad as in things where they may have less open indecency, but where they treat it all jokingly, and laugh at terrible sins—actually try to make them seem <u>comical</u>! That's what drives me furious. I wish they would suppress Byron's poems as they did Mrs. Woodhull's paper.[10] I'm sure they are worse. And as I undressed I wondered where Lord Byron was then; and whether he was sorry yet. He will have a dreadful time of it when he does begin to repent. As if it was any business of mine!

Jan. 29th

Wednesday. Went to Natural Philosophy, and though bright, it was so cold Edie cried all the way down to school. Went into the city with Emma, bought a

10. Victoria Claflin Woodhull (1838–1927) and Tennessee Claflin (1845–1923), freewheeling reformers and sisters, published *Woodhull and Claflin's Weekly* (1870–76) in New York, with sensational stories on everything from short skirts to legalized prostitution and free love. A special issue in November 1872 charged that the powerful New York preacher Henry Ward Beecher had committed adultery with Elizabeth Tilton (wife of editor Theodore Tilton). This resulted in the sisters' arrest and jailing for passing obscenity through the mails (*NAW*).

Lord Byron (1788–1824), English poet and author of *Don Juan*, had been a popular topic after Harriet Beecher Stowe wrote her controversial book *Lady Byron Vindicated* in 1870, revealing that he had committed a number of "sexual vices," including adultery and incest (see *NAW*, v. 3, 400).

corn colored and black necktie and a net,[11] changed some library books and came home.

Jan. 30th

Thursday. Began going to school all day. I don't think I shall be able to keep it up; but Mamma (gone to Maine) wants me to try.

Jan. 31st

Friday. After school came home with Edie and Emelia Sophia[12] dressed us for the sociable. We met Hattie Mann, by agreement, outside the church, but didn't go in for some time. I got so cold that at Hattie's suggestion I went into the dark empty church to get warm; but it was cold and I stole up to the pulpit and kissed the big bible Mr. Collyer read from, and came out. We finally went in, but the people did not come till later, most of them, and supper was not over till about 9, when we came away, just as the fun was beginning, after I had eaten too much and not had the jolliest possible time. I was introduced to a pleasant sweet looking girl, Nettie Young, whom I expect to like; and as Edith hunted for her rubbers I watched through the door the dancing that had just begun, and oh! to see Mr. Horne whirling about on one leg! We girls speculated on the probability of his having one of his awful headaches tomorrow. Came home in the dark with a small pen knife open in my hand in expectation of robbers and murderers, scared at every sound. Papa and Mamma got home.

FEBRUARY

Feb. 1st

Saturday. School. Edie in a sick and stomach-acheic condition after last night's disippation, and I—have collapsed, though not badly. Edith and I went down to Mrs. Sullivan's and took her the money for her last washing. Worked and read.

Feb. 2nd

Sunday. Went down to bible class, but Hattie Mann was not there according to appointment, though Carrie Littlefield was, and I sat in her pew at church. I didn't like the bible class much, nor particularly the sunday school afterwards. And as for the sermon after that, I did not understand much of it, and what I

---

11. A net was a piece of fine meshwork, probably used by Alice as a stole or head covering.
12. Emelia Sophia is Emma.

did in general I disagreed with. Emma was there. When I had walked about half way home (bearing a purloined hymnbook) I found I had forgotten my cloud[1] and had to go back for it. Read and made some candy. Edie was inspired by the sight of my proceedings to try too. Mine was a success; her's not much. *Newcomes.*

Feb. 3^d

Monday. School. *Newcomes* in the evening I believe but I have nearly forgotten what happened, which shows it was nothing important.

Feb. 4th

Tuesday. Mary Emma Ryder took me out to History with her. Lulu Mann came up home with me after school and made a call, and took home a couple of books.

Feb. 5th

Wednesday. Went into Boston and got *Margaret & Her Bridesmaids* again from the Library. That would be a very nice book if it did not come [with] the obey so strong. Shopped with Emma. Got a grey mohair for Spring, and a print for Summer wrapper, and went to Miss Randall and was measured. Came out on the same train with Emma, Mamma, Uncle Bo, Ruth Swan, and Lulu Mann and mother. *Newcomes.* New girl.[2]

Feb. 6th

Thursday. Left off Geography. Mr. Horne away all day. Edith has eaten too much fruit, and has diarhoea accordingly. Papa went to N.Y. sending by a Emma with great secrecy, a letter advising me to sleep with Mamma, because she felt lonely when he was gone. I didn't but Emma did. She finished *The Newcomes* in the evening.

Feb. 7th

Friday. Wrote a letter to Kitty, chiefly in school. Edith groaning with stomach ache. A delightful sea fog, in which I smelt the sea, and thought of M[artha's] V[ineyard]. Emma finished *The Newcomes* aloud.

---

1. A cloud was a light, loosely knitted woolen scarf worn by women.
2. The identity of this new domestic is unclear. From other letters of the period, it appears that several women had been hired during this time, including a Mrs. Spear. Alice does not seem especially attached to any of them, perhaps because she is enjoying the companionship of Emma and Edie.

Feb. 8ᵗʰ

Saturday. Found to my unspeakable consternation that we must have pieces to speak chosen by Monday, and this the first I heard of it, and it always takes me a week to choose my piece! Looked up pieces in my big book, and am divided in my mind between "Laus Deo" and "The Blessed Damozel."

Feb. 9ᵗʰ

Sunday. Went down to bible class, but Mr. Badger[3] was not there and there was none. There was a scrambling sort of Sunday school, and I fell in love at first sight with a bright looking little girl about 12 I should think whom I found on inquiry to be Bessie Johnson of the Industrial institution.[4] Did not stay to church. Worried as to what piece to speak, and looked over flowerseeds with Edith. Papa read *Middlemarch* aloud in the evening.

Feb. 10ᵗʰ

Monday. Am feeling rather badly. In the middle of supper Mamma bade me put some apples to bake for Papa. I didn't exactly feel like going down cellar in the dark, but went out. There was no oil in the lamps and I came back to ask where the candles were (I had asked something before about the oven) and Mamma jumped up and said it was less trouble to go for them herself, and went. She came back to table, and said before Mrs. Spear and Edie and Emma that She was so ASHAMED OF ALICE that she did not want any one to say anything or talk or something. I have forgotten what happened (besides school) in the first part of the day.

Feb. 11ᵗʰ

Tuesday. Took my design to school. After school walked over Milton Hill and back for exercise, and made my bed and Uncle Stone's and set the table, and felt virtuous.

Feb. 12ᵗʰ

Wednesday. Went into Boston, got *The Knickerbocker*, being obliged to return *Margaret and her Bridesmaids*. Returned books at Lorings, got my fitting over, went for note paper with Emma and to the P.O. (the Old South) for letters. Emma had her pocket picked and we suspected an officious old gentle-

3. The Reverend Henry Badger was the pastor at the Third Unitarian Society located near the Harris School.
4. The Industrial School in Dorchester was for destitute or neglected girls, who were given a basic education and taught housework and sewing skills.

man who seems to haunt the P.O. especially to give information to bewildered females.

Feb. 13th

Thursday. Mike has found a nest of young rabbits in the garden, and Edith has rabbit on the brain. They were hauled out of the hole by me (it is nearly the depth of my arm, which was nearly pulled out of the socket reaching after them) and they were duly examined. Toby is said to have eaten one, and Edie is frantic if he is seen out of doors.

Feb. 14th

Friday. More hauling over of rabbits. Church Sociable in the evening. I went with Hattie Mann, right from school, and sewed two baby sleeves of scarlet flannel with black dots—very pretty work, but it tried my eyes some, and stained my fingers badly. Hattie's were stained too, and we went over to Fanny Benedict's and washed them in vinegar. Hattie's came out, but mine wouldn't. Danced Uglemug watched the Virginia reel and waltzes and had a good time.

Feb. 15th

Saturday. Went into Boston with Edie. We joined Emma and we all went to see "Rachel the Reaper" and "The Gentle Savage" at the museum. Both were good I think, though Emma was disgusted with "The Gentle Savage."[5] I got *What She Could* at the Atheneum, *Margaret and her Bridesmaids* being out. Mr. Garrison and Colonel T. W. Higginson were in the office, and Mr. G. said the place was garrisoned and there was the Commander, and T. W. said they were prepared to dispose of pamphlets at reasonable rates.

Feb. 16th

Sunday. Went down to Bible Class, but there was none Mr. Badger being sick so went over with Hattie to Meeting house hill. The sermon was good but absurdly delivered. Saw who in the world but Nina Stone as I came out. She is here on a visit. Walked home through a snow storm. Emma slept with me, and

---

5. The Boston Museum was presenting two popular plays: *Rachael the Reaper*, a pastoral drama by Charles Reade, and *Ye Gentle Savage*, a localization of John Brougham's *Pocahontas*. Emma reviewed the performances for the WJ, signing her article "The Irregular Reporter," saying she liked *Rachael* but found the *Gentle Savage* to be "a farce, which attempting to be witty, succeeds only in being low. Its chief reliance for creating a laugh, is on . . . vulgar gyrations and display" (BDG: 27 Jan. 1873; WJ: 1 Mar. 1873).

Boston Museum.

I kicked and mauled her for some outrageous remarks whe made concerning "The Gentle Savage" yesterday.

Feb. 17th

Monday. Put turnip tops by the rabbit hole for the old mother to eat, and brought in the young ones to feed. Edie is really my thorn in the flesh.

Feb. 18th

Tuesday. School. Emma read *Middlemarch* in the evening.

Feb. 19th

Wednesday. Went over in the P.M. to the Chocolate factory with Mary Emma, Lulu and Hattie, but the expedition was rather a fraud, being made in rain and slush, and as I only got a little chocolate. *Middlemarch*.

Feb. 20

Thursday. Mrs. Spear's daughter came here to see her. I put the bookcase in order, and in so doing discovered the works and poems of Mr. Garrison, which I read in the evening with great interest.[6] The poor little rabbits are all dead; their hole caved in and crushed them. Mike showed me two of the frozen corpses.

Feb. 21st

Friday. Tomorrow is Washington's Birthday, and in honor of it we have had an explosion at school in the P.M. We read *The Character of Washington*; Mr. Horne read part of his "Farewell Address," and some of the scholars who had patriotic pieces recited them. A furious snowstorm arose while we were at it, and I was minus even an umbrella or waterproof. It snowed I think harder than I ever saw it, and I did not know what to do. But Mama sent Mike down with the sleigh, and we rode home. I never saw such a storm. When we turned the corner the sleet bit our faces painfully, and the wind blew like the Judgment Day. How the snow did whirl to be sure! We were nearly dead by the time we got home. It was truly magnificent. I went up into my den to watch the storm. When Papa got home he was coated and crusted with snow, and clean exhausted. He said the morning papers in the weather reports predicted a great storm. It seemed so good to be in the house!

Feb. 22

Saturday. Edie and I folded Papers for Papa. Clear and cold. Washington's birthday, and therefore holiday.

Feb. 23d

Sunday. Did not go to church nor anywhere. Great drifts on the roads reported. Read and loafed; got along pretty comfortably. Studied flower catalogues, etc. Read "Storming Heaven" again, but it did not do me much good.[7] Told Edie, who was bothering me, that I wouldn't speak to her till 3, and didn't, though she said provoking things to make me. Washed myself and my hair.

Feb. 24th

Monday. In the evening before supper I said I smelt smoke, but they thought it was a whimsy. I got through before the rest, and as I went to get wood for the

6. Alice was probably reading *Selections from the Writings and Speeches of William Lloyd Garrison* (Boston: R. F. Wallcutt, 1852). Garrison also wrote a slim volume of largely antislavery verse, *Garrison's Poems: Sonnets and Other Poems* (Boston: Oliver Johnson, 1843).

7. "Storming Heaven" is from Robert Collyer's book of sermons, *The Life That Now Is*.

library fire, the closet was full of a smell of burning. Papa and Mrs. Spear smelt it, and I was starting down cellar with a lamp to see if all was right there, when Mamma called out from the bathroom that the trouble was there. We rushed up to be nearly strangled with smoke. Mamma had hung some things over the stem of the gas, and they had caught fire, set fire to the wall and burnt off the rubber tube that goes to the gas stove. Mamma turned off the gas, badly burning her hand, and we all rushed. I collected the bed room pitchers, filled them at the sink, where all the faucets but one were frozen, and carried them up to the fire. Papa and Mike cut the wall open with an axe, and poured water down, and the fire was finally put out without much damage except to the one wall, and the filling the house [with] the old sickening smell of wood smoke.

Feb. 25ᵗʰ

Tuesday. Edith had tableaux in the evening with Papa.[8] They were of thrilling interest (anything but; that's ironical) and Papa and Uncle Bo and I, who were audience, applauded much and kissed a little. We then had *Middlemarch*.

Feb. 26ᵗʰ

Wednesday. Wanted to get *Margaret and Bridesmaids* again from the library, but Papa said he would get it for me, wanting me to stay and go riding with Mamma, which I did. We went in search of hay and I enlivened the journey by fighting Edith. *Middlemarch*. Studied for History examination.

Feb. 27ᵗʰ

Thursday. History examination in the morning. Went back in the P.M. to correct it, but found I had 100. Did not stay, as I haven't had Geography, but came home. Read *Margaret and her Bridesmaids*.

Feb. 28ᵗʰ

Friday. Grammar ex. in the morning, Arithmetic (100) in P.M. Read *Margaret & Bridesmaids*. Went to the sociable in the afternoon right from school. Sewed on the same sort of work, and had to go over to F. Benedict's to wash off the stains in vinegar with Hattie. The Benedicts have such a queer little house inside; little rooms opening out of one another, and the huge family packed like herrings in a a box. Hattie promised to dance Uglemug with me, but didn't. I

8. A popular form of entertainment in the nineteenth century was the tableau vivant, or living picture: a scene presented (often on a stage) by costumed actors who remain silent and motionless as if in a painting. Such tableaux were often presented at the church sociables Alice attended at Lyceum Hall.

was taken forcible possession of by a girl wh[en] Florrie dragged me away and told me she was an awfully acting girl, Mrs. Whitton's servant. Edie could not go because of her cold.

MARCH

March 1st

Saturday. Went over to Hattie's, played a game of chess, and beat her. Her mother taught us the Scholar's game, and gave me an item for Mamma. I like chess.

March 2nd

Sunday. Went to Bible class in the morning, and stayed to Sunday School. We went for a ride in the afternoon.

March 3d

Monday. It snowed hard. Gave Edie a music lesson and made some candy.

March 4th

Tuesday. Were driven to and from school, and the snow on Boutwell Ave. was up to the bodies of horse and sleigh. I am number 2. My eyes were bad in the P.M. I got another letter from Kitty, and implored Mamma to let me go to England. Edith intreated to the contrary, but Mamma seemed so favorable as to give me good hopes. I feared I had injured my cause by knocking down Edith who pulled Mamma down with her, but I guess not. What a perverse little creature I am! Now there seems a good chance of my going I am not so sure I want to.

March 5th

Wednesday. School, and a frantic scramble over spelling. Read, sewed, felt poetical, and thought about going to England.

March 6th

Thursday. Rode down hill with Edie, and tumbled off the sled about 5 times successively, to her great amusement.

March 7th

Friday. Had an unusually violent fight with Edie. A Mr. Allen came to examine us, and asked for a definition of History, and I said it was facts related in the order they occurred. Being asked if necessarily in order, I said I supposed the separate facts would be history, but not a history unless they were told in a string. Just one of my absurd speeches that are always popping out in spite of me! If there were a trap door under my seat I should certainly astonish the primary scholars by coming through now and then, for I am often ready to sink in my shoes. Mr. H[orne] charitably said it would certainly not be much of a history that was not strung on something, so I felt better. *Middlemarch.*

Mar. 8th

Saturday. Went into Boston, changed a book, and saw the Campbell's who are coming, and Miss Eastman.[1] Fathomless mud and water. Appointed with Lily Morse about the music lessons.

March 9th

Sunday. Bible Class; read, and fought Edie. Papa was "drunk" in the evening.[2] *Middlemarch.*

March 10th

Monday. A furious snow storm and one session. Made a lemon pie.

March 11th

Tuesday. Gray and fresh. Fought my way home from school after being kept in over an abominable sum in cube root which gave me head ache & backache and all over ache, against a magnificent March wind that almost upset me, and in the P.M. through a furious rain storm. Made Washington Pie.[3]

March 12th

Wednesday. Went with Edie to Carrie Morse's, and Lilla gave us our lesson. Agnes [Winny] came and was hugged. She looks miserably unwell.[4]

1. Mary Eastman, a former teacher at Antioch College, began lecturing for the MWSA in 1872 (*WJ*: 3 Mar. 1872). She became active in the New England Woman's Club, sometimes assisted in the *WJ* office and developed a close attachment to the Stone Blackwells.

2. Alice described the "game of drunk" in a letter to Kitty, saying that it consisted of: "Papa chasing Edith and myself around the table and tumbling back upon us in a tipsy manner, [with] . . . gesticulations on his part, and howls on ours." (ASB to KBB: 25 Mar. 1873, SL). Henry's game may have been his way of scoring a point for the temperance cause he and Lucy supported. It may also have been a way of releasing his own pent-up energy.

3. Washington pie was probably a cherry cream pie.

4. Agnes was pregnant at this time.

March 13

Thursday. Fought Agnes and Edith, and did my practicing. Papa did drunk surprisingly to Agnes's great amusement.

March 14th

Friday. Went to the sociable with Edith. They had a charade & music, but I did not enjoy it very much.

March 15th

Saturday. Was to have gone in to the dentist with Mamma, but it threatened a storm and I didn't. I believe I fought Agnes & Edith & practiced.

March 16th

Sunday. Went to Bible Class, and then to ride with Papa and Mamma & Edith. We set out for Quincy Great Head; but there seems a fate about that place—we are never able to get to it. This time we had to turn back for the wind, which beside being cold gave us all serious fears several times that it would upset the carriage. And Edie yelped and howled and rolled her self up in her waterproof all through the homeward journey. Made labels for flower beds.

March 17th

Monday. School again. Brought home a willow stick and made more flower seed labels. *Middlemarch*, after which Papa was drunk. Neither Edie nor I have yet got the penny Mamma offered as prize for a day of peace between us.

March 18th

Tuesday. Eyes bad. Shook in my shoes during the history, but did not miss. Mamma held a court in the evening to see if Edith and I were to have our pennies for yesterday, when we scrummaged about shutting the door. Papa was Judge, and sat in the big chair looking very absurd in the green lamp shade, which was put on to give him a Judicial aspect. Edie & I were prisoners at the bar, and Mamma was witness. After a sifting of the evidence it was decided that neither of us deserved our penny. I was much disgusted, for I think I deserved mine.

March 19th

Wednesday. Mr. Horne announced that we were to bring in letter compositions Saturday. Edith & I went to our music lesson.

March 20

Thursday. Snowed. School & practicing.

March 21ˢᵗ

Friday. Worked on my composition and was aggravated by Edie. Phebe [Stone] was here in the evening, and we had *Middlemarch* in the dining room.

March 22

Saturday. Went into Boston with Edith, and showed her the mummies.[5] There was no one else there, so Mrs. Foster showed and explained to us. Mamma came while we were there. The mummy case with the handsome carved face that reminded me of Miss Andrews and Aunt Marian, is that of an Egyptian princess. I think almost the most interesting thing there is a slender, dark, delicate woman's hand, with a little gold ring on the little finger. It has been cut off from some mummy, and lies in the glass case. It is said to be 4000 years old. I wondered how much the former owner of it cares for it now; whether she remembers the little gold ring; and how much I shall care what becomes of my hands and feet 4000 years after I die. I feel as if I should retain a certain interest in them; I always keep a tenderness for my old dresses. I got from the library the first volume of *The Ring and the Book*, the only thing in of Robert Browning's, and read at it by snatches, but am not ready to say what I think of it yet. I debated whether to come out in the cars or in the carriage with Mamma and Edie. I finally chose the cars, which was lucky, as Mamma and Edith lost their way and had rather a time of it. *Middlemarch* & <u>drunk.</u>

March 23ᵈ

Sunday. Bible class, and a long cold ride. Did half an hour's practising left over from yesterday. *Middlemarch.*

March 24

Monday. As we were playing <u>drunk</u> Papa and Edith plunged through the glass door. Crash went the glass, bang went Edith's head, howl went Edith. There was a great cut on her wrist, which we did up. I put her to bed, and she expressed her conviction that she should bleed to death in the night.

---

5. Alice took Edie to see a special exhibit of Egyptian antiquities on display at the Boston Athenaeum. The collection belonged to Samuel A. Way and had just been given to the Museum of Fine Arts (*WJ*: 27 July 1872).

March 25th

Tuesday. School. I find examinations begin Thursday. Practiced. *Middlemarch.*

March 26th

Wednesday. Went to music lessons, and came home through a pouring rain. My dress and cloak shed water like an umbrella when I came in. Read a *Harper's Magazine* as I waited for Edith and for Miss Morse to see a caller. Studied up my U.S. history, and studied and worried myself into a headache. Went to bed, slept ill, and dreamed I was Burgoyne, and doing the wrong events. I wish History was at the bottom of the sea.

March 27th

Thursday. History examination. 100 by the skin of my teeth.

March 28th

Friday. Grammar and Arithmetic. 91 and 90!!!! A sociable in the evening. Sewed, felt very dismal because of my bad examinations (what ever possessed me to forget the rule for present worth?) and watched Blue Beard with great edification.

March 29th

Saturday. Spelling examination. Went into Boston, returned *Middlemarch,* got the second vol. of *The Ring & the Book*, also another of his, and came home through such a rain!

March 30th

Sunday. No Bible class. Took a ~~long~~ walk to the Milton Chapel,[6] sat through the service and came home. There was a most magnificent wind, and I struggled violently and delightedly in the face of it, but as I came home it had somewhat decreased. Mrs. Howe came out here to supper & ~~lecture~~ sermon.[7]

6. Alice again was attending St. Mary's Episcopal Chapel at Lower Mills.

7. Julia Ward Howe (1819–1910), author, club woman, and suffragist, was a close associate of Lucy's. A founding editor of the WJ, she held leadership positions in the AWSA, NEWSA, and MWSA, and for nearly forty years served as president of the New England Woman's Club. She also helped establish the Association for the Advancement of Women, as well as the General Federation of Women's Clubs. Interested in religious issues of the day, she frequently preached in Unitarian and Universalist pulpits and for many years (beginning in 1873) held an annual gathering of women ministers in her home (NAW).

March 31ˢᵗ

Monday. School. I am No. 4. Agnes and I talked and confidentialized, and I enjoyed the possibility of an explosion. Because I think a good deal, and work myself up sometimes till I don't know whether to cry or swear, and there is no one to explode to. Miss Eastman came.

APRIL

April 1ˢᵗ

Tuesday. Miss Eastman overlooked my seeds, and promised to send me some snake cucumber seed. Potted my gourds and squashes. *Middlemarch*. Was kept in nearly half an hour over a worrysome sum, till Mr. H. declared he did not think he could see through it till he had had his dinner. I got it right in the P.M.

April 2ⁿᵈ

Wednesday. Drizzling and misty. Edith and I went to our music lesson. Agnes went away, poor darling, and this is the last day of school for the time being. Went over to Dr. Hall's church and heard Judge Putnam lecture on The passion play of Oberammergau, with Mamma.[1] Our bulbs came.

April 3ᵈ

Thursday. Our first holiday. Edith and I dug and delved in our gardens, practiced, and did some housework.

April 4ᵗʰ

Friday. Went into Boston and got the mail, and made the greater part of a crotchetted band for Agnes's prospective baby. A little girl called to see Edith. Read a new *Ledger* and some of Whittier's poetry. There is no one like Whittier after all.

April 5ᵗʰ

Saturday. Went into Boston again, got the mail and *Gates Ajar*. Mr. Horne came out on the train with me. I was glaring intently out the window when I found him standing in front of me and saying "Good morning." We shook hands, and he helped me out with my various huge parcels, and Mamma drove me home. Ironed. Have crotchetted a circlet of blue worsted, sewed a bit of black

---

1. Judge John Phelps Putnam gave this lecture several times in Boston during the Easter season, according to notices in newspapers.

silk (on which I had worked Mr. Collyer's initials) into it, and wear it around my arm for love of him. That was "The man Help," who once & again pulled me out of the slough of despond. *Middlemarch*.

April 6th

Sunday. Bible class. Went over in the carriage to the Milton Chapel, was let out at the door, and dropt into the nearest seat. The service had not begun. Left my prayer book on the ledge of the porch when I laid it down to put on my cloud. It began to rain as I began to go home, but the carriage met me half way. If I were ever to be any thing but a Unitarian, I think I should have to be an Episcopalian or Catholic; I don't think I could stop at any of the intermediate stations. But I shall never go in that direction. Papa had a very bad headache, and the reading of *Middlemarch*, after the first chapter, had to be turned over to Mamma.

April 7th

Monday. Asked Fanny Benedict to see about my Prayer book. Grey & cool. Am writing an article for the *Journal*,[2] and making a blue bag for Agnes.

April 8th

Tuesday. Finished the blue bag, and wrote some more on my Woman's rights piece. Papa read a chapter of *Middlemarch*, & then departed for N.Y.

April 9th

Wednesday. I don't know what in the world I shall do with my temper! In the end I am afraid I shall murder some one. Edith is excessively aggravating, and there are times when I should like to tear her to pieces. Now & then I do knock her down & pummel her. I hope I may not knock her down & murder her someday. But she fights so vigorously I should have time to recollect myself. Today my stomach is out of order, my feet cold, & I myself cross & with a strong desire to break windows.

April 10th

Thursday. Worked in the garden and about the house and practiced.

2. No article (signed) by Alice appeared in the *WJ* in the next two months. Although the next entry suggests that she was writing a piece on woman's rights, a close inspection of published articles on that subject does not indicate that any were written by Alice.

April 11th

Friday. Sociable. I decided to go, at the last moment, & wore my grey dress. Fought a duel in the dressing room with Emma Adams, with poker & shovel. After the combat we bled internally & writhed much. Addie Calendar & Carrie Littlefield both declared themselves desperately in love with Capt. Kidd. Came home before Edith, whom Papa afterward went for.

April 12th

Saturday. Went in to the dentist, and came out with Mamma through a heavy snowstorm. Mr. & Mrs. Horne and baby were on the platform, & Mamma offered to drive the two last up when our carriage came. Mr. H. said he would go on home and light the fire, and overtook me, I having started to walk up. We went on together, and the snowflakes were huge, as big as birds.

April 13th

Sunday. Stayed at home. Rather an unsatisfactory day. Did not read a sermon either. Stormy.

April 14th

Monday. School again. The school library is now ready, and I got out *Tom Brown*, but could not read it much, my eyes being worse than usual. *Middlemarch*.

April 15th

Tuesday. Am. History. Got through it somehow. Eyes very bad. Edith had Louisa D'Aubigny to tea. *Middlemarch*.

April 16th

Wednesday. Went down to music lesson. It is so provoking I should get nervous! A piece I can play perfectly at home I stumble on constantly. I think the evil spirit gets into my fingers down there, and I told her it seemed so.

April 17th

Thursday. English History. Miss T. is away, and Mr. H. has to take both classes. Mamma sent Edith and me down to Mrs. Sullivan's to pay her some money that is owing her, quite late in the evening, and it was very weird and windy and ghostly, especially where we came out upon the marshes. The only thing to make it perfect would have been to have had Capt. Kidd waiting for me down on the misty shore I was making for; and to have had my old Guardian instead of Papa's cane, and to have Edie keep quieter. When I left I whispered to Mamma that if I was assassinated she was to give my love to Papa & Mr. Collyer, which she promised to do.

April 18th

Friday. Went into Boston after school and got the mail and 1 vol. of *Tom Brown at Oxford* and to my utter dismay & amazement they said Papa had not yet returned *The Harveys*! 16 days out! He certainly has, and they must have forgotten to put it down. I shall make inquiries.

April 19th

Saturday. Papa got home. He has come very near being killed on the railroad. His train and a belated one met at the Stonington Junction and disputed which should go first. His train had the right of way, but the other conductor insisted and so Papa's conductor waived his right, and the other train went first, plunged over a washed away milldam in the pitch darkness, and a lot of people were injured, and the engineer and fire man and ten or twelve passengers burned to death, which was a very narrow escape for Papa, as his car was next the engine and would certainly have been smashed.[3] When I heard of it I went straight up to my den and down on my knees. I don't think I prayed but it seemed the right place to be. I didn't feel exactly in the right mood to go down to Carrie Littlefield's, and rehearse my part of Bessie in the Grecian bend,[4] but I went, and we rehearsed—all but Eva Dix. I got along some how and they approved of me, but I am not at all satisfied; quite the contrary. Papa came for me and took me home.

April 20th

Sunday. Went over to Chapel, walking with Fanny, whom I overtook. It was not as nice as in the afternoon, and there were few there. Rode over to Quincy Great Hill or Head with the folks. It is a glorious place—a great round hill with water all around it, and great cliffs that seemed almost like Martha's Vineyard. I watched my face in the blessed salt water, and heard the sound of it; but it was nearly spoiled by Edith's incessant noise and chatter, which gave me a headache.

---

3. Henry was returning from New York City when the accident occurred, about fourteen miles from Stonington, R.I., at 3:15 A.M. According to newspaper accounts, seven people were killed, and thirty injured. Many injuries were caused by the fires that quickly spread from heating stoves in the cars (*BDG*: 21 Apr. 1873).

4. Alice was rehearsing her part in a play or tableau for an upcoming church sociable.

April 21ˢᵗ

Monday. Got excused from school early to go in to Boston to hear Elizabeth Stuart Phelps read to the Ladies' Club. Got excused too early on account of mistaking the time, ran myself nearly to death, and found myself nearly an hour too early, so went and called on Mary Fifield. At her house I found a copy of Timrod's poems, which I read with great delight but found that he was a rebel and praised the Alabama to the skies![5] Went in, and heard the last few minutes of Elizabeth Stuart Phelps's reading, and got a look at her. She is not ugly, as I have heard, but rather handsome if anything, striking looking, with bright dark eyes. She seemed very earnest, and I was very glad to see and shake hands with her afterward, though she went right away.[6] Then there was discussion, and Dio Lewis defended trails,[7] and convinced me he was a humbug. One oldish lady behind me was very indignant and audibly expressed her wish that he had to wear one. And we went home.

April 22ⁿᵈ

Tuesday. I was to have rehearsed at Carrie's last night, but got home late and tired, forgot and didn't. But I went down this evening, was scolded, petted and told that the next rehearsal is tomorrow night at Mrs. Whall's.

April 23ᵈ

Wednesday. Went to Mrs. Whall's in the evening and rehearsed a Grecian Bend. I was introduced to several people, but had a bad headache and so could not enjoy anything. Mrs. Whall gave me camphor and everyone seemed to sympathize, and I got through it somehow. They rehearsed a gipsey piece

5. The *Alabama* was a Confederate ship. Henry Timrod (1828–67), a southern lyric poet, was receiving literary recognition with the publication of a new volume of his poems, edited by his friend Paul H. Hayne, *The Poems of Henry Timrod* (1873) (*DAB*).

6. Elizabeth Stuart Phelps Ward (1844–1911), popular writer, was best known for her phenomenally successful *The Gates Ajar* (1869), "a barely fictionalized argument that heaven will contain all that is loveliest and best on earth." Besides authoring fifty-seven books, Phelps also wrote numerous articles for magazines, contributing in the 1870s a series for the *Independent*, advocating dress reform, suffrage, and wider employment for women. Her mother, also named Elizabeth Stuart Phelps, was widely known as an author as well (*NAW*).

7. Dioclesian Lewis (1823–86), temperance reformer and pioneer in physical culture, was defending the use of trails, or trains, on women's dresses. Founder of the Boston Normal Institute for Physical Education, he was also noted for his "charming arrangements" for Turkish baths at 17 Beacon Street (*WJ*: 13 Apr. 1872).

before it, and made a great deal of fuss and chatter. I wanted to go home alone, but Mr. Whall said not if he knew it and escorted me.[8]

April 24ᵗʰ

Thursday. Rehearsal (dress) at church in the P.M. I went to Carrie's first, and was by her fixed into an overskirt. In the gipsey piece Mr. Whall did the man asleep, and his little dog lay down with him, and would persist in biting George Whall when he stirred him up to wake him. His barking quite spoiled the pathos, and Mrs. Whall had to keep him in her lap. Our rehearsal went off somehow, and at the last I caught sight of Papa in the audience. I had not dared look in that direction before, and I had to go and demand to know how long he had been there. It seems he had seen all that rehearsal and part of the one before. He then took me home.

April 25ᵗʰ

Friday. The great climax. Rehearsed at noon recess, but had to bolt for school before the others were through. Went home and dressed after school, and went down late. Got through supper somehow, and went and dressed with the others. The dressing room was full to overflowing, and it was such a scene of confusion! I did as well as I could, and was much praised for it afterward. I felt so queer when I was to come upon the stage! Something seemed to press up against my breasts and choke me. But I got through it. I have always got through things somehow. After it was over I went out to the audience and watched the gipsey performance. Papa and Mamma got there just too late to witness my performance! While we girls were larking around in the church Hattie Mann and Fanny Benedict demanded to be married, and I accordingly performed the ceremony in a disjointed and fragmentary manner from memory. The solemnity was rather marred by bride and bridegroom bolting before I could pronounce them man and wife, but it was great fun. As we came home Papa asked the name of "the young lady who poked boughs at me," and when I told him it was Lulu Mann he said she was "exceedingly pretty." Papa and Mamma got lots of compliments on my acting.

April 26ᵗʰ

Saturday. Rode into Boston with Mamma and Edith and Papa, and got two pairs of shoes—of which I am wofully in need,—a hat, and the second vol. of

---

8. The Whalls lived several long blocks from Alice's house, below Pope's Hill on Neponset Ave.

T[om] B[rown] at Oxford. Rode out in rather a bad state of mind, my one consolation being the fact that T. B. was in the bag. Nevertheless I felt very cross and uncomfortab[l]e. When I came in Edith and I were alone in the library and she began saying all the most hateful things she could think of. I stood it a while without answering, and then knocked her over. She went on worse than ever, and I did it again; and finally I gave her a kick, feeling as though I should like to kill her. Such a yell as she set up! I was sorry in a minute, and went upstairs and made my bed, but she groaned and snarled and whimpered and abused me all the evening. *Middlemarch*.

April 27ᵗʰ

Sunday. Read *Tom Brown at Oxford* in the morning, and felt so delighted I squirmed all over, and laughed, and would have liked to hug Tom Hughes. "T.B. at Rugby" would make me want to do that anyway.[9] What he says meets my views just—especially what he says about wild oats—and about all sorts of things too. What he says is so good and true and brave, and he says it so well and bravely and truly that I feel braver and better for it even when it does not especially apply to me. Went over to chapel in the P.M. Mrs. Beales was there, sat by me and found my places when I couldn't.

April 28ᵗʰ

Monday. Mike has caught the rabbit, and he and Papa have built him a hutch. When Edith and I got home from school we saw him—I should say her—put [her] into it, with a dish of water and an apple. He ran about and held up his poor little paws in a most touching manner, trying to get out.

April 29ᵗʰ

Tuesday. Emma Adams invited me to go rowing, and I gladly accepted, but she afterward recalled her invitation saying it was too rough and we had better wait till Thursday. So I walked over to Milton Hill instead, and meant to go farther, but a drop or two of rain made me turn about. I got home dry, though. That Milton hill is a lovely place—worth the three mile walk to see. Finished *Middlemarch*.

April 30ᵗʰ

Wednesday. School in A.M., Music lesson in P.M.

9. Thomas Hughes' *Tom Brown at Oxford* was a sequel to *School Days at Rugby* (1857).

MAY

May 1st

Thursday. Grammar ex. in A.M. and let out early so that the teachers might attend a lecture. History ex. in the afternoon. Rowed with Emma Adams.

May 2nd

Friday. Geography in the A.M. and I took the ex. by Mr. H's. advice, & got 52 the highest mark being 80, which Mr. H. said was very respectable considering. Arithmetic ex. in P.M. I scrabbled frantically through it, expecting every moment that Papa would call for me with the mail to take to Boston; thought I heard him below, and left, certain one sum at least was wrong, but not daring to stay and correct it. Met the carriage coming down the hill, papa having decided to go himself. To have spoilt my ex. for nothing was too bad. I am afraid I was cross to Papa, and I went home and cried. We had *Off the Skelligs* read aloud.

May 3d

Saturday. Spelling ex. I got 100 in that, anyway. Sent in a letter to be posted for Kitty. Read Mr. Garrison's writings, which I like. Very stormy.

May 4th

Sunday. Went over to Chapel in the P.M. Hot—very. Pasted things into my scrap book, practiced and washed. Skelligs. Papa's 48th Birthday.

May 5th

Monday. A singing lesson, and English History. Forgot the $.08 to pay for the ball in the A.M. But remembered in P.M. A year ago today! I remembered.[1]

May 6th

Tuesday. American History. Base Ball at recess. Walked over to North Quincy with Miss Jones[2] & Edith in the evening.

May 7th

Wednesday. Music lesson—a dreadful one. I never can play the piece in this world—never! Walked over to Milton Chapel after supper with Miss Jones, and on coming home we looked through the window and saw Mamma and Edith sitting in the library. Edith looked toward me, and I dodged out of sight. A

1. A year earlier Alice had heard Robert Collyer for the first time.
2. Miss Jones was a new domestic in the household.

moment after I heard a howl, and rushed into the house to find Edith with her face hidden holding onto Mamma and making a great ado. She said she had seen a great white face (Miss Jones's I suppose) crowned with a hat, glaring at her. We finally got her pacified.

May 8th

Thursday. Went in the evening to an entertainment at Mrs. Newhall's with Mamma. A Miss Pearson sang very prettily, and Miss Josephine Ellery read very well. But the singing made me think of dear Alice.

May 9th

Friday. Miss Jones and Edith went down to a sort of sociable at the church, so Papa and Mamma and I had our reading of *Off the Skelligs* in peace and pleasure.

May 10th

Saturday. Went into Boston (drove) and got *Wives and Daughters* from the library, and also Mamma and I chose me a shawl and silk dress.

May 11th

Sunday. Went over to Chapel, which was jammed and saw the Confirmation. Came home in the rain with an umbrella but no water proof, and got wet. An expression in *Wives and Daughters* rather struck me; Cynthia calls herself "A moral kangaroo" competent to a big leap of goodness occasionally, but not to a steady pace of it. It is an uncomfortable beast in my case. *Off the Skelligs.*

May 12th

Monday. Climbed trees with Miss Jones and Edie in the evening, and walked up and down with them on Train St.

May 13th

Tuesday. Got a letter from Nelly Hooper. The last part of it was religious, and stirred me up, and I sat down and answered it immediately, in excitement, stating my views. I stated them in rather strong language I believe, but I felt them strongly, and could not get the right words. I am so glad Mamma has decided to help Alice![3] Did not read above 15m.

3. Lucy apparently loaned Alice Earle money; in an 1875 letter, Lucy wrote that Alice Earle (then engaged) hoped to get pupils so that she could "earn something to pay me"(LS to ASB: 6 Aug. 1875, LC).

May 14th

Wednesday. Went to music lesson. Cut dandelion greens in the evening with Miss Jones and Edie. Got letters from Kitty and Aunt Marian. Went out walking after supper with Edie, and walked a mile and a half in 30m.

May 15th

Thursday. Promised to get to school at 1.30 to play base ball, but forgot. Played at recess and till school. Wrote to Kitty and Aunt Marian. After school walked to Milton Lower Mills, on over Milton Hill and home by way of Granite Bridge—about 7 miles I should think. Am at present in serene enjoyment of a good conscience and blistered feet.

May 16th

Friday. Went into Boston with Mamma after school to a meeting of the dress committee. Mamma agreed to stop at the school house for me in the carriage and wait five minutes for me at a quarter of three. We went up in the hall to recite where there is no clock, and I, haunted by visions of the carriage vanishing in the distance, tossed several frantic little notes over to Hattie to know what time it was. She saw the 3d or 4th and I saw no answer, but she said afterward Emma held up her watch. Finally in desperation I asked to be dismissed; Mr. H. said yes, and I flew down. There was the carriage, all right. We drove in, and I sat in the committee meeting, but found it stupid. I watched a youngish lady opposite who had a face I liked to look at, though I thought it had a slightly wicked expression, and reminded me of a Rebel. Mamma told me afterward that she was Mrs. Woolson[4] whose book I liked so. I had seen her several times and heard her, but from behind and I did not know her. It was rather stupid, but I talked a little to Dr. Safford after it, and got Lowell's[5] poems from the Library. Alice liked those.

---

4. Abba Goold Woolson (1838–1921), teacher, author, and dress reformer, was living then in Boston, where she chaired the dress reform committee of the New England Women's Club. In 1874, she edited *Dress Reform*, a book of five lectures (including one by her and one by Mary Safford) stressing the "physical discomfort and disease caused by corsets and other constricting forms of dress" and including detailed directions for making attractive substitutes. Alice may be referring to her just-published book, *Women in American Society*, a collection of essays portraying a young lady's evolution from "The School Girl" to "The Queen of the Home." (*NAW*).

5. James Russell Lowell (1819–91), American poet (*DAB*).

May 17ᵗʰ

Saturday. Edith and Miss Jones went to Barnum's menagerie;[6] I did not care much about going, so stayed and trimmed rosebushes.

May 18ᵗʰ

Sunday. We all went off on a picnic, and when, after a lovely ride, we had got out and lugged our baskets up a hill it began to pour with rain, and we finally dined under a tent of waterproofs. And then, the rain having stopped, Miss Jones, Edith and I rambled through the woods and loaded ourselves with moss, getting back to the carriage just in time to escape another shower. Then we rode to Hyde Park, and I, knowing they went to ask about Alice, and remembering the last time, felt nervous. . . . In the course of talk about Alice's prospects, Mr. & Mrs. Weld told us a great deal about Mr. & Mrs. Earle and Florence and Mr. Nicholson, whom she has married. It seems that after [s]he was taken to Europe he followed, and fairly besieged the convent to get access to her; finally heard a piano and recognized her playing. She came to the window and managed to speak to him. He said "Can I do anything for you?" and she managed to tell him how her mother was said to be very ill on her account, and she had promised to stay at the convent for the present. She said they must wait, and he then went home. Afterward she wrote home to her family that she should arrive on such a steamer and such a day; that Mr. N. would meet her and they were to be married, and invited them to meet her. None of them did but her brother George, and he did so, and stayed to the wedding; but all the Aunts and uncles and cousins took part with Florence, caressed and made much of her, taking part against Mrs. Earle. Nicholson Mr. Weld believes to be a fine fellow. He was accused of being the worst kind of fast, but appears to have done nothing worse than spending (as he confessed) a great deal of money very foolishly. I am so glad! Florence having been forbidden by her mother to see him at the house, met him in the park; and when Mrs. E. found out the scene ensued, and as F., despite imprisonment, refused to promise not to see or correspond with him, she was taken to Europe. Mary was married with opposition too, and both daughters I understand are disowned. Mr. E. is represented as a man with brains and talents, but a slave to his beautiful tigress of a wife. And they talked over Alice's position and about lending her the money, and I listened in breathless excitement, and when it

---

6. P. T. Barnum's traveling exhibition, or circus, was appearing at the Coliseum grounds for another week. Under "a vast canvas city" were "rare collections" of animals, a museum of 100,000 curiosities (including "Professor Faber's celebrated talking machine") and ring performances (*BDG*: 17 May 1873).

was over and Mamma was carried off by Mrs. Weld to see Mrs. Hamilton's baby,[7] and Papa and Mr. Weld began to talk of comparatively uninteresting things I pretended to read the *Independent* and covertly cried a little, what with excitement and trouble. And what Mr. Weld was telling about his daughter, though nothing compared to the Earle story, made me feel what Thackeray says about universal skeletons in closets. And about what Mr. Collyer says about loving being living. I have lived more, as regards strong feeling and excitement than in a year of ordinary living. Rode home with my mind full of all sorts of Earle-y and Earle suggested things.

May 19th

Monday. Got myself taken in to the ladies club—allowed to go, that is, for I went alone. I am always distracted with a variety of heroine worship. There are so many of them. Dr. Safford and Mrs. Woolson and Miss Eastman and a dozen more; but I think Dr. Safford is the ruling attraction. She spoke very kindly to me, and when I sat behind her gave me her hand, bidding me warm it. Prof. Agassiz[8] spoke his speak, and then there was discussion, and then general talk, and then the Club tea at which last there was much fun making, and I sat by Miss Eastman and was in clover. Very sleepy, though, on the way home . . .

May 20th

Tuesday. Worked among the flowers I believe, practiced a little and otherwise did nothing in particular that I remember.

May 21st

Wednesday. Weeded. There was a fire over away to the Westward, and Miss Jones, Edie, Mrs. Coe[9] & I watched it from Edie's den.

7. The Welds' daughter, Sarah Grimké Weld, was married to William Hamilton, pastor of the Unitarian Church in Hyde Park.

8. Jean Louis Agassiz (1807–73), eminent Swiss naturalist and educational reformer, had been chair of the natural history department at Harvard since 1848 (*DAB*). Agassiz had become embroiled in the question of coeducation and dress reform and was probably speaking on these issues at this meeting. At the time of his death in December, the *WJ* called on women to create a permanent memorial to him for opening his classes to women (*WJ*: 11 Apr. 1874).

9. Mrs. Coe, "a nice woman from Maine," served as housekeeper in the household. Her daughter, Annie, aged six, also lived there and became a playmate to Edie (LS to Margaret Campbell: 16 June 1873, LC).

May 22ⁿᵈ

Thursday. I had made all my arrangements to go into Boston and buy that thin paper so often forgotten by Papa, but on coming home found that Mamma had promised to get it. She brought it home and I wrote the beginning of a letter to Kitty.

May 23ᵈ

Friday. Finished the letter, and gave it to Papa with many charges to be sure and put on two stamps. Lo and behold, he did not post it [at] all! Music lesson. Walked down to Neponset and over the river. There was a beautiful rose crimson glow on the water.

May 24ᵗʰ

Saturday. Went into Boston, returned W*ives & Daughters* and got *Yeast* and *Stretton* again. Kept from reading after I got home. We read the *[Off the] Skelligs* on the Piazza till the mosquitos drove us in, and one of the horrid creatures kept me awake.

May 25ᵗʰ

Sunday. Slept late. Went off to the Codman School woods with Edie and got a quantity of columbines and black mould etc. and a great bunch of violets in a swamp not far from Milton. Read some of *Yeast*. Met Mary Emma Ryder & brother & sister, who had also been out after flowers.

May 26ᵗʰ

Monday. An unexpected History ex. Got 100 to my great surprise, though I had a name & date wrong. Muddled my brains with *Yeast*. Kingsley might well call it a problem—if it is true, as I suppose it is. But he doesn't believe in woman's rights, so I don't altogether believe in him, though he says some splendid good things. I like Tregarva immensely; but what a good thing it would be if every body would pitch in and do his best! But every body won't. I am so glad I am not responsible for every body! But I don't see through it.[10] Went out walking and muddling my brains, and saw Mary Emma as I came home. Took Mrs. Coe's little daughter to school.

10. Other readers have had similar difficulty making sense out of this book. Written by English clergyman, novelist, and poet Charles Kingsley (1819–75), *Yeast* deals with the injustice of extremes, especially wealth and poverty. Although Kingsley was an active Christian Socialist, this book reveals a deep conservatism underlying his most radical utterances (*DNB*).

The Frog Pond—Boston Common.

May 27th

Tuesday. All our class but four absent, so Mr. Horne had us go over our history papers, and let us go in half an hour. In the afternoon Hattie & Lonie were there also; they had all been into Boston to the drill;[11] and we had a Geography exercise. After which I went home with Hattie & played a game of chess. We both expected her to win, but I finally took all her men but the king, and still had two knights left. I felt quite conceited, for she has been playing all summer. I took the white pieces; I always like to get them, for it reminds me of Sir Lancelot, who found white & black knights fighting, and took sides with the black because they were getting the worst of it; but got unhorsed and wounded, although "the best knight in the world" they said. He found he had taken part with the devils against the angels, and of course had to go down.

11. During the Civil War a number of battalion drill clubs were organized in Boston; each year at this time, prize-winning high school drill teams put on a public program (*BDG*: 28 May 1873).

May 28th

Wednesday. Geography ex. Got 77. Miss Eastman was out here, and we got and fixed some flowers for the tea party tonight.[12] Then Edie and I put on our white dresses and we drove in. Miss Eastman said if she were I she would load herself with flowers each day when she came in, and scatter them in the street for the little children. The evening was rather a crush; I was introduced to lots to people, among them to Miss Alcott, whose looks greatly disappointed me. I didn't expect her to be handsome, but she is positively unpleasant looking, and I think laces.[13] Papa introduced me to Parker Pillsbury, and I spoke to him rather cordially, and found out after to my disgust, that he is a Woodhullite, by both theory and practice; and I wanted to wash my hands.[14] I wandered about seeking Mrs. Woolson, like a lost Hottentott; finally caught sight of her, and heard her talk a little. Saw Mr. Garrison and Mr. Higginson, and both saw and heard a young Mr. Charles Ames, whom I greatly liked, though he is not handsome.[15] He is like both Harry Spofford and Charley Blair. They took a good deal of money and when it was all over we drove home—six in the carriage. We had some supper—most indigestible—while there. Got to bed about 12 P.M.

It's salt[i]er then I thought—the world, I mean.

May 29th

Thursday. Grammar & Arith. ex. I am feeling excessively uncomfortable, for I wrote a note to Mary Emma asking her to set down her answers so that we could compare them after school, and she thought I wanted to ask about the

12. The event Alice attended was a special subscription festival held at Wesleyan Hall, on Bromfield St., sponsored by the NEWSA for the support of their work. The event featured music plus talks by well-known suffragists and raised $1,700 (*WJ*: 24 and 31 May, 7 June 1873).

13. Louisa May Alcott (1832–88) was a prolific author of books describing American nineteenth-century domesticity, seen through the eyes of young women of the day. She acquired celebrity status with the publication of *Little Women* (1868–69). An active member of the New England Woman's Club, she apparently did not subscribe to recommendations of the club's committee on dress reform, given Alice's observation that "she laces" (wears a corset) (*NAW*).

14. Parker Pillsbury (1809–93), outspoken and uncompromising reformer, had been a close associate of Lucy's when the two often lectured together on behalf of Garrison's American Anti-Slavery Association. He had aligned himself with more radical reformers after the war, including Woodhull (*DAB*).

15. Charles W. Ames (1855–1921), later a publisher (see *NCAB*, v. 27, 114), was the young son of liberal Unitarian minister Charles G. Ames, a featured speaker at the festival (*DAB*).

examination, and wouldn't take it till I assured her to the contrary. Honorable of <u>her</u>, of course; but the idea of suspecting that I would do such a thing! I am feeling really very badly about it. And I made an insane and idiotic mistake on the last question, so that I shan't get but 90; and it's hot and mosquitoey, and Edith is a plague and Annie Coe an outrageous bother. And my music lesson (to which I went from school) was not very satisfactory. And yesterday or day before I made a vow not to read more than 15 min. each weekday while school lasts, out of school; not that I want to go back on that—no indeed. Alice Earle's father has telegraphed to Papa not to send Alice the money till he gets a letter from him which is on its way. Someone has told him and there is trouble brewing I expect. What a queer business this is!

May 30ᵗʰ

Friday. Sick in A.M. with diarrhoea and stomach ache; petted a poor little squirrel Edith found half dead under a bush. Rode into Boston with Mamma and Edie and Annie Coe; but Mr. Earle's letter had not come. On the way in Mamma accused me of having known about Alice's affairs before; and I was driven to all sorts of prevarications (<u>not</u> lies) to keep from confession. I said I had had my suspicions but Alice had kept very quiet about her family affairs. On the heels of this we find a letter from Alice —a sad one, poor thing—telling about Florence, inclosing that article from the *Golden Age*, and saying that she had formerly believed it to be false, and <u>had told me so</u>, but now knew it to be true, as Florence said so.[16] There was a sweet situation for me! But I had forgotten her telling me, and said so. She said she enclosed a letter which we could not find; and I came home in some excitement, and lay awake and thought of her till near midnight. The squirrel ran up Mrs. Coe's sleeve, and she tried to pull it out by the tail and pulled half its tail off. Drove home with Papa, Annie Coe driving.

May 31ˢᵗ

Saturday. Went into Boston to the anniversary of the Ladies Club, in Freeman Pl. Chapel; but it was very stupid, except Mr. Garrison's and Mamma's speech—mostly reports. Afterwards a lunch, also very stupid, chiefly compliments.[17] Drove home.

16. No article identifying Florence Earle was discovered in a check of issues from the *Golden Age* during this period.

17. The New England Woman's Club held their program at Freeman Place Chapel (across from the Athenaeum). Members then walked one block to their club rooms on Tremont Place and enjoyed their last luncheon before disbanding for the summer (*BDG*: 29 May 1873).

JUNE

June 1ˢᵗ

Sunday. We went out riding, and the light hurt my eyes so I had to cover them. Played croquet.

June 2ⁿᵈ

Monday. I am No. 1!!! We are to be raced through the Rebellion in a week! Played croquet with Miss Jones and Edie, and got myself knocked on the head with a mallet. Miss Jones was swinging about hers, while disputing a point of order.

June 3ᵈ

Tuesday. School, croquet and practicing. Went down to Hattie Mann's in the P.M. and played croquet.

June 4ᵗʰ

Wednesday. Sent in a huge bunch of lilies of the valley to be divided among the girls in the printing office. I think it is such a pity the flowers should all be in one place and the people in another! We have more flowers than we know what to do with. Edie's last day here. She sent her goodbye to Miss Morse by me. Played croquet with her, and let her beat the last game, it being the last.

June 5ᵗʰ

Thursday. Edie left in the morning early. Went out walking toward Dr. Means' church. Mr. Horne wants me to write a valedictory composition. Oh!!

June 6ᵗʰ

Friday. A letter from Alice—the one she didn't inclose. Of all the mournful stories I ever read! Truth is stranger than fiction, and sadder too. Poor Alice! brave still though, my dear dearer dearest! Rode with Papa and Mamma with my head full of it. It tells all about her unhappy life, poor thing! I want to kiss her & cry over her.

June 7

Saturday. Most of the class absent at rehearsal. Those left had a grammar ex. Went into Boston and got *Old Margaret* & *Alice Vale* dodging between showers.

June 8th

Sunday. Rode over to the Quincy granite quarries with Papa and Mamma, and he & I climbed up to the top, saw the view and got 5 leaved ivy & ferns, also Solomon's seal & I an armfull of ~~columbines~~ wake robin—one huge specimen nearly half as long again as my arm, measuring from root to leaf tip. It is a lovely romantic place & I mean to go again.

June 9th

Monday. Went into the last meeting of the Ladies' Club, in which they were to give the last (for the present) handling to dress reform; but Dr. Safford has gone west, and Mrs. Churchill & Mrs. Wells said some atrocious things on the wrong side, and aggravated me greatly;[1] and I was not very successful with the flowers I had brought to give to the dirty little children in the street,[2] and there was another letter from Mr. Earle, and poor little Anna [Lawrence] is worse, so altogether I was so ferociously cross when we started to drive home with Papa as to make him laught at me. Mary Emma Ryder called in the evening to arrange about going tomorrow.

June 10th

Tuesday. Went in to the last festival rehearsal with Mary Emma. At her wish and against my judgment we took seats far back; but the music was splendid.[3] We both smelt fire during the rehearsal, but it came to no open confession. Got *Hereward [the Wake]* having time before the train went. Mr. Horne said to my delight that he didn't think it would be worth my while to go to school the P.M. so I didn't—having had no dinner & it being past time.

June 11th

Wednesday. A great splurge about having Papa bring his newspaper clippings into my den. Went to my music lesson, but they had company and Miss Morse put it off till tomorrow.

---

1. Elizabeth K. Churchill (1821–81), was a suffragist from Providence. Kate Gannett Wells (1838–1911) was an affluent antisuffragist reformer from Boston who sought to preserve traditional female social functions. Active in various kinds of moral reform and social philanthropy, she was also a member of the New England Women's Club and the national director of the Association for the Advancement of Women. In 1874 she was elected to the Boston School Committee (*NAW*).

2. It was rather common for flowers to be distributed among poor and working class people in Boston, thanks to various fruit and flower missions whose members took bouquets (as well as fruit, jellies, and eggs) to needy areas.

3. The sixth annual musical exhibition of Boston high schools and grammar schools took place the next day at the Music Hall (*BDG*: 11 June 1873).

June 12th

Thursday. Having decided to make my composition as ridiculous as possible & put in Hattie, I threatened her vaguely as to future vengeance.[4] Went again for my Music lesson. Miss Morse was sick.

June 13th

Friday. Read *Hereward* in school. Afterward went and took my last music lesson for the time being, and bade Miss Lily good bye.

June 14th

Saturday. Went up to Gardner with Mamma to see poor little Anna, my scruples about losing Monday's lessons being put down by Papa's saying that he thought she might die any day. Took a cake of maple sugar with me and gnawed it in the cars till Mamma took it away from me & threatened to throw it out of window when I tried to reclaim it. We drove into Boston to take the train, and in the carriage Mamma told me all sorts of queer things about boys—how if you show them any attention they immediatly think you want to marry them, and that they would like to marry you. How very inconvenient! Anna was very glad to see me; got up from the sofa and came and put her arms round me—and when I held her she felt so thin & fragile & breakable that I felt like a monster for being so brutally big and strong—like a bull in a china shop—as if I were all out of the order of nature. I slept with Emma, and we lay awake late, she telling me about the Vineland Swedenborgians, whose church she attended while there and who seem to have interested & nearly converted her. From what she told me, a good many of their doctrines seem very good indeed—almost like Mr. Collyer—while others I utterly disagree with.[5] This is the anniversary of about the wickedest thing I ever did in my life. She forgave me, but I doubt if I shall ever forgive myself.

June 15th

Sunday. Emma & I wheeled Anna in a baby wagon down the road to see me pull brake roots, which were afterward put in pickle. Climbed up Drs. Hill and visited the pine grove going up and the beech going down, climbed the latter,

---

4. Alice was writing her valedictory speech in which she would include humorous references to Hattie Mann.

5. Emma is referring to Vineland, N. J. Followers of the Swedish scientist and theologian Emanuel Swedenborg (1688–1772) founded a religion in his name that claimed direct mystical communication between the world and the spiritual realm and Christ as the true God.

stood on top of the hill with Wachusett on one side and Monadnock on the other.[6] Walked in the woods across the road with Emma in the evening.

June 16th

Monday. Went home—drove out with Papa.

June 17

Tuesday. A good many scholars absent. Drove out to Squantum and had *Off the Skelligs* in the evening.

June 18th

Wednesday. I am to be Mrs. Starch in "Using the Weed" which they are going to have at exhibition. It was arranged today. Mr. H. spoke of having Florrie [play] Starch, but all the girls in chorus declared I should do it best, so I am to have it.

June 19th

Thursday. Stayed after school to rehearse, and set the girls into fits by the way I did Starch.

June 20th

Friday. Am in great worry and trouble of mind about my diploma examinations and my composition.

June 21th

Saturday. Mr. Horne made an electric battery, which wouldn't work at all nicely, and we stayed a good while after school watching his attempts to set it going. He finally gave it up in despair and dismissed us. But he explained about telegraphs, which was very interesting. Rehearsed. *Off the Skelligs.*

June 22nd

Sunday. Papa, Mamma and I drove over to Squantum, and Papa and I went out rowing. It seemed harder work than rowing with Emma, perhaps because the oars were longer, for coming back with short ones it was easier. We landed on the farm school island—some wild looking boys came to meet us. I went up for a moment into a lovely larch grove. The boys helped us get the water out of

6. Wachusett is a mountain in Mass., and Monadnock a mountain in N.H.

our boat; we launched it; Papa gave them some money and we rowed back to Mama.[7]

June 23ᵈ

Monday. Mr. Horne made the battery work, had the boys stand in a ring and shocked them. Then the girls. It was funny to watch the way they behaved. Diploma examinations.

June 24ᵗʰ

Tuesday. History ex. for diplomas. Gave in my composition which I have worried through with, much to my own dissatisfaction.

June 25ᵗʰ

Wednesday. Mrs. Coe ironed and starched me a wrapper of hers, and made me a cap and we had a dress rehearsal down at the school house in the evening. Rehearsed.

June 26ᵗʰ

Thursday. Rehearsed before the other scholars from various rooms to make us used to an audience. Afterward Mr. Horne heard me read my composition.

June 27ᵗʰ

Friday. Exhibition. Mary Emma read her composition, which was good, but ended up with a personal compliment to Mr. Adams, a thing I always dislike. Songs and recitations, and we, "the dialogue girls" as Mr. Horne called us, went off to our various dressing rooms. Such a flurry as took place in those little closets! I did my part satisfactorily, Hattie gave that inevitable rising inflection to "Unhappy child!" of which we have been trying to break her, but the audience applauded, Lulu and Annie did excellently, and it all went off very well.[8] When I came to read my valedictory I did not dare look at the audience except at the girls now and then to see how they were taking it, and felt my legs rather shaky, as at Agnes's wedding; but I don't think my face showed it at all. I heard Mr. Adams chuckling, which was inspiring, and I think I heard Mr. Horne laugh also; the audience laughed plenty, and when I stole a look at Hattie she had her fan before her face and was blushing in the most satisfac-

7. It is not surprising that Lucy stayed on shore. Overweight and suffering from rheumatism for some time, she usually avoided activities that required any physical agility.

8. Alice was one of nine graduating girls who appeared in the dialogue "Using the Weed," as part of the Harris School exhibition, held at Lyceum Hall (*BDG*: 27 June 1873).

tory manner. I went back to my seat while the audience applauded, and find that the sensation of being clapped is very pleasant. Mr. Adams complimented me on my valedictory in his speech which was embarrassing; and said there were a number of things which it was customary to say on such occasions which were very true etc. and the only objection to which was that every one had heard them before; and that he for one was very glad to see that old fence broken through. It's perhaps the first, but I don't mean it to be the last old fence I shall break through. Mamma and Papa were invited to make speeches and did it. Papa's was simply buncombe, though he denies it indignantly; but it was; regular 4th of July buncombe. Mamma's was good, but she made a tremendous mistake as to the best scholar being the best base ball player, for it is exactly the reverse, as I have several times told. And all the school was aware it was a mistake—Agnes told me so afterward. I got complimented after it was over by various people, and Eddy called me "a naughty girl." I am glad he is not offended by what I said about him; it was all meant in good nature.

In the evening we had a little party at Mr. Horne's. First we sat out on the piazza and talked, while Mr. Young across the way watered his houses and yard with a hose. I wish we were not too high up for that—the constant plash was very refreshing. Afterward we went in and had ice cream and cake, and a good deal of fun afterwards. The Rev. Annie or as we called her, Robert Phips, she having been Miss Roberta in the dialoge, Capt. Paul Louis Mann (Lulu who was Miss Pauline, and whose real name is Louise) and I, had a free fight with our diplomas as weapons and I fear scandalized Mr. Horne by the noise we made. I have at last distinguished between Mr. Horne's wife and his sister. After a good deal of fun we broke up and went home. During the evening Lulu and I vowed eternal friendship, and she pledged herself that if my husband was caught by the military she would save his life, and I promised that if <u>she</u> was ever taken prisoner by Capt. Kidd, I would have her let go. Won't I plague Kitty about that!

June 28th

Saturday. Went down to Hattie's and played a game of chess with her. She stalemated me. Lulu came in while we were at it, and we three went up to the school house and got our dialogue things which we had left there. Mr. H. was there, working over papers. Felt uncommonly miserable after all the excitement.

June 29th

Sunday. Uncle George arrived. Felt rather miserable.

June 30th

Monday. Poor little Anna is very much worse. Sent in flowers to the printing girls, and dozed on the lounge. Hannah was raving drunk.[9]

JULY

July 1st

Tuesday. Mamma left to go to Anna . . .

July 2nd

Wednesday. Went in to the reception. It was not very pleasant, except the getting our bouquets. Several people made us speeches; Ralph Waldo Emerson was one, but we could not hear him. Also Phillips Brookes, who made a good speech but whom I consider an unctuous priest. He was much cheered. Then we filed across the platform, got our bouquets, passed down into the basement and were fed; after which I went home, as the hall where they promenaded was crowded and I was tired.[1]

July 3[d]

Thursday. Took a long ride with Papa and Uncle George. We three sat on the house top in the evening.

---

9. Lucy had complained several weeks before that her "strong Irish woman . . . gets drunk every week but . . . is much better than most of those who are sober, when she is sober, that I have kept her along" (LS to Margaret Campbell: 16 June 1873, LC). On this occasion Hannah had indulged in sour cider stored in the basement. Henry drove her to her daughter's with a note from Lucy saying she need not come back. The same day she "reappeared, said she had taken the pledge, and begged for another trial" and was taken back (ASB to KBB: 7 July 1873, SL).

---

1. This annual festival, given for the graduates of the Boston public schools, was held in the afternoon at the Music Hall. Nearly 1,300 scholars were seated according to their school in the balconies, with the girls attired in white dresses with brightly colored sashes. According to one paper, the speaker's platform was almost hidden from view by "a profusion of pot plants and floral devices." Ralph Waldo Emerson (1803–82), American essayist and poet, "regretted that the standard literature of the day was so inferior to that of his childhood." Phillips Brooks (1835–93), Episcopal clergyman and nationally known orator, claimed that Bostonians never cease to be scholars (BDG: 3 July 1873; DAB).

The organ in the Music Hall.

July 4ᵗʰ

Friday. Anna died, at one oclock in the afternoon. Rode over to West Roxbury with Papa and Uncle George. We left Papa to go into Boston by the horsecars and drove home. He got back to supper.[2]

July 5ᵗʰ

Saturday. Went into Boston with Papa, and we went to the office, where we found a letter from Mamma saying that Anna died yesterday. As near as I can calculate it, she was dying while we sat at dinner. Then I went and changed several books, and went out home. Sadie joined herself to me at the station, and I did not care for her in the least—rather disliked her if anything. How I did worship her about a year ago! Uncle George drove us up from the station, and when I got safely into the house I cried a little for dear little Anna. And felt

2. Because Alice did not learn of Anna's death until the next day, this entry was probably written at the same time as her entry for 5 July.

like a wretch because I didn't feel worse—though I did feel badly, and could have cried a deal if I had encouraged it a little. We drove out to Squantum. Papa taking me much against my will. He wanted to go out rowing, but could not get any but a sailboat, so we came home again.

July 6ᵗʰ

Sunday. Walked over to Milton to the chapel. It seemed rather right to be in church while they were burying Anna. Washed out some blue and white cloth (horribly dirty) and hung it up in the bathroom to dry.

July 7ᵗʰ

Monday. Fixed the blue cloth into a covering for a box to make an ottoman for my den. I think it looks well. Mamma got back in the evening, and told us the particulars about Anna's sickness & funeral. I wonder how she feels now.

July 8ᵗʰ

Tuesday. Went into Boston with Papa & Mamma and got a book. Mamma and I looked at pictures, and Papa got another copy of *Two College Friends* for Kitty, which was duely sent by Uncle G. who left this day.[3] I had commissioned Papa to get *Magdalen Hepburn* also, but he could not get it and got *Margaret Maitland* instead. But he is to return it. Drove out home.

July 9ᵗʰ

Wednesday. We are canning cherries, but I have nothing to do with that. Made some cakes and got supper. Lulu called, and we made an appointment to bathe together tomorrow. Papa has a hose, and waters the garden with it, while some one pumps. He read *Story of a Bad Boy*.

July 10ᵗʰ

Thursday. Mamma drove me down to Lulu's and we had a nice bath. I was allowed, after some protest to wear the blue Adirondack suit in.[4] I swam, and ducked, and splashed, and paddled. Then Mamma drove me home.

3. George Blackwell left for an extended visit to England and France.
4. The Adirondack suit may have been an old hiking outfit of Alice's, probably knickers and a long loose fitting top. Women usually wore navy, black, or gray wool bathing dresses (with skirts reaching well below the knees), along with long bloomer-type pants to the ankles. Bathing hats and shoes were also worn.

July 11ᵗʰ

Friday. Wrote to Uncle Bowman telling him to expect me to morrow, and took it into Boston and posted it. Changed books, and came out with a whole armful of Thomas Hughes—two vols. were *T[om] B[rown] at Oxford,* one *The Scouring of the White Horse.* Picked currants with Papa to make jelly. Papa read *Story of a Bad Boy.*

July 12ᵗʰ

Saturday. Read T. B. at Oxford, and rather loafed about before dinner. In the afternoon went up to Uncle Bowman's. No one met me, as I thought likely, my letter having been mailed so late; so I left my cloak and umbrella at the depot and walked up with my bag. I was scared by a rather bad looking man with a stick who walked behind me, and momentarily expected to feel the said stick knock me over the head; so I finally sat down on a stone when we came near a house, and began to mop my face. He then asked me where I was going, and offered to carry my bag, saying it was rather a hard load for a girl of my size; but I declined with thanks, saying it was not very heavy, and he went on, while I followed at my leisure.

July 13ᵗʰ

Sunday. Walked with Phebe to see Uncle Stone salt the cows and mounted a rock with her to be out of the way of an unpleasant black bull, that pawed, bellowed, and eyed us with disfavor. We came around by the Hemlock Hill, and the great rock on top of which Mamma used to skip rope. Went up with Phebe and saw the sea of purple hills and the sunset.

July 14ᵗʰ

Monday. Phebe has undertaken to find me something to do to stop my reading: churning; and I churned in the cellar till the butter came.

July 15ᵗʰ

Tuesday. A telegram came to know if I had arrived safely. I telegraphed back "Arrived alive and well & right side up. Will write." Wrote accordingly, and picked a quantity of gooseberries. I remembered there used to be a small bush of them in a certain clump of rocks, and found it had spread & multiplied greatly. Went up the hill and saw the sunset—and the golden gate. And thought all sorts of things that I could not write—Pilgrim's Progress—and working and resting—and the finish and end of it.

July 16th

Wednesday. I lost my net when I went up the hill last night, and this morning went up again and looked for it. I did not find it, but got a quart of thimble berries. Toward evening helped Mrs. Van water her garden.

July 17th

Thursday. Made candy after Anna's recipe. Aunt Martha & Aunt Woodward got home.[5]

July 18th

Friday. Made cocoa candy after a recipe for chocolate ditto which I found in Godey.[6] Played croquet with Phebe & beat her.

July 19th

Saturday. Cloudy still. Ate the cocoa candy & hunted eggs. Phebe read the *Woman's Journal* aloud to me to our mutual satisfaction, since our views coincide.

July 20th

Sunday. Went away out into the North Pasture with Uncle Bowman to salt the cows and came home very tired. He pointed out several sepulchres on the way; said a cow died once among certain rocks and we saw the bones; and that a horse was buried where some rank grass grew. Wrote home, and went up with Phebe to see the sunset.

July 21st

Monday. Phebe routed me up early by request, that I might ride down with the milk with her; which I did. We went over to the Rock house, Phebe & I, taking with us Mrs. Browning's Poems which we frequently stopped to read. In the rock house she read me the "Rhyme of the Duchess May" & murdered it rather, but it gave us mutual satisfaction. There was a bird's nest on the side of one of the rocks of the rock house, and I was bound to look into it, which I succeeded in doing by scrambling with frantic efforts onto the rock & looking down. There was one young bird in it. I picked a delicate spray of leaves as a

5. These aunts were probably relatives of Bowman's wife, Samantha Robinson, whose mother's maiden name was Woodward.

6. *Godey's Lady's Book and Magazine* was a popular illustrated magazine devoted to fashion and domesticity.

trophy to send Sir Robert[7] and came down, stained with black mould. We saw also the <u>oven</u>, a hole in a rock.

July 22nd

Tuesday. Drove down with Phebe for the milk and got a letter from Mamma telling me I had better come home now. Went up with Phebe, Aunt Martha & Tip to drive the cows; Aunt Martha saw them home, and P. and I went on to the top of the hill; found quantities of delicious thimbleberries, prospected for our house, and saw the sea of purple hills, the sunset & the golden gate. For the last time this visit, sat at the foot of the old tree, and heard the wind, high, high overhead in its branches. I love that tree.

July 23d

Wednesday. Came home, Aunt Martha coming with me at Mamma's invitation, expressed in her letter.

July 24th

Thursday. Made raspberry vinegar. Cousin Clara is here, and is nicer than I expected—kind, and seemingly rather nervous.[8] Papa & I being on the roof, he said he could recite more poetry [but we] kept it up, and the match is not over.

July 25th

Friday. Mamma, Papa, Clara, Aunt Martha and I went to Nantasket beach on the Rose Standish.[9] Papa and I went into the water and had a nice bath. We ate where we did on our former trip, got a great basket of sand for potting this fall, and came home on the 3.30 boat. All the way out, and till I had had my bath I was so sleepy I did not know how to hold my head up. Mamma thought it was my liver, and threatened a blue pill. I was too sleepy to think much of anything, but rather supposed it was because I got up so early at Uncle Bo's. Got home tired.

---

7. A reference to Robert Kidd, alias Kitty.

8. Clarinda ("Clara") Barlow (b. 1835) was the unmarried daughter of an older sister of Lucy's (Eliza Barlow), who died when Clara was a baby.

9. Nantasket Beach is a spit of land separating Hingham Bay and the ocean, about ten miles by water from Dorchester.

July 26th

Saturday. Drove in with Papa, saw Clara off at the Worcester station, and went to the dentist who sees to Dr. Moffat's patients.[10] The teeth whose (bad grammar) filling I have been so dreading are pronounced perfectly sound, but he found and filled a cavity in a molar, and treated one as a man & a brother, not as a mere pair of jaws. The filling did not hurt much, but an extraordinary newfangled india rubber gag or muzzle which he put onto me did some what. Got *The Athelings* & 2 vols. of *Vanity Fair*, and drove out with Papa through clouds of dust. We got a postal card from U[ncle] S[am] saying that F[lorence] would arrive by a certain train, naming no day. Papa met the train, but she was not there, and after some uneasiness, much puzzling & consultation we decided that we could do nothing, and began reading *Vanity Fair* aloud in the evening. I like Colonel Dobbin.[11]

July 27th

Sunday. Drove out with Papa and Mamma. We broke a shaft; spliced it, drove on & broke it short off in trying to turn in one of those no thoroughfares Papa loves so to go into, so surely as he sees a sign "no passing through." I believe he would turn out of his way to do it. Luckily this happened near a livery stable; and Papa procured a man who spliced it very cleverly, while it rained & rained. Played for Papa in the evening. *Vanity Fair.*

July 28th

Monday. Flo arrived. I saw the queerest fog bank coming in from sea when I was on the house top watching. Went shopping in Boston with Mamma. We mutually begged each other to put on our tombstones

> "Died of shopping with an unreasonable mother"
> "Died of shopping with an impracticable daughter."

July 29th

Tuesday. Read & played croquet with Florence. Rode out to Squantum with her, Mamma, & Mike, who was rather oderiferous as usual.

July 30th

Wednesday. Read and played croquet. Went up onto the roof with Florence; and while there she confided to me the fact that she was engaged to be married,

---

10. Drs. G. T. Moffatt and L. D. Shepard shared an office at the Hotel Boylston, on the corner of Boylston and Tremont.

11. William Dobbin, a character in *Vanity Fair*, is a tall, lumbering, but forthright and faithful young man.

---

and that I might ask her mother if I didn't believe it—which I scarcely did at first; but she soberly affirmed it. His name, as she further divulged, was Ziba Osborne; and she told various other particulars. It seems very queer to think of Floy as engaged—our Floy, that I've played with in the sand at Martha's Vineyard, and talked to, and chattered unutterable nonsense with ever since I could chatter at all! Probably she won't marry him though—her mother has made her promise not to do so before she is 18, and she says she doesn't mean to till she is 20.[12]

July 31st

Thursday. Read and played croquet. I think also tried unsuccessfully as usual to write a notice of *Marjory Fleming*. I would like to say a good word for it, for it is really the prettiest little story I have read for ever so long, and the author's kind heart seems to beat through the whole of it. It gives one a curious feeling to be reading the letters & diaries and thinking the very thoughts of a child who has been dead nearly 70 years—it is like groping about among old fashioned furniture, ancient historical furniture, only more so. I should like to see those pictures of Maidie.[13]

AUGUST AND SEPTEMBER

Aug. 1st

Friday. Read and played croquet. Aunt Sarah arrived unexpectedly in the evening, and the sight of her in her black dress brought back the thought of dear little Anna very strongly. She will always be little Anna to us I suppose, even 50 years hence if I should live till then. There was a thunderstorm in the evening and Flo and I sat on the lounge in the dark and she told me about Ziba and his proposal, etc. It seemed so queer to have Flo telling me her own love story—our Floy! We sat late talking, and finally went to bed.

Aug. 2nd

Saturday. Drove into Boston, all of us, with Aunt Sarah. We showed Flo the mummies & pictures, and we did some shopping and on the way out called on the Miss Goddards. The one who talked to us was a very sweet looking elderly

12. This was the first of several of Florence's "engagements."
13. *Marjorie Fleming*, by John Brown, was the true story of "pet Marjorie" (or "Maidie"), a precocious Scottish girl, told partly through the letters and diaries she wrote before her death in 1811, at the age of eight. "Those pictures" is a reference in the book to portraits of Maidie painted by her older sister.

Beacon Street Mall.

lady in a pleasant shady room, such as I am hoping to set up housekeeping in with Kitty when we are two old maids and live together. Aunt Sarah has adopted a boy and came to Miss G. to see about adopting a girl.[1]

Aug. 3ᵈ

Sunday. At supper (mine just finished), Papa said to Mamma that "I fear we have given birth to a compound of <u>fanaticism</u> and <u>idiocy</u> mingled with <u>intense intolerance!</u>" Oh me! And all because I object to saying "yoolyoose kiza" for "Julius Caesar" according to the Continental pronunciation, and last night and this morning I have been in woe over the prospect of being compelled to do so at the Chauncey Hall school.[2] But I would rather be slaughtered— almost; and I <u>wont</u> I <u>wont</u> I <u>wont</u>—unless I have to. And he quoted "But I count the gray

1. Sarah's adopted children do not appear in any published Stone genealogy. Like many "adoptions" of the period, the arrangement was probably only a temporary one and was made informally—in this case through the Goddard sisters, who probably had connections with a Boston orphanage.

2. Lucy and Henry did not believe Boston's high school for girls provided adequate preparation for college and probably chose Chauncy Hall for Alice because they knew girls could excel there. The *WJ*, for instance, had carried a story about the achievements

barbarian lower than the Christian child." Upon which I called him the gray barbarian, and he denied my claim to be called the Christian Child. F. and I went to the Milton Chapel, but it was hot, and not many were there. Papa drove us over, and met us with the carriage as we were walking back.

Aug. 4th

Monday. Packing and disorder. Mrs. Spofford & Florence came unexpectedly.[3] I was delighted, but ashamed to be caught dressed as I was. The two Florences and I played croquet; little F. is very bright and well mannered. I think she will come to something—an agreeable woman probably. We had *Vanity Fair* read aloud on the roof, and then Papa told F. & me a most absurd story after Mamma went down by moonlight. I wrote a letter to Kitty and in a private inclosure told her of Floy's engagement, and like a goose told F. I had done so. This caused difficulties between us and made a very uncomfortable state of things. I reopened the letter and tore up the enclosure.

Sept. 12th

Friday. The days between this and the last entry are recorded in another diary.[4]

On this day I was disturbed in my mind on account of unbelief, doubts and faithlessness, and got comfort from reading *The Life that Now Is*.[5] Mamma saw that I had been crying, and wanted me to tell why, as did Papa, but I couldn't. I said it was nothing she was to blame for, as she seemed to suspect she had hurt my feelings; only a little private worry of my own. Feeling much better after a bit of sharp and appropriate rebuke which I came across in the sermon, and duly took to myself. I rode into Boston, changed a book and

---

of Mary Livermore's daughter Etta who had recently won a gold medal for scholarship at Chauncy and had tied (with another young woman) as top scholar of the entire school (*WJ*: 8 Feb. 1873).

Because of a devastating fire that occurred a few months before Alice enrolled there, the school was temporarily located in a former church on Essex St. awaiting the completion of new school quarters on Copley Square. Known today as the Chapel Hill–Chauncy Hall School (after a merger in 1971), it is located in Waltham, Mass.

3. Harry Spofford's mother and sister had probably been vacationing at Martha's Vineyard.

4. This diary has not been located. Alice wrote it while vacationing in the White Mountains and planned to send it on to Kitty, who had been vacationing in Switzerland during the same period. Apparently they both planned to exchange vacation experiences (ASB to KBB: 1 and 5 Sept. 1873, LC).

5. A book of sermons by Robert Collyer.

---

bought *Marjorie Fleming* for Kitty, or had Papa buy it. We rode out again, and before doing so I had some soda water. *Vanity Fair* in the evening.

Sept. 13ᵗʰ

Saturday. Tried to mark drawers with very bad success. However, my clothes will now be known as well perhaps by large blurrs as by distinct names. Picked up my dinner, Mamma and Papa being gone. Read *The Surgeon's Daughter.*

Sept. 14ᵗʰ

Sunday. Got into bed with my parients and while there was presented with a pair of gold studs, a hand glass (to see myself as others see me, if I can, Mamma said) a silver fruit knife and a silver thimble.[6] At breakfast we had honey, peaches and candies. Read Mr. Collyer's sermons, and in the afternoon rode over with Papa and Mamma to Mr. Garrison's. He treated me very kindly, but said things about Gen. Butler which made me glower darkly at him not withstanding.[7] Socked our wheel in trying to turn around "to go a new way." *Vanity Fair* in the evening.

Sept. 15ᵗʰ

Monday. Went into Boston with my parents and took dinner at a little restaurant with Miss Person and follower.[8] Was taken to the Chauncy Hall School by Mamma, and exhibited to Mr. Ladd and Miss Smith, the teacher of mathematics. Was much interested and somewhat appalled by the sight of a great hall full of boys.[9] I am to begin tomorrow.

6. This was Alice's sixteenth birthday.

7. General Benjamin Butler (1818–93), Union general and controversial Massachusetts politican identified with the "radical wing" of the Republican party, was serving as a member of Congress (1866–75). As an abolitionist and advocate of woman suffrage, he found support among the Stone Blackwells' circle of friends; but he was also regarded as a maverick and was personally disliked by some. After two unsuccessful bids for governor of Massachusetts, he was elected, as a Democrat, in 1882, for one term (*DAB*). Alice complained that her own family was politically "at variance" over Butler. "I am savagely Butler; Papa is Butler at home, & dubiously neutral abroad; my female parent violently anti-Butler. . . . She and Papa and I constantly disagree" (ASB to KBB: n.d., LC; internal evidence suggests that this letter was written in July 1873).

8. Miss Person, "a pleasant young lady . . . accustomed to keeping books and to newspaper work" became the office assistant at the *WJ*, after Mrs. Hinckley left to have a baby (LS to Margaret Campbell: 16 Jan. 1873, LC).

9. William H. Ladd was coproprietor of the school and head of the rhetoric and elocution department. Sarah Smith was head of the mathematics and natural history departments. During the previous term, 250 boys and 14 girls had been enrolled in the lower and upper divisions of the school.

Sept. 16th

Tuesday. Found myself, on going to school, the only girl in a Latin class of small boys, among whom I towered up like a watermelon among peaches. They blundered abominably, and I found the Continental pro[nunciation] even worse than I expected. I got along pretty well with the girls, especially little Georgie, who is out of sight ahead of me in her studies. They showed me the orchestra gallery, a favorite resort, the charms of which are enhanced by the danger of Mr. Cushing[10] catching sight of the top of our heads. A dirty, cramped hole, but seemingly much liked. A dirty, vast, confused medley it seemed to me, and I did not like it. I never knew what lesson came next, and found that I had nothing to do a large part of the time, which was very stupid. I came home by the 3 o'clock train, so tired I could hardly have got up energy enough to run and meet Kitty even.

Sept. 17th

Wednesday. I liked it better at school, but it is very unpleasant that I, who would about as lief have a garter snake near me as a boy, should be the one girl in class of from 20 up to the 50's. A pale, dark haired and eyed, gentle acting girl named Miss Turner[11] is with me in the algebra, and she very kindly explained it to me at lunch, as it was all Greek to me. I think I shall like her. Not so tired, perhaps because today I did not go up to the office for letters.[12] Was shown my French teacher and had a lesson set me.[13]

Sept. 18th

Thursday. School as usual. Nothing particular. I am getting a little more used to it. Papa brought me a letter from Flo, which I tore up as directed. I feel very uneasy about her; she says there has been an explosion about P. Augustus.[14] I am afraid she will get into very hot water if she doesn't look out. *Vanity Fair*.

Sept. 19th

Friday. Recited to my odd old French teacher, who calls me "Mees Blackwell," and said "Vary well" when I had recited. Was thankful to remember there was no school Saturday. *Vanity Fair* and a fight with Papa.

10. Thomas Cushing was coproprietor of the school and senior principal.

11. Alice followed the custom of the school by referring to most female students (especially those who were older) as "Miss" and to boys by their surnames.

12. Alice had to walk some fourteen blocks out of her way, if she went to the WJ office after school before taking the train home.

13. J. B. Torrichelli was Alice's French teacher.

14. An alias for Ziba Osborne.

Sept. 20th

Saturday. A music lesson. Miss Person and Lucy Chadburne came out to spend Sunday. Poor little Miss P. will get good from it I hope. She needs it. It must be horrid to be always shut up in the city. Flo sent me a letter sealed & stamped, requesting me to direct it to her at Finderne in a gentleman's hand and post it.[15] Which I did. I said F. had made a most extraordinary request of me, being in much amazement & bewilderment, but when Mamma wanted to know what it was I didn't think it quite fair to F. to tell her. But when I had directed it behind her back she declared she knew what it was; that F. wanted me to direct a letter to a boy, and that it was very wicked; and I interrupted and said it was only to herself at which Mamma expressed great relief. Went down to Field's Corner and posted it.

Sept. 21st

Sunday. We drove over (without Mamma) to the Quincy Granite Quarries for ferns, and got a variety of treasures. There was a quantity of young men on the top, which was a nuisance as they lay behind rocks and poked up their heads like turtles to look at us; but we didn't stay there long. We drove home by the dragons.[16] Miss Person went back to the city.

Sept. 22nd

Monday. After school fell to work and potted a quantity of geraniums. A very odd thing happened at school; I brought in my French exercise, and laid it on Monsieur's table when demanded; during the lesson discovered a mistake I had made, and when we were through asked for it back to correct it; but it wasn't in the pile of books, or anywhere to be found. Going back upstairs I found it in my desk. If I had not so distinct a remembrance of handing it in I might know what to make of it; as it is, I well nigh believe in spirits.

Sept. 23d

Tuesday. Georgie Townsend and I stayed in the lunch room after the rest went, turning out the gas lest Mr. Cushing should make a raid upon us, and then spouted poetry to one another to our mutual satisfaction, till my conscience misgave me that I ought to be reciting. Wrote part of a letter to Kitty. Mamma in bed with a bad cold.

15. Finderne is about three miles southeast of Somerville, N.J., where Florence and her family resided.

16. These are unidentified but may have been rock formations in the quarry area.

Sept. 24th

Wednesday. School. Practiced. Mamma up and better. My eyes bad.

Sept. 25th

Thursday. School. Felt very tired and didn't practice. Eyes bad. Mamma wants to write to Mrs. Spofford and tell what I said about Harry, and I am willing, if Mrs. S. doesn't tell him. Mamma says she is very wise, which I believe, and won't; so I don't mind. But I am disgusted both with Harry and myself; with myself for not keeping my unruly member quieter, and with him for taking jokes seriously, being hurt without reason, and taking offence where none was meant.

Sept. 26th

Friday. School and French lesson. Brought home some French to translate. Called on Mary Emma [Ryder].

Sept. 27th

Saturday. Music lesson. Agnes [Reed] came up, and we gave her grapes and pears. She said it seemed like Paradise up here. I am to row with her on Saturday.

Sept. 28th

Sunday. Did not go to church. Read, and played hymns to Papa in the evening. *Vanity Fair.*

Sept. 29th

Monday. A letter from Kitty. Rode home with Mamma.

Sept. 30th

Tuesday. Rainy. School and practicing much as usual.

OCTOBER

Oct. 1st

Wednesday. As I stood in the lunch room studying my French, waiting till it should be time to go to French, Mr. Herbert[1] came in from the orchestra gallery to my dismay, and said "Ah? How is it? Recess?" I explained the state of

1. To distinguish between the two Mr. Cushings, Alice referred to Herbert Cushing as Mr. Herbert.

the case, and on demand the state of the case which made me be absent from Latin in the morning, and he said "Ah!" and departed! Mamma and Papa away, and I had supper & chocolate in solitary state, and got nervous in the evening, with the library and fire and silver basket all to myself. Walked to N. Quincy.

Oct. 2nd

Thursday. Knew my Latin well, which was lucky, as Mr. Demerit[2] was in a very bad temper, and several small boys caught it severely. Battalion Drill again. I am determined to practice at home till I get as limber as old Mr. Cushing.[3] My pride in my suppleness is greatly taken down. Passing by the door of Room 2 I saw Mr. Herbert sitting with a large green blinder over one eye, which made him resemble a prize fighter. Made inquiry and found that he wears it to keep the sun out of his eyes.

Oct. 3d

Friday. School and practicing much as usual. Walked over to N. Quincy. We had fun in French class, till I hid my face in my book for laughing. The professor is rather given to jokes in his queer English, and one boy had his lesson abominably, which produced laughter. Read extracts from Carlyle's *Past & Present* to Mamma.

Oct. 4th

Saturday. Went out rowing with Agnes Reed. Her father showed me the divers and pile-driving. The divers are laying a wall under water. Only one was at work, and he, in his hideously absurd dress, looked like the Little Master in *Sintram and His Companions*, to my thinking. We had a nice row, I rowing all the time, sometimes with one oar, and a good while with both, while Agnes sat in the stern and laughed at my awkward gambols and splashing. It was jolly but fatiguing. A large ship bore down on us, and we rowed desperately to get out of the way; but the ship ran aground in the mud, and we rowed toward and circumnavigated her.

Oct. 5th

Sunday. Kitty's birthday. Last night I calculated Swiss time, and drank her health ten minutes after midnight by it, while it was yet the 4th with us. Made grape jelly, till I hated the sight and smell thereof.

2. Edwin Demerritte.

3. Herbert Cushing trained the boys' drill team at this time; the much smaller girls' team was probably led by older Thomas Cushing, organizer of the first Chauncy team in 1861.

Oct. 6th

Monday. Came out on the 3.35 train, after changing *Mt. Washington in Winter* for *At the Back of the North Wind*. Miss Eastman came out, and in the evening a little informal meeting was held at our house, about the formation of a Woman's Suffrage political club.[4] I went to bed at about 8.15 while the people were still arriving.

Oct. 7th

Tuesday. Rainy. School much as usual. Military drill. Practiced.

Oct. 8th

Wednesday. School. Picked petunia seeds; practiced. *Vanity Fair*. Talked a few minutes with Chase.

Oct. 9th

Thursday. A letter from Nelly Hooper. She has misunderstood me, and says things, or rather insinuates things about Robert Collyer and Tom Hughes, for which I shall give it her severely. Mr. Cushing being a saint and Mr. Ladd an angel, they have given us holiday, till next Tuesday. But there's a compo to write.

Oct. 10th

Friday. Wrote to Nelly, and gave it her. Got the long-expected letter from Kitty, and she asked 14 questions and seemed in as great fits over Flo's engagement as I could desire. Answered the letter.

Oct. 11th

Saturday. Rode into Boston with Mamma, and found Emma in the *Journal* office. Changed book, and bought sealing-wax and went with Emma and Miss Eastman to hear Brougham.[5] Didn't like it much; couldnt hear very well. Was rather amusing though. Home with Emma.

---

4. A number of woman suffrage "political clubs" were being organized at this time throughout Massachusetts, each dedicated to electing friends of suffrage to the legislature by systematically distributing tracts and newspapers, holding public meetings, and signing individual pledges of support (*WJ*: 6 Oct. 1872).

5. John Brougham (1810–80), Irish-American playwright, read from his writings at a matinee recital at the Music Hall (*BDG*: 11 Oct. 1873).

Park Street Church.

Oct. 12ᵗʰ

Sunday. Wrote out my composition for the first time. Went into Boston with Emma to hear Mr. Murray.⁶ The sermon made Emma cry. He was talking of his father's death and burial, and I knew she thought of Anna. I believe Mr. Murray is a good man. After sermon we got some lunch and then attended a spiritual meeting, which was very stupid, as there were no manifestations. After which Emma trapsed about in search of Maud Lord, towing reluctant me after her. Miss Lord had left the city but we found plenty of other mediums, and got very tired.

Oct. 13ᵗʰ

Monday. Finished my composition and walked to N. Quincy.

Oct. 14ᵗʰ

Tuesday. Gave in my composition. School & practicing.

6. William H. Murray was the pastor of Park Street Church (Congregational) at Tremont and Park streets.

Oct. 15th

Wednesday. Said my piece to Miss Ladd, in No. 3. She said I had such a good clear voice that she should think I would make a beautiful reader; which flattered me exceedingly, it being Miss Ladd. Went and called on Mrs. Smith. She was very glad to see me, and we talked away very sociably. She set me going; and told me various things, and about some cases in the house, and I exploded, in a milder manner than usual, but happening to look up caught sight of my face in the glass and was startled to see how flushed I was. And Mrs. S. when I told her how mad it made me, hearing of such things, said "Ah, this will all come out in good work some day."[7] Amen. I had to run for the 3.35 train. She is rather sentimental sometimes as I said, but good, and devotes herself to fighting the wickedest thing in the world; so I heartily respect her.

Oct. 16th

Thursday. School and practicing. No letters. Emma somewhat blue and my cold bad.

Oct. 17th

Friday. School, of course, and practicing ditto. Went up to the office, and while there Mamie Molineux and mother came in. Mrs. M. wanted to inquire whether the Technological Institute is open to girls.[8]

Oct. 18th

Saturday. Emma and I went into Boston to write wrappers under Papa's orders, which we did.[9] Mr. Campbell came in. He had a presentiment something had happened to Mrs. C. and was anxiously expecting a letter from her. . . . Raced for our train, did the distance in 13 minutes, and caught it.

Oct. 19th

Sunday. Emma & I went in to the Spiritual Meeting for the second time, with our sealed questions, which we duly gave in, keeping a wary eye upon them to

7. Alice was visiting the office of the New England Moral Reform Society at 6 Oak Place. The society helped "dissolute" girls and young women find temporary homes and assisted them financially until they could find repectable employment. Mrs. P. W. Smith was editor of the society's monthly magazine, the *Home Guardian.*

8. Although Ellen Swallow (1842–1911), pioneer woman chemist, had received a B.S. from MIT in 1873, she did so as a special student (NAW). The institute did not begin accepting women into its regular courses until 1878.

9. Emma and Alice were writing individual names and addresses of WJ subscribers onto strips of paper, which were then wrapped around the newspapers for mailing.

see that they were not tampered with. The answers were scrawled and nearly illegible, and did not apply, convincing us that this medium at least is a humbug. I asked if Kitty was a habitual medium, and was told to seek and I should find; and whether mediums did eventually lose their strength of mind, and was told to come in faith and receive a reply. We mutually assured each other that it was humbug, and went home convinced of that pleasing fact. We had to wait some minutes for the station to be opened, and while promenading slowly under the station roof away from the rain, were insulted by some idle youths there congregated.

Oct. 20th

Monday. Wet. School of course.

Oct. 21st

Tuesday. My letter came at last. Emma said it had, and while I was rummaging Papa's satchel for it, I was horror-stricken to find therein the letter to Kitty which I gave him to post the other day. I blew him up, and departed. Kitty is worried about Flo, and vexed that she did not tell her, and hurt, what's worse, and I am troubled about it. I thought Kitty would be mad, and therefore vexed & savage, but not that it would hurt her feelings.

Oct. 22nd

Wednesday. School. Wrote to Kitty, and felt unhappy in my mind. *Vanity Fair.*

Oct. 23d

Thursday. Mamie Molineux invited me to spend Friday afternoon with her. Which invitation I gladly accepted. Mamma, Emma and I pulped grapes in the evening. Felt miserable and faithless again.

Oct. 24th

Friday. I have been to see Mamie Molineux. Oh, it was so ridiculous! She showed me her cats, and her mother, and various curious and beautiful things of which they seem to have a great stock, and as we were at the window examining a drawer of lovely Californian pebbles, when Mamie exclaimed "There's Arthur Chamberlain coming!" "Coming here" cried I, jumping up in alarm, and seeing a boy coming along the street. "Yes," said she; "don't you want to see him? He won't want to see you either," and with much laughter from Mamie I retired to her little study and was there shut in, while she went to let him in. He was taken into the parlor, and every now and then Mrs. M. or Mamie would come in to me and sit down and laugh. It seems that he is as direfully afraid of girls as I am of boys, but not of Mamie, as she is his old friend and playmate. But as he came along, so Mamie with much laughter confided to me, he thought "Suppose Miss Rand should be there!" Miss R. is the other girl in our class. The thought was fearful, but he proceeded. But when he reached the corner he thought "<u>Suppose</u> Miss Blackwell should be there?" He wavered, but came on—and caught sight of me at the window. He decided not to run away however, and his courage was rewarded by finding I had fled. I recovered courage as soon as I found that he was shy too, and apparently my flight produced the same effect upon him. But he would not come down to supper, and retreated to my place of refuge, the study, where I caught sight of him crouched over a book when I came upstairs again. I instantly stole away and concealed myself behind the stairs, out of sight of the study door. Mamie came up behind me, and went and closed it, and then came to me, laughing intensely. I rushed into the parlor with a tragic gesture—and started back in horror at the sight of an old gentleman seated at the farther end of the room and looking at me. I retreated, horror stricken and told Mamie. I thought she would have laughed herself into a fit. She told her mother, who laughed likewise (it was Mamie's grandfather I had seen) and I received directions for my way and went. But it was too absurd, the whole thing. I wonder how we shall look when we see one another Monday! Probably we shall not see one another. I walked across to the South Boston Depot, took my train when it came and got home after dark.

Oct. 25th

Saturday. Potted with Mamma and took my last music lesson of Lily Morse. "We parted; sweetly gleamed the" sun, and I am really sorry to have seen the last of her, though the practicing was a dreadful bore. *Vanity Fair*—Mamma slept through it.

Oct. 26th

Sunday. We took a long ride over toward the Blue Hill[10] to see Autumn colours.

Oct. 27th

Monday. Fiercely rainy. Did <u>not</u> try to stare Arthur Chamberlain out of countenance and took no special notice of him.

10. An elevated, parklike area in Milton.

Oct. 28th

Tuesday. School, of course, much as usual.

Oct. 29th

Wednesday. Miss Rand and I had our compositions corrected. Miss Newhall[11] said mine was very good, and asked me where I got the quotation "He that hath his own world hath many worlds more." In arithmetic we hardly recited at all, for Miss S[mith] and the boys somehow got switched off upon the subject of honesty and dishonesty as concerned in the passing of railroad tickets and picking up of money, and engaged in a violent discussion which lasted till the bell rang. I wholly agreed with Miss Smith but so did not all the boys. Went up to the office and inquired when I could catch Mr. Fisk; Miss Person said he wouldn't be in till 3.30. I made up my mind to wait for him and go without my dinner, but he came in much sooner. He promised that if I would come in the next day he would show me his panorama of "Athens" and give me all the information he could.[12]

Oct. 30th

Thursday. Went up to the office after school. Mr. Fisk came in prompt to time, loaded with pictures and the panorama, which we spread out on the floor. As a preliminary he presented Miss Person and myself with two lovely little carnelian crosses. He showed and explained and talked away volubly, and every now and then raced up to his room to get something illustrative of the case in point. He gave me no end of pictures for my parents, and lent me a beautiful great book from which to extract information, with many charges to be careful of it. He sat down and let himself be questioned like a lamb. And finally, I told him my essay would astonish my teachers, and he gave a [high] shriek of laughter, and scuttled away.

Oct. 31st

Friday. Recited Scott[13] to Mr. Ladd for the first time. It was awful. I am much more afraid of him than of Mr. Cushing; Mr. C. gets into fearful rages sometimes, but Mr. Ladd's cold sharp saw-like temper and unvarying savageness is a great deal worse. Got some composition paper.

11. Lucy Newhall is listed in school catalogs as an assistant teacher of German, mathematics, and history. During the 1873–74 school year she appears to have been assisting in the history department.

12. Phocius Fisk was living in attic rooms above the *WJ* office, the same rooms that the Campbells had lived in earlier (LS to Margaret Campbell: 16 June 1873, LC).

13. Sir Walter Scott (1771–1832), Scottish poet and historical novelist.

NOVEMBER

Nov. 1st

Saturday. Wrote at my composition. Went down to Field's Corner for a walk.

Nov. 2nd

Sunday. Wrote at my composition. Went after sweet acorns for a walk, but did not get many. Papa had a Woman's Rights politician come up to see him.

Nov. 3^{d}

Monday. Did not feel very well, and ate no breakfast. Gave in my composition. Walked over to Neponset.

Nov. 4th

Tuesday. I am to be alone most of the rest of this week. Therefore coming home from school I bought chocolate, with which to comfort myself evenings. Bought a new watch key, and punched Mr. Cushing. I ached to the first time he invited us girls to try our strength on him. This time he repeated his offer. I didn't quite dare speak before all of them, but when we had broken ranks and were going out, I said to him "I think I could hurt you, Mr. Cushing." He very readily planted himself before me, but looked at me and said "You needn't hit but once, though; I don't know but you are stronger than the others." So I hit him, and knocked him backwards—as we all go when he says "Backward—march!" He said I was stronger than the others. I said I hoped I had not hurt him and he said "Oh no." Mamma being away, I took the opportunity to put a large mustard plaster on myself, having a pain in my chest. I did not raise blisters this time, though.

Nov. 5th

Wednesday. Began to correct my composition with Miss Newhall, but we did not have time to finish. We had a difference as to the using of a capital, and she quoted Carlyle at me, but I denied his being an authority. He uses words that would condemn any composition, I'm sure; "beautifuller," for instance. But his authority was on my side, for as Miss N. said, he begins nearly all his nouns with a capital, and I wanted to spell "bay" with one. The girls at recess discussed the relative beauty of the various boys at school in a way that surprised me greatly. I wonder if boys talk such stuff about us? This one was "as handsome as he could be;" that one "not exactly handsome, but very pretty;" one "perfectly elegant," and another "so cunning!" as if he had been a sweet infant of six months old. I couldn't help thinking that if I had been a boy I should not have been flattered to have the girls talk of me so.

Nov. 6th

Thursday. We drilled with guns for the first time. It was very pretty to see the "veterans" go through the manual alone. Florence Schenck, when they go into the position to charge bayonets, looks like the pictures of the Goddess of Liberty, being of a full figure, whether real or make believe I don't know. Mr. Cushing is very particular not to have the boys see us drill, and generally locks the doors. Today he didn't—one at least, and while we all stood drawn up, with our guns, in line, the door opened, and young Leland came in—a young man whose bright eyes and dapper appearance always remind me of a frog. As soon as he was heard at the door handle Mr. Cushing threw himself into position to charge him with his gun the moment the door opened. He dropped the letters on a seat and Mr. C. drove him out.

Nov. 7th

Friday. Finished correcting my composition with Miss Newhall. Emily Ladd stood by and listened to part of the correcting, and told me afterward that she was going to get and read it. Florence's 17th birthday.

Nov. 8th

Saturday. Mamma did not come. In the dusk sat over the fire and sang doleful ballads and meditated, and enjoyed myself in a quiet way, "taking my pleasure sorrowfully after the manner of my nation."

Nov. 9th

Sunday. My parents came home, or rather I saw them for the first time.[1] I took a short walk with Papa.

Nov. 10th

Monday. Miss Smith made me put a question on the blackboard for the first time. I did it with fear and trembling but got it right.

Nov. 12th

Tuesday. Misconducted myself in school. While we were eating our lunch I sat by the door, and drew out the key and hid it in my pocket. The lower half of the door of course was locked, so "When they would have gone, they found no way to go." I stood apart and watched while they all clustered around the door and

---

1. Lucy and Henry had been speaking on behalf of the MWSA, at suffrage conventions in three Massachusetts cities. They had probably arrived home the night before, after Alice was asleep (*WJ*: 1 Nov. 1873).

Florence precipitated herself against it, till to my horror I caught sight of Miss Smith on the other side of the door, shaking it. I thought that if the authorities were up it was about time to be rid of the key, which I accordingly dropped among the feet of the girls, and then suggested that it might be on the floor. There it was found (of course) upon search, and I got off without suspicion. Being still evilly disposed, and Georgie Townsend having rooted out a placard with "Clothes Room" printed on it in large letters, I pinned the same upon the door of the janitor's bed, which is a ward-robe by day.

Nov. 13th

Wednesday. The day Miss Barney and I ought to have spoken our pieces, but we both declared our determination not to speak till we were called for. Poor Miss Rand has a felon on her finger.

Nov. 14th

Thursday. Drill again. Mr. Cushing said we should take our guns to the lunch room and the veterans should each drill a raw recruit in private. We marched upstairs in line, carrying our guns, to the uproarious delight of the primary scholars, who glared upon us as if we were the King of China.

Nov. 15th

Friday. At recess we tried to have a little private drill, plastering with paper the chinks of the door from the curiosity of the primary and passing scholars. I have learned one new motion at least. The boys read miserably, vilely, at French translation, all but Puer[2] and maybe one more. After I had read, one boy remarking that I had not read to the end of the lesson, the professor said that I had read enough, and as well as all of them put together.

Nov. 16th

Saturday. Mamma went away. I went in to Boston with her, and when she had left, started from the office to call on Mrs. Smith. As I came down Tremont Alley a gentleman entered at the other end, and grinned cheerfully at me. It was Uncle George![3] I could hardly believe my eyes at first; but it was he. His steamer had unexpectedly changed its destination, and came to Boston instead of N.Y. We agreed to meet at a certain train, and I went down and called on Mrs. Smith. We talked as usual. U. G. found fault with me at supper for calling him "Sir," as not proper in families, and when I brought out my French lesson

2. Probably Chauncy student C. H. Poor.
3. George Blackwell had just arrived in Boston after a four-month stay in Europe.

to translate, made me read to him. He denounced my French professor as an Italian who had taught me the Italian pronunciation, and took me up on nearly every word till I leaned back in my chair and laughed myself almost into a fit. He finally took to perusing my French reader on his own hook.

Nov. 17th

Sunday. Displayed Uncle G. triumphantly to P[appa] & M[amma], who had arrived in the night. A violent storm in the midst of which Uncle G. started for N.Y.

Nov. 18th

Monday. In French the boys made a botch of their translating, and when I had done my reading he said "This I call translating; this is not guessing but translating, and giving the meaning of every word, and very good meanings, too."

Nov. 19th

Tuesday. A storm. Mamma did not want me to go to school, but I was bound & determined to go. Finally she said that if I went, I went without her consent and against her judgment; and if I was prepared to go on those terms, I might go. I went. My conscience troubled me all day, and I begged pardon when I got home, but Mamma had about made up her mind she had been mistaken, as the storm had subsided. A letter from Floy to say her engagement is about broken off. Mamma left in the evening.

Nov. 20

Wednesday. Boy's declamation. Went up after school to the Atheneum to consult the Encyclopedia about my composition. Found lots of information.

Nov. 21st

Thursday. Drill again. Brought out papers. Miss Newhall read me some poetry by one of the boys, and proposed I should write a poetical composition sometime.

Nov. 22nd

Friday. My first quarrel at school. When I got there in the morning I found the girls congregated in the dressing room whispering, and soon found that they were all abusing Mamie Molineux because she had reported some boys who were annoying the girls while drilling after school, to Mr. Cushing. He rushed upstairs two steps at a time, seized a couple of the wrong boys, marched them downstairs and marked them a double penalty. The girls all sided against Mamie, and talked about tale-bearing. At recess I heard Mamie's side of the story. She sat by herself in the door of the balcony, and we ate our lunch at the table. She went out afterwards, and the abuse of her continued. Florence Schenck headed it, and raked up all sorts of old stories against Mamie, and accused her of meanness and no end of things. She lost her temper or she wouldn't have said them. I had defended Mamie from the beginning, and told I thought she must be mistaken. When she repeated her statement in a still more violent manner, I lost _my_ temper and told her flatly that I didnt believe her. We both cooled down afterward, and made it up. Miss Rand, Florence, Georgie Townsend and I stayed in the lunch room after the others left, and back bit our teachers to our mutual satisfaction.

Nov. 23ᵈ

Saturday. Wrote on my composition. Miss Person and Mr. Miller came out and spent the evening, I being alone. And he talked predestinarianism, a thing I hate. I held up my fist by the lamp shade, and said I could smash it or not, as I chose. He said I couldn't smash it. Of course that wasn't to be borne, and I immediately struck it. It crashed but did not break. He afterwards denied having said what he did, and begged the question and twisted about like an eel. I hate him. If Miss P. marries him she will throw herself away.

Nov. 24ᵗʰ

Sunday. Took a ride and wrote on my composition.

Nov. 25ᵗʰ

Monday. Gave in my composition. Prof. Torrichelli addressed the French class as "Gentlemen" adding with a grin "and ladies." The class giggled, and I, being the only girl, turned red.

Nov. 26ᵗʰ

Tuesday. Snowy and soppy. Miss Newhall lent Freeman's History to Miss Rand and me that we might read up about the return of Godwin.[4] Mamma went away. Alone studying in the evening.

4. This text was probably written by Edward Augustus Freeman (1823–92), a British historian and author of both scholarly books and textbooks, best known for his work on the Norman Conquest.

Nov. 27th

Wednesday. At French the boys, according to the Professor, had made dreadful work of their exercises. Emerson said he had spent an hour over his, and several declared it was no use, that they could not write exercises, and would not try any more. Torrichelli suddenly appealed to me, to my great consternation, and demanded to know how I wrote mine. I said I couldn't without a dictionary, and he gave the class a lecture. Miss Rand and I being desperate to know what our Latin lesson was I screwed up my courage and asked Crossby, who was sitting in the desk in front of me. He told me with much politeness, and I am beginning to think that a boy, a small one at least, is not such a formidable creature as I thought. Georgie Townsend and I chalked and black-leaded each other. After school I went with Mamma and bought a dress.

Nov. 28th

Thursday. Thanksgiving day. Made mince pies in the morning, and took a walk with Papa to Neponset, along the railroad and home by the Granite Bridge station.

Nov. 29th

Friday. Mary Fifield and Lulu called in the evening.

Nov. 30th

Saturday. Mamie came out by invitation and spent the day. We chattered, and she gave me her version of Florence Schenck's slanderous stories. We took a drive, but it was cold. She said she had had a lovely time, and I was very glad to hear it, for Papa & Mamma were away, and I don't in the least know how to entertain company. I hope she meant it.

DECEMBER

Dec. 1st

Sunday. Looked over Vick's catalogue and discussed with my parents the question of my taking extra Latin.

Dec. 2nd

Monday. Actually spoke to another small boy—Emery—this time about the lesson in Scott.

Dec. 3d

Tuesday. When we assembled to deferred Scott, and were spending the time before Miss Ladd appeared chiefly in frantic inquiries of one another, chiefly

about the meaning of words, I actually exchanged a few words with Brewer—
the biggest boy I have ventured to speak to yet.

Dec. 4th

Wednesday. I had to leave out one sum, not having time to finish it, to my
great disgust, as it is the first time it has happened. When I came in to French
lecture and sat down, Brewer turned round and showed me the place, and
afterward picked up my pencil when I dropped it. Went to be measured for my
dress.

Dec. 4th

Thursday. A hard headache, owing I think to worrying over English History
and Latin. Went and was fitted and brought home my dress.

Dec. 5th

Friday. As I was leaving the hall after being checked I heard someone calling
to me, and found it was Mr. Demerit, who came out from his hedge of benches
and smilingly informed me that my father had spoken to Mr. Ladd about my
rushing off without breakfast in the morning and that instead of reciting with
my class, if I would come to him after school with a well-prepared lesson, he
would hear me then. I thanked him and rushed up to the Journal office raging
and exploded to Mamma. Got *The Boy in Grey* from the library and drove home
with Mamma.

Dec. 6th

Saturday. Went into Boston with Mamma on various errands. Changed a book
at the Public Library, and came up to the office, where I joined Mamma, and
we went to buy Christmas presents. We got two pairs of vases and a kitchen,[1]
and I, having had some dinner, went up to the Atheneum to look up pictures to
describe in my composition. And the first person I came upon in the rooms was
that Cushing boy, of all persons in the world. He held out his hand and said how
do you do, and I made some absurd and incoherent remarks in answer, being
much taken aback. It makes me mad with myself to think how I behaved,
though I suppose he did not notice it. I afterwards noticed several other boys in
my class in the rooms, all there for the same purpose that I was. I'm afraid I did
not pay very good attention to the pictures, for I felt dreadfully uncomfortable. I made my notes, however, had a little more conversation with the
Cushing boy, and came out home, where I acted so absurdly that Mamma,
whom I had of course told about it, finally asked me point blank, after regard-

1. New Englanders often referred to dutch ovens as kitchens.

ing me suspiciously, whether it was meeting those boys that had made me feel so. I said I supposed it was; for I was in constant fits of inward laughter remembering how absurdly I had behaved. I wish I was not such a fool!

Dec. 7th

Sunday. Wrote up my diary, and read *Shields*, and went over to Milton Chapel, which I regret, as it made me uncomfortable. Took two short rides with my parients, and finished translating my French.

Dec. 8th

Monday. Went up to the Atheneum after school to study up about painting in the Cyclopedia.

Dec. 9th

Tuesday. Went up to the Atheneum picture gallery with Miss Turner, but the light was so bad we might nearly as well have stayed away.

Dec. 10th

Wednesday. A note from Florence. Went up again to the Atheneum to study the Encyclopedia.

Dec. 11th

Thursday. Willie Emerson made such a fool of himself in history that I am disgusted with him. Mr. Herbert came in and supervised our drill, and after it was over the girls rushed upstairs and congregated in the upper hall, cursing him with gestures of fury.

Dec. 12th

Friday. Examination in Arithmetic. Found to my horror, upon consultation with Miss Rand that one question at least I had wrong.

Dec. 13th

Saturday. Everybody away. Tried to write at my composition, but did not get on very well.

Dec. 14th

Sunday. Wrote at my composition, and finished copying it after 8 PM. Drove over to the quarries to get evergreens for mottoes for tomorrows explosion.

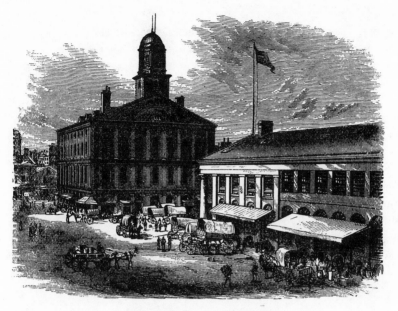

Faneuil Hall and Quincy Market.

Dec. 15th

Monday. After school went up to the office, where I found the long expected letter from Kitty awaiting me. As I plunged at it one of the ladies said "How her eyes brighten up!" I read it waiting for my dinner at Marston's, and finished it in Faneuil Hall, whither I then went to our tea-party. I saw my teacher Miss Smith outside the door and she spoke to me. Emma and I sat in the gallery. Wendell Phillips and Mr. Garrison & Mrs. Livermore & Stephen Foster & Fred Douglass and a lot more of our folks spoke. Wendell P. is much finer looking than I thought him at first sight. Mamma made the most eloquent speech I ever heard from her. I came across Mrs. Woolson in the audience, and had a few words with her. She looked as nice and sharp & wicked & charming as ever. There was a tremendous crush at supper and Emma, Miss Person & I were squeezed flat. We waited till every one was gone, and then drove home. I was frighted half out of my wits by our being nearly run over by a fire-engine which came tearing upon us around a corner. I got a few words from Mr. Garrison near the last, as he was going away. We all thought it had been a great success.[2]

2. To celebrate the centennial of the Boston Tea Party, the NEWSA threw their own tea party at Faneuil Hall, so that New England women could protest the fact that, after one

Dec. 16ᵗʰ

Tuesday. Miss Smith complimented Mamma and her speech very highly when she met me at school in the morning. I agreed with her, and told her I was proud of my mother. She said I ought to, or to that effect, and kissed me, of which I was glad, as I like her. Miss Newhall also complimented the speech in her fashion, as we came upstairs. In the evening Mamma, Emma & myself went to the other women's tea-party—the non-suffrage one—but found it very stupid, that is I did, and was glad to come away and get home.[3]

Dec. 17ᵗʰ

Wednesday. It's very aggravating to be asked inconvenient questions! Miss Rand was telling Miss Turner how a friend of hers (Miss R's) had accused her (Miss R) of being self conceited, and Miss T. said she thought she was not, and appealed to me for my opinion. Now I do think she is conceited—very—but I said I thought she didn't look like it, that being the best way I thought of to get out of it.

Dec. 18ᵗʰ

Thursday. Stephen Foster was in the office when I came in, and Mamma introduced me to him. He was much delighted at several things which I very innocently happened to say—once at finding I was a Butlerite, and again at a comment I made upon something Papa said, and he talked very pleasantly to me as we went with Mamma down to Marston's for dinner.

---

hundred years, they still were being taxed without representation. Those in the audience paid twenty-five cents for admission and twenty-five cents for refreshments, with proceeds going to the work of the NEWSA. The idea for the party was Lucy's, and she was largely responsible for organizing the immensely popular event at which both women and men suffragists spoke, including Wendell Phillips (1811–84), Frederick Douglass (1817?–95), and Stephen Foster (1809–81), all leading abolitionists and old associates of Lucy's (see DAB). Julia Ward Howe, Margaret Campbell, Henry, and Lucy also gave speeches. One newspaper agreed with Alice's assessment of her mother's contribution, saying that hers was the most stirring speech. Music and light refreshment were offered; however, the crowd was so large that servers ran out of tea. The evergreens that Alice had collected the day before were woven into a huge motto, displayed at the rear of the speaker's platform: "Taxation without representation is tyranny" (BDG: 16 Dec. 1873; WJ: 15 Dec. 1873).

3. This was the Boston Ladies' Centennial Tea Party, and like the suffrage party the evening before, it also filled Faneuil Hall, featured speeches, music, and tea, and was the leading story on the first page of Boston newspapers. There was a noticeable difference, however: at this event only male dignitaries gave speeches, and women served only as hostesses (attired in colonial dress) (BDG: 17 Dec. 1873).

Dec. 19th

Friday. Had the signs wrong in half my algebra examples. They were a new kind and Miss Rand wouldn't let me see hers, saying she hadn't time. She often insists on seeing mine when I am dreadfully hurried, and I was quite mad with her. I wanted to cry in class, but was bound I wouldn't till I could do it privately, and then I didn't care to. I told Miss Smith and Miss Ladd about it after I had got over it, while I was flinging on my things to go home, chattering wild nonsense as usual, I suppose, for Miss Smith laughed and Miss Ladd looked at me with amiable amusement, as if I were an interesting wild kangaroo from the Carribee Islands. No letter from Kitty.

Dec. 20th

Saturday. Spent the morning in Boston, shopping Christmas presents with Emma. Got Vol. 1. of *Pendennis,* and *Ravenshoe* to read on the way to New Jersey. Read *Pendennis* in the afternoon, and am delighted with Laura and like Warrington too thus far.

Dec. 21th

Sunday. Went with Emma to hear Mr. Murray preach, but there was a choral service instead. Read *Pendennis.*

Dec. 22nd

Monday. Did the arithmetic for 2 days in advance at school, and went and got the 2nd vol [of] *Pendennis.* Then went to 6 Oak Pl., being bound to have the next number of the *Home Guardian* before going south, if possible. Mrs. Smith said the magazines had not come from the printers, but she was expecting them every minute, so I waited, and read *Pendennis.* Was furious because Laura did not marry Warrington, with whom I am decidedly in love. He was worth six of that miserable, misanthropic, dandyfied Pen. Got my Guardian, and left.

Dec. 23^{d}

Tuesday. Went into Boston with Papa, and was put into the cars and started for N.Y. Rode all day, got there, and found Uncle G. waiting for me. He took me to 20th St. and I had my first view of the new house.[4] Was put to sleep in a queer little room with 2 windows.

---

4. In March Emily Blackwell had purchased a "cozy" house on 20th St. so that Nannie and Neenie would not have to be brought up in the infirmary (ASB to KBB: 22 Mar. 1873, LC).

Dec. 24ᵗʰ

Wednesday. At breakfast presented the spoons, knives and forks sent by Papa to the N.Y. family. Went up and saw the nursery. Went out to Somerville with Aunt Ellen and Nannie. Uncle Sam met us and drove us up, and I had a confab with Flo.

Dec. 25

Thursday. F. and I found peanuts, etc. in our stockings, and devoured them. After Uncle G. and Aunt Emily arrived, bringing Nina, we were allowed to assist at the stripping of the tree, to which the children had had free access all the morning. It was a scandalous breach of custom, and they had made themselves acquainted with the destination of nearly every interesting looking article, and had not kept 'hands off,' though strictly ordered to do so. However, the giving of the presents caused great commotion. When a rather soft package was given me, I pinched it, to judge of its contents by the feeling, to the alarm of Uncle G., who was standing by me, and cautioned me not to squeeze it; whereby I guessed he knew what was in it. It proved to be a beautiful necklace and bracelets of little pearly Venetian shells, strung together with tiny beads. I found afterwards that they were from him. I had also a copy of Scott's poems, a breast pin to match my sleeve buttons, a pair of skates, comb, penholder, pencil, etc., and a little book from Edie. Also a knife. After the presents were given, Uncle G., who had misbehaved somewhat during the process, proceeded to make a pest of himself generally, stealing our presents, especially a bunch of bananas which belonged to me, and over which we had violent battles. He found me pretty strong, I think. Finally he cast F. and Edie & myself in a heap on the floor amid hideous remonstrance; but his hair was in great disorder, and he had to retire and brush it carefully over the bald spot, before he could appear at dinner. After dinner he went away, and finally Christmas was over. At dinner U[ncle] S[am] asked me where I should be spending Christmas if I could choose. I promptly said Rome.

Dec. 26ᵗʰ

Friday. A snowstorm. Drove down to Somerville with U. S. and Aunt N[ettie]. In the evening, while F. and I sat over the fire, she said, after we had confabbed awhile, that she knew it was very dreadful, but she didn't believe in woman's rights! I saw she expected me to be horrified and explode, so I asked cooly why. She said she didn't want to vote. I asked her if that was any reason why I shouldn't, and she said that it wasn't the voting she minded so much, but that she thought married women oughtn't to have professions, etc; went over the usual rigmarole in fact, and said that the sentiments expressed in *Only a Girl* a most aggravating book which Aunt N. & I had joined in abusing, were hers exactly. I didn't take the trouble to argue much with her, but told her she would come around when woman's rights became fashionable; which remark she took with great good humor. Wrote to Kitty.

Dec. 27th

Saturday. Hoped for a letter from Kitty but got none. Flo & I got out the old Planchette[5] which Aunt M[arian]. used to use, and tried it secretly in the evening, in the parlor, with closed doors. But it wouldn't go for us; only scratched a little.

Dec. 28th

Sunday. We had meeting—one of U. S.'s pleasant home meetings. It took me so long to choose what to learn, that I did not know it very well. It was that splendid bit about the Lord being—"A very present help in time of trouble"— and the wilderness & solitary place "blossoming as the rose," etc. Also we were besieged in the dining room, F. & I, and had a tremendous time.

Dec. 29th

Monday. Read, & chopped up head cheese for Aunt Nettie.

Dec. 30th

Tuesday. Flo showed me Aunt Elizabeth's letter, which she had accused me of bringing on her. It was a very nice letter. Miss Anthony's lecture was in the evening,[6] and everyone went down to it but Gracie and either Agnes or Ethel, I forget which. Gracie had been lotting[7] all the week on having me that evening to tell her stories. She is a dear little thing, Gracie, though just at the awkward, scraggly age, and with a voracious appetite for fairy stories. I was afraid I might not know enough to fill up the evening till bed-time, but as it turned out, we sat up till ever so much o'clock, telling & listening. I like Gracie.

5. A planchette is a small triangular board with a pointer supported by two casters and a vertical pencil, which is said to spell out messages from the spirit world when the operator's fingers are placed lightly upon it.

6. Susan B. Anthony (1820–1906), leader (with Elizabeth Cady Stanton) of the National Woman Suffrage Association, based in New York City (NAW). Although she had once been a close associate and friend of Lucy's and Antoinette Brown Blackwell's, the suffrage split in 1869 was both the cause and effect of a bitter and personal break between Anthony and the Stone Blackwells. Brown Blackwell, however, retained ties to Anthony throughout this period.

7. To lot upon means to depend on or hope for.

Dec. 31st

Wed. Miss Anthony was there. She and Aunt N. talked gossip in the parlor, and Miss A. took notice of me in quite an embarrassing way, and also of Flo, and asked me about Mamma. I don't much like Miss A. She strikes me as being tall, sharp, dictatorial, conceited, pugnacious & selfish. Also plucky, undoubtedly. Got a letter from Mamma.

THE JOURNAL FOR 1874

JANUARY

Jan. 1, '74

Thursday. Said Goodby'e to Aunt N. & went into N.Y. with U. S., Flo and
Agnes. We ate our New Year's dinner (the pudding was kept for supper) and
then Uncle G. proposed that we should go to Central Park. It is not so pleasant
in winter, with the snow cleared off the paths, but we went and saw the wild
beasts,[1] and I made up my mind, not for the first time, that I could not possibly
have been a Christian Martyr. There was a great crowd in the monkey room
and it smelt horribly, so I was glad when we left it, though the monkeys were
very queer, and one fellow with a small body and legs and tail of startling
length moved about constantly, looking like a great black spider. We looked
through the windows of the building where most of the beasts are, and had a
very good view. There were two small elephants eating hay, and tigers, and a
lion who seemed restless, and roared. He did it in gaping, apparently, not in
anger, and it was not very loud, but it shook the windows against which we
leaned. U. S. quoted—"The lions do lack and suffer hunger," and Papa said
he—the lion—had "a noble countenance;" but I thought him a very ugly beast.
We had gone up in horsecars and omnibuses, but we walked back, all down 5th
Avenue, and I don't think I shall ever forget it. This was the first time I had
ever been in N.Y. except just to pass through, since I was quite a small child. It

1. The "Menagerie" (whose quarters were in the Old Arsenal, located near the entrance to the park on Fifth Ave. and 64th St.) housed a collection of wild animals. In
winters the exhibition was especially large because many traveling shows went into
winter quarters there.

was a gray unpleasant evening, and U. S. and U. G. led Agnes between them. There were also Flo, Papa and I. It was very interesting. There were the beautiful brown stone fronts, and it was frightful the sums they said it cost to buy and live in them; and we passed A. T. Stewart's great marble palace, and the cathedral, which is most beautiful, unfinished though it is.[2] Also a great number of churches, in all sorts of queer styles of architecture, many very quaint and nearly all hideous, which must have cost and cost huge sums. Uncle S. wondered how much real piety had to do with the building of them, and Papa called them Synagogues of Satan, and Uncle G. said several things; but Lowell's "Parable" was running through my head all the evening, especially the two lines "With gates of silver and bars of gold Ye have fenced my sheep from their Father's fold"[3] and I felt decidedly sad and savage.

Papa and I admired and criticized the buildings, told which we liked and should like to live in, and which we disliked, and argued and disputed and disagreed with each other, and finally we stopped before one most beautiful large brown stone front, and burst out into unanimous exclamations of rapture. The lights were just beginning to be lighted, and shone faintly through the curtains—real starry lace—that hung in the tall clear windows. It <u>was</u> beautiful. Uncle G. quietly remarked, "That's Madam Restelle's."[4] We went on, quenched most effectually, I feeling queerer and queerer. There were flocks of little beggar children with whining voices, who sallied out upon us; and a little boy sat by the railing, with a fiddle laid across his knees, crying. Papa made some remarks about his doing it for pretence (not to <u>him</u> of course) and joked about it; but I felt more like crying than laughing. It was such a contrast somehow. The lamps were all lit before we got home, and the basement of one great hotel seemed to be open to the street, the great sheets of glass which fenced it out were so clear. Passing another, with a row of lighted windows, I saw two black figures in relief against two of them, looking out. It struck me very much, I don't know why; but they were doing the same thing,

2. The group was admiring St. Patrick's Cathedral (on Fifth Ave., between 50th and 51st streets) and the home of the New York "merchant prince" Alexander Turney Stewart (1803–76), located on a spacious lot at Fifth Ave. at the corner of 34th St. Built of Carrara marble and referred to as "the Palace," it was considered the most opulent house in town at the time (DAB).

3. These lines are from James Russell Lowell's poem "A Parable."

4. Ann Trow Lohman (1812–78), better known as Madame Restell, was a notorious New York City abortionist whose arrests and extravagant living attracted much publicity. She lived with her husband in a four-story brownstone at 52nd St. and Fifth Ave., choosing the site, it was said, partly to annoy the archbishop, who was erecting St. Patrick's Cathedral nearby (NAW).

close together, looking out at the same things, and both visible to us, and neither visible to the other, nor knowing what the other was doing. Well, that queer walk came to an end at last, and we had supper with plum pudding, and Floy and I went to bed in the little room at the head of the hall, and heard the people go reeling home, singing, under our windows; and I thought, "New Year's calls."

Jan. 2nd

Friday. Read, and explored the house a little, looking out from the garret windows at the houses, and wondering what was going on behind those walls and inside all those back windows. A city is a queer thing! Also took a short walk or saunter with Floy.

Jan. 3d

Saturday. Went home with Papa. We had to wait—45 min. I think it was—for a horsecar, and missed our train. We took the next, but there was a very heavy fog, on account of which the train went slowly, and it was late when we got home & Mamma welcomed and fed us.

Jan. 4th

Sunday. Read, and walked over to Neponset.

Jan. 5th

Monday. Went to school again. There was talk about the Exhibition, which is to come off on the 28th.

Jan. 6th

Tuesday. Rainy. Had my composition corrected, and got Clough's *Bothie [of Toper-ma-fuosich]* from the Library.

Jan. 7th

Wednesday. Torrichelli told Willie Emerson, who had misbehaved about his exercise as usual, to "Go & repent;" at which there was a general grin. Was not very well, having a bad cold. Was given ginger tea.

Jan. 8th

Thursday. Was kept at home from school, to my huge disgust. Rode to So. Boston with Mamma.

Jan. 9th

Friday. Still kept from school, but drove into Boston & went to the Atheneum.

Jan. 10th

Saturday. Tried to write my composition.

Jan. 11th

Sunday. Ditto.

Jan. 12th

Monday. Mr. & Mrs. Campbell, Jr.[5] came and stayed over night. I didn't like either of them.

Jan. 13th

Tuesday. Papa went to N.Y., and had intentions of consulting Aunt Emily about me. I knew they would overstate my sickness, so I sent along a private letter to Aunt E., giving my views of it.

Jan. 14th

Wednesday. A snowstorm.

Jan. 15th

Thursday. Dr. Sewall was brought out to see me. She questioned me, heard me cough, said I had bronchitis, and that the odd appearance on my cheek was a herpes, (English, a cold-sore) which would disappear presently. She left a prescription.

Jan. 16th

Friday. Began to eat. Took a new medicine, washing away the taste with cider. Had salmon for supper.

Jan. 17th

Saturday. Same as usual; medicine, reading and toasting myself over the fire.

Jan. 18th

Sunday. Took a sleigride, and had theological arguments with Miss Titcomb, the dress-maker, who holds all sorts of queer opinions. She says people have no souls, only bodies; that when we die, we are dead. That at Judgment the bodies of the righteous will be resurrected and made immortal, whereas the wicked will not be resurrected at all. A very queer doctrine, which she supports with much Scripture. Certainly an improvement on universal damnation.

5. Margaret and John Campbell's son and his wife.

Jan. 19th

Monday. Read and took medicine.

Jan. 20th

Tuesday. Read, and disputed theologically with Miss Titcomb.

Jan. 21st

Wednesday. Miss T. started a new argument against the doctrine that animals have souls; namely that there would not be room in heaven for all the elephants. I told her she didn't know the size of an elephant's soul, forgetting that she doesn't believe in souls. Seems to me the elephant argument is like the anti-Woman's Rights argument that the townhouses would have to be enlarged to hold the women.[6]

Jan. 22nd

Thursday. Had a short argument with Miss T. on the subject of corsets, and stopped, finding that I couldn't keep my temper. Rode over to Meeting house Hill with Mamma. Foggy.

Jan. 23d

Friday. Took a long ride over by Lower Mills with Mamma. They persist in taking me out. Agnes Reid called to see what had become of me, having not seen me on the train lately, and a letter came from Mamie Molineux, inquiring after me and saying she hoped I should come to exhibition. And it seemed quite pleasant to think that people missed me.

Jan. 24th

Saturday. Sent an answer to Mamie's letter saying I would try to come into school Monday and find out about it. Rode down to old Mrs. Woods's with Mamma to get some more cider for me. She stayed some time, as he wanted to talk to her about his old wife who died quite lately, and I sat in the carriage, and was cold. Worse, & took a bath.

Jan. 25th

Sunday. Much better.

---

6. Alice is using town house according to common nineteenth-century usage in the U.S., meaning a house where the business of a town or city is transacted in legal meetings. Opponents of woman's rights apparently argued that the limited size of a town house precluded the presence of women at town meetings.

Jan. 26th

Monday. Cried because they would not let me go into school as I had meant to do. It was clear but very cold, and I suppose it wasn't best. Got over it and was amiable. Curled the feather in my hat for exhibition.

Jan. 27th

Tuesday. Mr. Ladd sent a letter to Papa with instructions and tickets for tomorrow, and I'm to go.[7]

Jan. 28th

Wednesday. Mamma took me in to the Exhibition. We drove to Music Hall, and when we got in couldn't find the girls' dressing room. It was nearly time, and I was wild lest we should be late. Rushing to one door I found myself face to face with the boys, marshalled in rows, drawn up waiting for the word of march. I asked them where the girls were, got some confused directions, and finally found their dressing room just as they were going to start. I tore off my things, exchanged excited greetings, got into line, and found myself at last seated in the balcony, at the end of the upper row of girls, with Miss Mansfield by me. The boys were to sit on the platform, and they marched on, slowly and precisely. It was a very fine sight, as Mr. Ladd had told us it would be. Finally they all got seated in rows, after facings and doublings and twistings many and wonderful.

Then the performances began. Several small boys gave "Agricultural addresses" and Stanton Day recited "The troubles of a little boy" with great applause. There was reading by a row of boys, and one of them imitated the roar of a naughty young one to perfection. Newton Mackintosh spoke a piece very cleverly; Willie Emerson spoke "the Saving of St. Michael's," very well too I believe, and various other boys spoke. There was a funny dialogue in which the settees of boys represented a Lyceum Society discussing the question whether newspapers was a cuss or a blessin', and another dialoge about chicken stealing, in which my prime abomination, Alden, acted the Dutchman, Mr. Henzrust. He did it very well too, and was so disguised that I shouldn't have known him. Marion Endicott was in this piece, and did finely; so was that Jones youth, representing the Judge. But when Curtis Guild came forth and made his speech or piece or declamation or whatever they call the thing, I got furious. It was an abominable tirade against England. I squirmed in my seat, I punched Miss Mansfield, I darted withering glances at the platform, and

7. The tickets were for the annual Chauncy Hall School exhibition.

longed for something to throw at him. I uttered suppressed grunts of wrath. We didn't beat the English so easily that we need pretend to despise them now, and if we hadn't been English ourselves we couldn't have done it at all. And what can one think of a boy who libels his grandmother? I wondered if the Cushing boy, whom I had picked out early in the afternoon, felt as angry as I did. Then that piece of Longfellow's about Agassiz was read, and we adjourned to the dressing room again. (Oh! I forgot to say that Mamie Molineux delivered an oration in Greek, took a medal, and distinguished herself, to my glory and satisfaction.)[8] The prizes were given last of all. Newton Mackintosh got two, one for drawing and one for composition; Alice Chapin also got one for composition. Wilmarth having been elected the Cock of the School in short, that fact was proclaimed, and the boys rose and gave him three cheers, to my huge disgust. They also cheered the takers of medals, seeming to me to cheer loudest for those whom I particularly detested. (I had been in terror all the afternoon lest Mamma should appear and seize me, as she had meant to take me home before the end, but she didn't.) More greetings in the dressing-room, from Mrs. Molineux, Miss Smith and the girls, and also some of the other teachers. Then we went home.

Jan. 29ᵗʰ

Thursday. No perceptible ill effects from yesterday. Made gingersnaps, and got a circular from Kitty, containing a Martha's Vineyard summer plot.

Jan. 30ᵗʰ

Friday. Wrote to Kitty, and sewed on drawers.

Jan. 31ˢᵗ

Saturday. It snowed. Had on mustard plasters and was given a dose of the vile bitters prescribed by Dr. Sewall.

8. Curtis Guild's declamation was from a speech of his father's, "at the reception of Capt. Winslow." Curtis Guild, Sr. (1827–1911), was an author, editor, and antiquarian. Young Curtis later distinguished himself as Republican governor of Massachusetts (1905–07) and ambassador to Russia (1911–13) (see DAB for biographies of both Curtis Guild Jr. and Sr.). Longfellow's poem "The Fiftieth Birthday of Agassiz" was read by a chorus of four girls and five boys. Mamie Molineux's declamation was listed in the program as "Original Greek Version of W[endell] Phillips on American Civilization" (Order of Exercises at the Forty-Sixth Annual Exhibition of Chauncy-Hall School, 28 Jan. 1874).

FEBRUARY

Feb. 1ˢᵗ

Sunday. Read and took doses.

Feb. 2ⁿᵈ

Monday. Sewed on drawers, and wrote on the private attempt which I have in hand at present. Miss Bass, our new girl, came.

Feb. 3ᵈ

Tuesday. Great snowstorm. Discussions with Miss T[itcomb] and an attempt at singing in the evening.

Feb. 4ᵗʰ

Wednesday. Miss T. and I make the house ring with our discussions, to Mamma's great amusement. Only as I won't admit the authority of Scripture and she won't admit the authority of anything else, we have no common ground to go upon, to our mutual regret. Fought her.

Feb 5ᵗʰ

Thursday. Upset Miss Titcomb into a snowdrift, by instigation of the devil. We were out on the piazza, and by a sudden impulse I pitched her over the edge. She went down the bank of course, and lay wallowing and laughing in the snow at the foot. Her legs went up. I fled into the house, and afterwards apologized, but had difficulty in making my peace.

Feb. 6ᵗʰ

Friday. Disputed with Miss T. concerning the immediate coming of the day of Judgment. Papa read aloud a book about New Zealand.

Feb. 7ᵗʰ

Saturday. Sewed on drawers. Tried to wear a pair of flannel over ones which Mamma has had made for me, and read *My Wife & I*.

Feb. 8ᵗʰ

Sunday. Made cakes. Papa insisted on taking me for a sleighride. Of course I objected, but the sun was bright and the snow deep and I enjoyed it. We took the cross road over beyond the river, and found it so blocked up by huge drifts that the sleigh came near upsetting. However, we got through and rode home.

Feb. 9th

Monday. Went into Boston with Mamma and bought a lot of neck-ties, and got from the Athenaeum the 2 first vols. of *Mademoiselle Mathilde*.

Feb. 10th

Tuesday. Discussed much with Miss T. and sewed a little on drawers.

Feb. 11th

Wednesday. Made gingersnaps, and went down to see Mrs. Hinckley's puppy. Was perfectly delighted with the charming little wooly beast. They keep it in the cellar and she took me down there to see it. The cat regarded it with fear and distrust, but it would not pay any attention to her and did not seem to see her. It is chubby and unsteady on its legs, and absurd & fascinating.

Feb. 12th

Thursday. Drove down to the coalyards with Mamma.

Feb. 13th

Friday. Began to go to school again. Had uncommonly good chances of staring at the Cushing boy, which I improved.

Feb. 14th

Saturday. Took a long walk over Neponset bridge and home by the drunken house. It is so good to begin to feel strong again.

Feb. 15th

Sunday. Read Jules Verne's *From the Earth to the Moon*, and found it very amusing indeed.

Feb. 16th

Monday. Mamma came up in the morning and insisted on my putting on underdrawers. I was furious at the time because I didn't want to do it, but afterwards I felt worse because Mamma had told me I needn't wear them, which she couldn't deny, than at the discomfort of them. Began going to school taking my regular lessons. Walked over to Neponset after school, which I mean to make my daily constitutional.

Feb. 17th

Tuesday. English History and drill at school, and walked over to Neponset.

Feb. 18th

Wednesday. Said my piece to Miss Ladd. Going down the hill on my way to Neponset, I saw something black in the field and got over the fence to look at it. It proved to be poor Toby, dead. I suspected both Mike and Mr. Putnam's dog, but on the whole I believe he died in a fit.

Feb. 19th

Thursday. Called on Fanny Benedict. She was at home on account of Neuralgia. She told me about the tea party or some such thing—a charity or religious one—which she had been at lately, and the look of the house, with the picture of a cross on the wall, gave a sort of Catholic atmosphere to the place which was very pleasant to me.[1]

Feb. 20th

Friday. Mrs. Coe and Annie called. I went up on the roof and saw the sunset.

Feb. 21st

Saturday. Made gingersnaps, and kept eating all day. Bad for my stomach.

Feb. 22nd

Sunday. Washington's birthday. Played for Papa, fought him, and washed some of my laces.

Feb. 23d

Monday. Went to Mamie Molineux's, by invitation. She and her mother sat down and we were talking very cosily. They told me about Alice Chapin, who they say disbelieves in Woman's Rights, the immortality of the soul, and various other things, and holds very odd opinions generally. That accounts for her looking so unhappy. And while I was there, that boy, Arthur Chamberlain, called again! I couldn't escape this time for Mrs. M. brought him right in, and spread herself between us with a pretence of protecting us mutually and preventing damage. I was dreadfully flurried, but after the introduction was fairly over, I also wanted to laugh. For while I went on talking to Mamie, I glanced at him in the chair where he had been put, and sat as if in the stocks, with his eyes cast down and his large flat face crossed by his wide mouth, the corners of which were turned up in a sort of helpless smile. O it was comical! I

---

1. Because Alice had attended St. Mary's Chapel with Fanny Benedict, it is likely that the Benedicts were Episcopalian.

tried to speak to him now and then, and before the end of the visit we mutually recovered somewhat, and held several conversations. It appeared, in answer to my question whether he liked cats, when Mamie's came upon the scene, that he 'admired cats,' and we petted it. I recovered first, but felt dreadfully queer. Also the subject of compositions arose. Finally he said he must go, and mentioned the time. I found it was much later than I supposed, and I had only just about time to catch my train. So I flew down and got on my things, and we left at the same time. And as our ways lay side by side as far as Dover St. of course we had to go together. So we started off, and I know I heard Mamie and her mother laughing as they watched us from the door. I silently made a vow that I would shake Mamie when next we met. We got along pretty well however, and parted at Dover St. very politely. I walked on to the So. Boston depot laughing internally. I gave Papa and Mamma an account of my visit driving up home.

Feb. 24th

Tuesday. Shook Mamie on the stairs. She was shaking enough with laughter, but protested that it was wholly accidental, and she had nothing to do with it. Walked to Neponset.

Feb. 25th

Wednesday. A snowstorm. Went and got my *Home Guardian*.

Feb. 26th

Thursday. Miss Smith found a new way of testing our memory on the squares of numbers. She called up two scholars together and called various squares to see which could answer the quickest. Several pairs had been called up, and it suddenly occurred to me "What if she should call me up with that Cushing boy!!" And she instantly did that very thing! She said, "Miss Blackwell, and Cushing." I got up reluctantly, and she said "Don't be distressed, Miss Blackwell," which made me feel worse. I didn't answer the first question at all, I was so flurried, but I recovered myself and kept up with him pretty well through the rest. I think she shortened it for my benefit.

Feb. 27th

Friday. Eyes troubled me. Got *John Halifax* from the Athenaeum, and heroically refrained from reading the same.

Feb. 28th

Saturday. Wrote out the first rough draft of my composition and then read *John Halifax*. Found soon after Mamma left for town that she had left the humorous for the paper.[2] Papa had laid it on my conscience to make sure it went in, and Mamma had promised to see to it. I put on my things, went and met the sleigh on its way back from the station, caught the next train, took it in to Mr. Upham, hurried to the office and told Mamma I had done so, and caught the train home. She said it was not necessary it should go in that day.

MARCH

March 1st

Sunday. Finished my composition and read *John Halifax*.

March 2nd

Monday. School again. Realized for the first time the width of the Cushing boy's mouth, as he turned around on the broad grin at something or other.

March 3d

Tuesday. Miss Turner asked me how I managed to come to school and do my lessons, yet keep well, and whether I thought it was my loose dressing. So I gave her my views somewhat. Took a walk, but got into what seemed to be a blind st. and had to retrace my way—a thing I hate.

March 4th

Wednesday. Made gingersnaps and fixed my laces.

March 5th

Thursday. Went down and called on Mrs. Hinckley and walked over to Neponset. I knew the Cushing boy was apt to blush upon slight occasion, but today Miss S[mith] said, "Why Cushing, what are you doing?" And I looked and saw what seemed to have been a slight squabble. He said, "I was trying to get Guild's paper for him." Miss Smith said Guild would get his paper all in good time, and the lesson proceeded. But I, looking at him, saw his neck turn red clear down to the collar, which flush gradually disappeared. I've read of peoples blushing clear over their necks, but I think this is the first time I ever saw it.

March 6th

Friday. Went up to Newburyport after school, getting dinner at Marston's. I had hardly got my things off before Miss A[ndrews] took me up to see her nice

2. The "Humorous" was a regular column in the *WJ*, with amusing stories and jokes.

little schoolroom, just fixed up, and evidently the pride of her heart for the time being. Mr. Hale came to supper and spent part of the evening. I slept in my old room, Miss A. in the little ante chamber. She said next morning that I talked in my sleep, on metaphysical subjects and in very long words, but couldn't remember what I said.

March 7ᵗʰ

Saturday. At breakfast Miss A. gave me a sketch of her scholars, whom I saw when they came. I sat through the session, and it was delightful. Several of them were very interesting seeming children, and I fell in love with little Lily something, who reminded me of Anna. She had a "pale face, star-sweet," and I longed to kiss her before she went away, but could not screw my courage up to it. Another was Montie, and the two little "Southern ladies," with bracelets of twisted gold, sent them by their parents in India. Miss A. is good at teaching. The history lesson was verbal, and the children much interested. They clapped their hands over the victories, especially the taking of Quebec, and were in lamentations when the lesson had to be ended. I came home in the afternoon. I do love Miss Andrews.

March 8ᵗʰ

Sunday. Made candy.

March 9ᵗʰ

Monday. Mrs. Hinckley came up with Sancha.[1]

March 10ᵗʰ

Tuesday. Had a second attack of bronchitis, and coughed tremendously in school, to my shame and confusion of face.

March 11ᵗʰ

Wednesday. Still coughed dreadfully. Got excused from declamation on account of it, fought Marion Endicott in the lunch room (she is strong and pugnacious, but I can beat her) and signed a note, with Miss Rand and Hattie Turner, to accept the boys' invitation to picnic. Read *Past and Present*. Emma [Lawrence] came.

March 12ᵗʰ

Thursday. The three boys, Hunt, Guild & Emory invited us three girls to a private conference on the picnic. All stray boys were ejected from the room

1. Sancha was Mrs. Hinckley's dog.

with great parade, and the general arrangements were settled, but not anything of much importance done, except to dispute as to whether we girls should pay our own fares; which we agreed to refer to Miss Smith.

March 13ᵗʰ

Friday. Was explicitly given leave to come with the 2ⁿᵈ French class next time. Guild & Co. appealed to Miss S. about the fares. Mr. Ladd made us an oration at List-call, telling us that news had just come of the death of Charles Sumner. I was very much startled, but took home the news to Mamma after school. "Well," said Mamma slowly, "I don't know that Woman's Suffrage owes much to Mr. Sumner," or words to that effect.[2] Called on Mrs. Hinckley.

March 14ᵗʰ

Saturday. Rode into Boston with Mamma.

March 15ᵗʰ

Sunday. Went with Emma, Lucy Chadbourne and Miss Bass to see Summer lying in state in the Statehouse. There was a great crowd, and we were pretty well squeezed, though we heard that in the afternoon it was much worse, and ladies and children fainted. The coffin was nearly buried in flowers—a great cross of calla lilies at the head, and an inscription in violets on a white ground (we couldn't read it, but found afterwards that it was "Do not let the Civil Rights Bill fail") at the foot. A dove was suspended over it, and colored guards stood at the doors, and inside the inclosure of ropes. We were only allowed to pass round and go out, and then went to hear Phillips Brooks preach. Had to stand through the service.[3]

2. Charles Sumner (1811–74), Republican member of the Senate from Massachusetts (1851–74), was the first prominent political leader to urge emancipation. Author of the Fourteenth Amendment (1866), providing equal suffrage for black and white males, he believed women must "wait" for the franchise, despite strong appeals from suffragists that the bill also include the franchisement of women (*DAB*). The Stone Blackwells personally appealed to him in Washington, hoping that their old antislavery associations would strengthen their case for women as well. Unsuccessful as they were, they still supported the amendment, whereas Stanton and Anthony did not—a difference that contributed to the suffrage break in 1869. Lucy accepted Sumner's belief in the primacy of black suffrage at the time, saying, "I think God rarely gives to one man . . . more than *one* great moral victory to win. . . . If Mr. Sumner 'don't want to be in this fight,' as he told me, in my heart I yet say, 'God bless him.' Our victory is sure to come, and I can endure anything but recreancy to principle" (see Hays, *Morning Star*, 185, 203).

3. The Episcopal congregation served by Phillips Brooks was without a building after the 1872 fire destroyed Trinity Church on Summer St. Until their new edifice on Copley

Statehouse.

March 16th

Monday. Emma and Miss Persons went to see the Sumner procession and were much squeezed. Looked out the address of the Cushing boy. Mamma took me to Dr. Sewall's office to consult about my cough, but she had gone South for her own health, and her assistant said that it would no doubt be good to take me south, but she did not think it necessary.

March 17th

Tuesday. Oral examination in Arithmetic. A letter from Mr. Cushing was read. Coughed to that extent in the night that Papa and Mamma came flying upstairs in white drapery, with a dose and mustard plaster to administer to me.

Square was completed in 1877, Phillips preached to packed crowds at Huntington Hall, the large public auditorium at MIT.

March 18th

Wednesday. Mamma wanted to keep me from school, but I was allowed to go in on the 9.03 (I think) after Dr. Fifield had seen me, and sounded my lungs and arteries with what <u>seemed</u> great thoroughness. He said I lacked blood, for all my rosy face; that my lungs were all right, the left one very good, the right not quite so good, but nothing the matter with it. Went to French with the 2nd Class at last, and was rather disappointed in it. Felt unwell, and told Mamma and Emma when they came into school that I was willing to go to Washington.

March 19th

Thursday. Emma went to Washington, and my whooping-cough developed itself.

March 20th

Friday. Can't go to Washington because Mamma thinks it would be wrong to expose the babies on the cars to the cough. Am much disappointed for I had looked upon my going as a settled thing, and had got eager for it. Was taken with Mamma when she went to carry Mrs. Crimmins home.

March 21st

Saturday. Fried potatoes and rode with Mamma.

March 22nd

Sunday. Refused to ride; stayed at home and fried potatoes with great success.

March 23d

Monday. High wind and cold. Cough violent. Ate my supper with the expectation of seeing it again before morning. Expectation not fulfilled.

March 24th

Tuesday. High wind, cold and clear again. Fried potatoes, and read *Reports and Realities*.[4] Papa is non-suited with old Gosse.

March 25th

Wednesday. Still too cold to go into Boston. Made Welsh rabbit.

---

4. *Reports and Realities*, published by the Rosine Association of Philadelphia, reported on their work combating prostitution between 1847 and 1855.

March 26ᵗʰ

Thursday. Rode into town with Mamma. Got my *Home Guardian,* and 2 vols. of *Adela Cathcart* from the Atheneum. As we were riding home, Mamma told me what Miss Andrews had told Miss Bass about me, when she was coming here—that I was the most conscientious and truthful child she ever knew. That she had also made her expect to find me hard to get acquainted with, in which respect she was mistaken.

March 27ᵗʰ

Friday. A new calf was announced, and I saw it in the pen. Rode into town with Mamma and got 3ᵈ vol. *Adela Cathcart,* and *Daisy Chain.* We were too late to look for a puppy. Duke fell down.

March 28ᵗʰ

Saturday. Fried potatoes and read *Les Miserables.* Hunted up the other volumes. In the evening I was reading away, and just as my favorite Enyolras had put a pistol to the head of Le Cabuc and given him one minute to say his prayers, Papa made me stop to listen to that stupid biography of Scott. I went to bed with the white cold face and flying hair of that young executioner before my eyes.

March 29ᵗʰ

Sunday. Finished *Les Miserables* and made French rabbit.

March 30ᵗʰ

Monday. Read, and plagued Miss Bass.

March 31ˢᵗ

Tuesday. Began to read *Les Miserables,* taking it regularly & not skipping a word. Papa called me the names recorded on the back of Fantine.[5]

APRIL

April 1ˢᵗ

Wednesday. Got *Kenelm Chillingly* from the Atheneum, and went with Papa and Mamma to look for a dog. We saw a room full of them. There was a majestic

5. Alice was probably beginning the second volume of *Les Misérables* by the French writer Victor Hugo (1802–85). It is unclear whether Alice read the French edition or the English translation. Fantine is a female character in the book.

but sleepy St. Bernard and a Scotch colley with a beautiful face. The man had not the sort of puppy we wanted, but promised to look one up for us.

April 2nd

Thursday. Went with Papa to another animal place, where a lean black puppy with a white tip to his tail, was waiting for us by appointment. I had known my heart would warm to the first puppy I saw, and it did. He had a sweet face, and we bought him despite his thin body & ugly tail, for $15. and took him home in the carriage. I took him down & compared him with Sancha. He is much the slimmer. They wanted to fight. His name is Major.

April 3d

Friday. Fed Major & took him walking twice, 2nd time without a string. He kept breaking his string to follow me. Made a cream cake.

April 4th

Saturday. Snowed in A.M. Read Victor Hugo, fed Major, and took him walking. We met Mr. Horne, who asked Major's age, and predicted that he would be a monster.

April 5th

Sunday. Rode with Papa and Major.

April 6th

Monday. Rode in Boston and bought dresses. Saw Mamie Molineux.

April 7th

Tuesday. Read *Cosette* & wrote on T. S. Gen. Lee lectured.[1]

April 8th

Wednesday. Walked with Majie and rode with Miss Bass. Not having much confidence in her driving I drove myself, but made her promise not to tell Mamma. If Mamma finds I drive at all I shall have to keep going down to the station.

---

1. "Cosette; or the Detectives Pursuit" was an episode in *Les Misérables*. General E. M. Lee was in the area lecturing on "Woman Suffrage in Wyoming" (*WJ*: 11 Apr. 1874).

April 9th

Thursday. Worked and read *Lord & Master*. Raged at the ending thereof. To have one of my favorite male characters turn out to be a woman in disguise, and Guy confess himself a disreputable character, was too enraging.

April 10th

Friday. Wrote on T. S. & made gingersnaps.

April 11th

Saturday. Had a headache. Took a cold drive with Miss Bass & Majie.

April 12th

Sunday. Cold ride with Papa to the lands beyond the river. Pared his toe nails.

April 13th

Monday. Rode with Miss B. & played with Major, who chased chickens.

April 14th

Tuesday. Walked to Neponset and back in a great hurry. Miss Bass being unwell, I did the dishes.

April 15th

Wednesday. Went to Miss Randall's. Letter from Kitty.

April 16th

Thursday. Rode with Miss Bass. The horse would stumble, & wouldn't go fast. Mamma returned from an ovation, bringing a beautiful great bunch of flowers and part of a great cake called "Lucy Stone cake."[2]

April 17th

Friday. Arranged the books and fried potatoes.

April 18th

Saturday. Passed most of the day in going down to the station for Aunt Nettie, who did not come.

April 19th

Sunday. Went down early in the morning and got Aunt Nettie.

2. This ovation is not described in the WJ.

April 20ᵗʰ

Monday. Went into town to hear Aunt Nettie read a paper before the Ladies' Club.³ In the midst of it had to slip out to cough. Began to whoop on the stairs. Fear I made an awful noise for the stewardess rushed out to ask if she could do anything for me. We drove home.

April 21ˢᵗ

Tuesday. Walked with Major on our street.

April 22ⁿᵈ

Wednesday. Guided Aunt N. about Boston and showed her the Atheneum.

April 23ᵈ

Thursday. Read, and showed some of my verses to Aunt N., of which I immediately began to repent.

April 24ᵗʰ

Friday. Went to school again.

April 25ᵗʰ

Saturday. Rode into Boston, changed books, got a couple of hats and went with Mamma & Aunt Nettie to get an outer sack. We went to three or four places, and I tried on ever so many, but though they were full ladies' size they were no end too narrow in the back, and I have got to have one made to order. I am bloated with pride on account of my broad back.

[No entry for Sunday, April 26]

*[April 27]*⁴

[Monday] Went to a party at Miss Rand's, Miss Turner meeting me at the office by appointment. The party was rather stupid. There was talk of forming a club. Many healths were drunk at tea (in water). Mamie & I agreed that we would not drink to "Fair Harvard" if proposed. Got very full of water and drank the last toasts from an empty glass. Papa came with the carriage for me, and I sang college songs of a rather rowdy character most of the way home.

3. Antoinette Brown Blackwell read a paper, "Work in Relation to the Home," at the New England Woman's Club. The *WJ* had been featuring a series of seven articles by her on "Sex and Work" (running from March and to end in June), which would later be published in her book *The Sexes throughout Nature* (1875) (*WJ*: 18 Apr. 1874).

4. This final entry appears earlier as "April 15." It has been crossed out and a marginal note added: "This should be for the 27ᵗʰ—on 15ᵗʰ went to Miss Randall's. Letter from Kitty."

AFTERWORD

In the weeks and months following April 1874, Alice predictably chalked up academic honors and was popular with her classmates. When she graduated from the Chauncy Hall School in 1877, she won the gold medal for English composition, a skill she had continued to develop by frequently writing short articles and reviews for the *Women's Journal*.[1]

In 1877 she enrolled at Boston University, one of only two young women in a class of twenty-six men. Being in a decided minority was not new to her, thanks to her Chauncy Hall experiences. As in earlier school days, she lived at home and commuted into the city for her college classes. Her decision to attend a local college may have been influenced by a need to stay close to her mother; perhaps she wanted to assist her, or perhaps she feared she would be homesick. Whatever her reasons, by her junior year she confided to Kitty a growing concern about her mother. In a letter written when her father was away again (overseeing his latest business interest, a beet sugar company in Maine), she said:

> It is a heavy load for poor Mamma—the Journal every week, the general supervision of the suffrage cause in Massachusetts, and the care of this big place, indoors and out—planning what we are to eat three times a day, keeping an absentminded daughter clothed and in running order, seeing that the geraniums are covered up if the evening threatens frost, that the

---

1. Alice began writing occasional reviews for the *WJ* shortly before stopping her journal; her initialed review of the January "Vick's Floral Guide" appeared in the issue of 18 Apr. 1874.

Alice Stone Blackwell, c. 1885. (Library of Congress)

various fruits are picked at the right time & kept without spoiling, etc. etc. adinfinitum. I should think she would go cracked; but she pursues the even tenor of her way and shows no sign of breaking down.[2]

It was no surprise, then, that after her graduation in 1881 she began to assist her mother in organizing suffrage work, as well as in writing and editing the *Woman's Journal*. Alice brought with her superb qualifications for both jobs, having been elected president of her class and to Phi Beta Kappa. And by using her pen as a "brighted weapon," she had already produced ample published evidence of her writing ability. By 1884 she was officially listed on the mast-head as "Editor," along with Lucy Stone and Henry Blackwell. Referred to now as "the daughter of the regiment," she carried on her mother's work, but also began to carve out a life of her own.

2. ASB to KBB: 28 Sept. 1879, SL.

In 1887 she also took on the sole editorship of a new, small weekly newspaper called the *Woman's Column*, devoted exclusively to coverage of the suffrage movement. For the next eighteen years, this broadside was sent to hundreds of newspaper editors with the intention that its ready-made suffrage stories would be reprinted in more popular newspapers and thereby aid the cause. Alice's stories in both papers attracted notice. "When you tackle anybody, something gives way," she was told once by an admirer. And a Boston editor who opposed woman suffrage conceded that Alice Stone Blackwell was the only woman in Massachusetts who could write a paragraph.[3]

Perhaps her most significant nonwriting achievement during this period came in the late 1880s when she acted as a prime mover in bringing together the two suffrage factions that had split off from one another in 1869. With her mother beside her, she began a series of meetings with "plucky" Susan B. Anthony and Anthony's protégé, Rachael Foster. Alice's ability to diffuse former animosities (possibly aided by her new friendship with Anthony's niece, Lucy Anthony) facilitated negotiations for a merger. This was consummated in 1890 when the first meeting of the National American Woman Suffrage Association took place in Washington, D.C.[4] Both Henry and Alice participated in the sessions, but Lucy was ill and unable to leave home.

By this new decade, Alice found herself watching helplessly as her mother's physical decline manifested itself in what often seemed like simple exhaustion. It had been going on for several years: Lucy would rally for special events, somehow look and feel energized, then collapse, recover, and begin again. Finally, late in the spring of 1893, after returning home from the Columbian Exposition in Chicago, Lucy found no restoration even after a full summer's rest. This time she suffered not only from exhaustion but from an inoperable stomach tumor. She died in October, with Alice at her side. Among her last words were those directed to her daughter: "Make the world better."

Alice spent the rest of her life trying to do just that. She began by following her mother's footsteps and taking over the major editing responsiblity for the *Woman's Journal*, while her father continued to write regular columns and take care of the financial aspects of the paper. Also like her mother, she held offices in all the major suffrage organizations, including a twenty-year post as secretary of the NAWSA. In spite of her uneasiness on a podium she began to speak for suffrage. Not blessed with as pleasing a voice as her mother's, she was nonetheless a persuasive speaker and could engage in well-argued debates. A distinguished lawyer once said that he attended suffrage

3. *NAW*, v. 1, 157.
4. Lasser and Merrill, *Friends and Sisters*, 231.

Alice Stone Blackwell as editor of the *Woman's Journal*. (Library of Congress)

meetings whenever he could because he considered her rebuttal speeches the "ablest presentation of controversial matter he had ever heard."[5]

By the time the Nineteenth Amendment was ratified in August 1920, Alice had taken on a number of new causes close to her heart—causes well outside her mother's experience. She had discontinued her connection with the *Woman's Journal* in 1917 when it merged with two other papers. After her father's death in 1909, she lived alone, supporting her modest lifestyle with her invested savings. With both energy and time to spare, she threw herself into a number of humanitarian and social reforms, many of them radical for her day. Although she often used her voice, her pen became her most effective weapon in her work as writer, editor, and translator. In her efforts, she broke through many "old fences"—just as she predicted she would in her journal on the night of her Harris School graduation.

Active in many progressive organizations (including the Women's Trade Union League, the National Association for the Advancement of Colored People, and the American Peace Society), she was, not surprisingly, often involved in women's reform. She believed that women would lose their identity as an "autonomous moral force in politics" if they worked only within the traditional two-party system. To offset this, she helped found the League of Women Voters in Massachusetts and remained an active force in the organization. When a detractor pointed out that woman suffrage had not brought about the millennium afterall, she coolly replied, "There is a great deal of human nature in women." [6]

In 1935, when she was nearing eighty, she wrote and spoke against an attempt by the city of Boston to prevent married women from holding city jobs. The Massachusetts Women's Political Club endorsed the action on the ground that married women with jobs were being dragged from "true womanhood" and their proper place in the home. The Club also denounced the League of Women Voters as a "bolshevik" organization for defending married women's job rights. Alice responded in a lengthy newspaper interview, saying such thinking was "a step in the direction of fascism." Whether to hold a job, she continued, is a decision for individual women, not the law, to make.[7]

At about this same time she helped establish the Boston Evening Clinic and Hospital, located then at 452 Beacon Street. She served as vice president of the board and was immensely proud that Boston had a place where poor people

5. "Alice Stone Blackwell," *Bostonian* (a publication of Boston University), April 1950, M37, reel 5, Blackwell Family Papers, SL.

6. *NAW*, v. 1, 157.

7. *Boston Traveler*, 6 May 1935, M37, reel 5, Blackwell Family Papers, SL.

could be hospitalized as well as secure good, free medical treatment after working hours. Boston newspapers covered the dedication ceremonies; pictured in the midst of Governor Curley and a number of distinguished looking men was Alice—small, wiry, and determined-looking, her gray hair in disarray. [8]

Alice called herself "a socialist in opinion, but not a party member."[9] Distrusting parties, she most assuredly had independent ideas about almost any political issue. She supported the short-lived Non-Partisan League in the Midwest and in 1924 endorsed the radical Progressive candidate for president, Robert La Follette. A committed civil libertarian and fighter against anything smacking of political oppression she took increasingly stronger stands against what she believed were the reactionary abuses of human rights that followed World War I. She spoke and wrote against the misuse of the Espionage Act, the deportation of radicals, the suppression of free speech, and the growing incidents of racial discrimination at Boston University (where she sat on the Board of Trustees). At least one Boston paper refused to print her letters because of the controversy they produced. Seemingly unperturbed by the reactions she was producing among Boston conservatives, she went on her provocative way, confessing only to her journal in April 1920 that she "dreamed last night I was to be hanged on a charge of 'Red' activities." [10]

This dream did not seem to deter her from actively supporting Italian anarchists Nicola Sacco and Bartolomeo Vanzetti, who had been arrested that same month for murder. Convicted the following year in a highly publicized trial, they were put to death in 1927. Alice remained convinced of their innocence and believed, like many other liberals and radicals, that they had been tried for their political views rather than for any actual crime. She avidly supported their long defense and carried on a voluminous correspondence with Vanzetti during his years in jail.[11]

One of the causes that Alice cared most about was helping Armenian refugees, an interest that came about after a friendship and brief romance with a young Armenian theological student in 1893. From him she learned of the Turkish atrocities against his people, and after his death several years later she devoted the rest of her life to helping the Armenian community in the United States. For years she operated an informal employment service for needy Armenians. At one point when she was collecting money to feed Arme-

8. *Boston Post*, 13 May 1935, M37, reel 5, Blackwell Family Papers, SL.
9. Samuel Warman, *The Alumni* (n.d.), M37, reel 5, Blackwell Family Papers, SL.
10. *NAW*, v. 1, 157.
11. Ibid.

nian children she sold all her valuable rugs from Pope's Hill to contribute to the cause. Such acts of generosity did not go unnoticed by the Armenian community. When she was honored on her seventy-fifth birthday at a dinner sponsored by the International Institute, prominent Boston Armenians presented her with a large Oriental prayer rug, and she was ordered never to dispose of it.[12]

As Alice immersed herself in the lives of her new Armenian friends, she learned of their country's literature and poetry, which led her to the writings of other oppressed peoples. These works opened up a new world for her—a world she sought to share with her customary literary enthusiasm. She likened Spanish-American poetry, for instance, to "a large garden, full of flowers of every kind and color" with "bouquets" for every taste.[13] There was more at stake for her, however, than sheer literary value. She believed greater world understanding could be achieved by sharing the human experiences and longings expressed in these up-to-then "foreign" works. Fired by both her love of letters and her belief in a common humanity, she began her avocation as a translator.

From 1896 to 1937, she translated into English the works of Armenian, Yiddish, Russian, Hungarian and Spanish-American poets. In doing so she made hundreds of foreign poems available to English-speaking readers for the first time.[14] She relied on her many foreign friends to provide her with literal translations of the original poems in English or French. Working from these she then made her own compilations and more finished transcriptions, publishing them in a number of articles and well-received books. Her last effort, *Some Spanish-American Poets* (1929), made the works of such now-distinguished poets as Rubén Darío of Nicaragua and Gabriela Mistral of Chile available in a collection that pioneered the effort to provide readers with the original poem on the page opposite its translation. Alice strongly believed in this format and dug into her own purse to reimburse her publisher for the extra costs involved. Her inital investment paid off, for the book was such a success that it was reprinted in 1937.[15]

12. News clippings, M37, reel 5, Blackwell Family Papers, SL.

13. Alice Stone Blackwell, comp. and trans., *Some Spanish-American Poets* (New York and London: D. Appleton, 1929), xvii.

14. See her *Armenian Poems* (Boston: Roberts Brothers, 1896); a new and enlarged volume of this was published by R. Chambers in 1917; *Some Spanish-American Poets* went into a second printing in 1937 when it was published by the University of Pennsylvania Press; a second edition of her translations of Yiddish poetry appeared in *Songs of Grief and Gladness* (Boston: Williams, 1917); and *Songs of Russia* (published by Alice Stone Blackwell, 1906).

15. Samuel Montefiore Waxman, *The Alumni* (n.d.), M37, reel 5, Blackwell Family Papers, SL.

One of her most publicized books was politically motivated. Provoked by czarist injustices, she helped activate the Friends of Russian Freedom in 1904 and became a friend and supporter of the Socialist revolutionary Catherine Breshkovsky when she visited the United States the same year. Breshkovsky had been imprisioned and exiled in Siberia for twenty years before her release and triumphal tour of the United States. On her return to Russia, she was once again exiled, this time until the czarist regime fell in March 1917. She served briefly as a member of the Preliminary Parliament until the Bolshevik take-over in October. Alice's correspondence with Breshkovsky led to the publication in 1917 of her only edited book, *The Little Grandmother of the Russian Revolution: Reminiscences and Letters of Catherine Breshkovsky*.[16]

The book that provided her with the deepest sense of personal satisfaction, however, was her biography of her mother, published in 1930. She had known since the age of sixteen that she would write it, confiding to Kitty in 1872: "Did I ever tell you that I am going to write Mamma's biography when I am older, and am collecting all the facts and stories about her that I can, for that purpose? Mama objects, but she will not be able to help herself if I persist and I shall make her correct and revise it herself. I am uncommonly proud of being Lucy Stone's daughter."[17]

Her actual research and writing began after her mother's death. It was no easy task to go through the vast collection of antislavery and suffrage records, correspondence, and speeches that she had in her possession. For nearly forty years she intermittently labored over the book, finding it more difficult to complete than any project she had ever undertaken. Although her mother is the overwhelming presence in the book, her father also figures prominently. In the final section she pays tribute to him, expressing pride in his "unswerving support" of her mother's life work and her gratitude for his valuable contributions to woman's suffrage. Her recollections of him at the end of his life are reminders of her journal descriptions of him written thirty years earlier: "He was active to the end. Most men of his age lean upon their children. To the very last, I leaned upon him. He was so vigorous physically, so alert and youthful mentally, that he was more like a brother than a father. However late at night I got back from a lecture trip, he was always waiting at the station to meet me and to carry my suitcase up the hill."[18]

Never one to indulge herself with unnecessary expenses, Alice moved out of the family house and into smaller quarters on Monadnock Street in Dorchester soon after her father died. She refused to sell the family home at 45 Boutwell

---

16. This book was published by Little, Brown.
17. ASB to KBB: 29 Oct. 1872, LC.
18. Alice Stone Blackwell, *Lucy Stone*, 293.

Street; instead, in 1919 she turned it over to the first of several charities. At one time the grounds were used by poor Russian and Jewish women for vegetable gardens. Eventually, Pope's Hill became divided into sections by the addition of new streets lined with houses on small lots. In the 1950s, after a long period of neglect, the old homestead was torn down. In its place now stands a two-story frame duplex; to the side, however, remain the original granite gateposts that once marked the entrance to the long driveway and Alice's garden.

Her old neighborhood is virtually unrecognizable. Harris School, old First Parish Church, Lyceum Hall, and most of the neighboring homes Alice used to visit are all gone. Commercial Point has fulfilled its name: billboards and two large gas tanks now dominate the landscape around Dorchester Bay and old Tenean Beach. Although Fields Corner and Harrison Square both exist in name, they have merged as a conglomerate of commercial strips, with little sense of two distinct neighborhood centers.

Parts of Boston, on the other hand, remain much as Alice found them at the time of her journal. The Athenaeum, although enlarged, still has the same reading rooms and galleries she enjoyed. Boston Common, St. Paul's Church, the State House, and King's Chapel all stand just as they did when Alice made her book-collecting rounds. Tremont Place is now filled with multistoried office buildings, but around the corner a "new" Tremont Temple (1896) stands on the site of the old hall. Inevitably, the Public Library on Boylston Street ran out of room for books and in 1895 moved to distinguished new quarters on Copley Square—quarters Alice continued to enjoy for another fifty years.

The later lives of other people who figured in Alice's journal often followed predictable courses. Among her Blackwell cousins, Florence married and became a Methodist lay minister, and both Edie and Agnes became doctors. Much to everyone's surprise, however, Emma Lawrence married Alice's Uncle George in 1875, when Emma was twenty-four and he was forty-three. Alice developed an especially close relationship with her Aunt Nettie after Lucy's death. They often appeared together at suffrage conventions, and Alice enjoyed long visits with her during which Brown Blackwell would reminisce about Lucy and their work on behalf of woman's rights. Alice often took notes during these times and later incorporated many of these reflections in the biography of her mother. In November 1920, Alice joyfully celebrated the fact that her aunt, then ninety-six, was finally able to cast her vote for president, although she must have been horrified to learn it was cast for the Conservative Republican candidate, Warren G. Harding.[19]

19. Elizabeth Cazden, *Antoinette Brown Blackwell* (Old Westbury, N.Y.: Feminist Press, 1983), 267.

Alice's cousins, daughters of Samuel and
Antoinette Brown Blackwell. Front row, left
to right: Agnes, Edith, and Ethel; back row:
Grace and Florence. (Schlesinger Library,
Radcliffe College)

Kitty Barry served as Dr. Elizabeth Blackwell's daughter, accountant,
housekeeper, and right-hand woman until Dr. Blackwell's death in 1910. She
retained her residence in England until 1921, when at the age of seventy-four
she finally joined sixty-four-year-old Alice in Dorchester. At about the same
time Kitty officially changed her name from Barry to Blackwell. Together,
amid a jumble of books, newspapers, and memorabilia, the two lived out
another of Alice's journal prophesies, in which she likened the pleasant shady
room of the elderly Goddard sisters to "such as I am hoping to set up housekeeping in with Kitty when we are two old maids and live together." After
1935, following the loss of most of Alice's invested savings (from the dishonest
handling of her trusted business agent), the two were supported by an annuity
fund set up on Alice's behalf by such distinguished Americans as Carrie Chapman Catt, Dorothy Canfield Fisher, and Eleanor Roosevelt; several thousand
admirers and friends contributed to the fund.

Alice outlived Kitty (who died in 1938) another twelve years and spent her
last years in a modest Cambridge apartment. In 1945, five years before her

Alice Stone Blackwell and her aunt Antoinette
Brown Blackwell riding in a suffrage parade,
c. 1910. (Schlesinger Library, Radcliffe College)

death, in recognition of her work as a humanitarian and writer Boston University awarded her an honorary Doctor of Humanities degree, commending her for her fight for woman's rights and "her defence of the underprivileged and the oppressed the world round."[20]

When Alice died in 1950, at the age of ninety-two, Boston recognized the loss of one of its most enduring reformers; her obituary appeared on the front page of city newspapers. At her memorial service, held, appropriately, at the Arlington Street Church,[21] friends and associates spoke of her accomplishments and personal qualities. They recalled her affirmative nature, candor, and independence, her penetrating intelligence, and her ability to laugh at

20. Reel 36, Blackwell Family Papers, LC.
21. Alice never strongly identified with any one church or denomination, although she generally found Unitarian churches most compatible with her religious needs.

herself[22]—qualities so apparent in her girlhood journal begun some seventy years before, when she decided to "sift herself out."

Aside from her books and published articles, her most visible memorial is on display in the Bates Reading Room of the Boston Public Library.[23] It is a marble bust of Alice, which was presented to the library in 1961 by the League of Women Voters. Exhibited along both sides of this lofty, vaulted room are busts of some twenty other prominent Bostonians. Not surprisingly, the one closest to Alice's is that of Lucy Stone, the only other woman in the collection.[24] Both Alice and her mother would be proud to know they can still be seen together—side by side—in this public place of honor.

22. Reel 5, Blackwell Family Papers, SL.

23. The Boston Evening Clinic and Hospital also has on display a large oil portrait of Alice by Carnig Eksergian. Done about 1905, it was commissioned and presented to her by her Armenian friends.

24. Anne Whitney (1821–1915) sculpted the bust of Lucy Stone for the Columbian Exposition in 1893; Frances L. Rich (b. 1910) sculpted the bust of Alice in 1960.

APPENDIX 1

Books and Periodicals Referred to in the Journal

The following information, presented by title, was obtained from the *National Union Catalogue*, the *Union List of Serials*, and the Online Computer Library Center, Inc. (OCLC), as well as by consulting catalogs of the Boston Public Library and the Boston Athenaeum. Book publication dates are based on selecting the earliest full date, excluding "18—" entries. If publishers from two or more countries listed the same year of publication, selection was based on matching the home country of the author with a publisher in the same country.

Adela Cathcart by George MacDonald (1824–1905). 3 vols. London: Hurst and Blackett, 1863.
Alec Forbes of Howglen by George MacDonald. London: Hurst and Blackett [1865].
Alice Vale: A Story for the Times by Lois Waisbrooker. Boston: W. White, 1869.
Annals of a Quiet Neighborhood by George MacDonald. London: Hurst and Blackett [1866].
The Antiquary by Sir Walter Scott (1771–1832). London: Longman, Hurst, Rees, Orme and Brown, 1816.
At the Back of the West Wind by George MacDonald. London: Strahan and Company, 1871.
The Athelings, or the Three Gifts by Margaret Wilson Oliphant (1828–97). 3 vols. Edinburgh and London: W. Blackwood and Sons, 1857.
Austin Elliot by Henry Kingsley (1830–76). London and Cambridge: Macmillan, 1863.
Battles at Home by Mary Greenleaf Darling (b. 1848). Boston: Horace B. Fuller, 1871.
The Bothie of Toper-ma-fuosich, a Long Vacation Pastoral by Arthur Hugh Clough (1819–61). London: Chapman and Hall, 1848.
The Boy in Grey by Henry Kingsley. London: Strahan, 1871.
A Brave Lady by Dinah Maria Mulock Craik (1826–87). London: Hurst and Blackett, 1870.

The Cameron Pride, or Purified by Suffering by Mrs. Mary Jane Howes Holmes (1825–1907). New York: G. W. Carleton, 1867.

The Character of Washington by Edward Everett (1794–1865). Boston: Little, Brown, 1868.

Christian's Mistake by Dinah Maria Mulock Craik. New York: Harper and Brothers, 1865.

Christie Johnstone by Charles Reade (1814–84). London: Richard Bentley, 1853.

Condensed Novels, and Other Papers, edited by Bret Harte. New York: G. W. Carleton, 1867.

Constance Lyndsay: Or the Progress of Error by Mrs. Charles Granville Hamilton. New York: Harper and Brothers, [1849?].

The Cruise of the Midge by Michael Scott (1789–1835). Boston: Allen and Ticknor, 1834.

The Daisy Chain: Or, Aspirations, a Family Chronicle by Charlotte Mary Yonge (1823–1901). London: J. W. Parker, 1854.

David Elginbrod by George MacDonald. London: Hurst and Blackett, 1863.

Elsie Venner; a Romance of Destiny by Oliver Wendell Holmes (1809–94). Boston: Ticknor and Fields, 1861.

The Essays of Elia by Charles Lamb (1775–1834). London: Printed for Taylor and Hessey, 1823–33.

Estelle Russell by Mary Allan-Olney. New York: Harper and Brothers, 1870.

From the Earth to the Moon: Passage Direct in Ninety-seven Hours and Twenty Minutes by Jules Verne (1828–1905). Translated from the French by J. K. Hoyt. Newark, N.J.: Newark Publishing, 1869.

The Gates Ajar by Elizabeth Stuart Phelps Ward (1844–1911). Boston: Fields, Osgood, [1868].

Geoffrey Hamlyn by Henry Kingsley. London: Chapman and Hall, 1874.

Glenmahra: Or the Western Highlands by Sir Randal Roberts (1837–99). London: Chapman and Hall, 1870.

Godey's Lady's Book and Magazine. Philadelphia, 1830–98. Monthly.

Golden Age. New York, 1871–75. Weekly.

Good Words for the Young. London, 1868–72. Yearly.

The Great Rebellion: A History of the Civil War in the United States by Joel Tyler Headley (1813–97). Hartford: Hurlbut, Williams, 1863–66.

The Guardian Angel by Oliver Wendell Holmes. Boston: Ticknor and Fields, 1867.

Harper's New Monthly Magazine. New York, 1850–1900.

Harper's Weekly. New York, 1857–1916.

The Harveys by Henry Kingsley. London: Tinsley Brothers, 1872.

Hereward the Wake: "Last of the English" by Charles Kingsley (1819–75). London: Macmillan, 1866.

Hide and Seek by Wilkie Collins (1824–89). 3 vols. London: R. Bentley, 1854.

Home Ballads and Poems by J. G. Whittier (1807–92). Boston: Ticknor and Fields, 1860.

Home Guardian, published by the New England Female Moral Reform Society. Boston, 1838–92. Yearly.

The Household. Boston and New York, 1868–[1930]. Monthly.

Illustrated London News. London, 1842–present. Monthly.

In School and Out: Or the Conquest of Richard Grant by Oliver Optic [William Taylor Adams], (1822–97). Boston: Lee and Shepard, [1863].

The Independent. New York and Boston, 1848–1928. Weekly.

Insects at Home: Being a Popular Account . . . Describing Their Structures, Habits and Transformations by John George Wood (1827–89). New York: Scribner's, 1872.

Is It True?: . . . An Authentic Account of the Discovery and Description of a Sunken Vessel, . . . Supposed to be That of the Pirate Kidd, Including an Account of His Character and Death, at a Distance of Nearly Three Hundred Miles from the Place by Merritt Sanford. Lynn, Mass.: Kimball and Butterfield, 1845.

Isaac T. Hopper: A True Life by Lydia Maria Child (1802–80). Boston: John P. Jewett, 1853.

Ivanhoe; A Romance by Sir Walter Scott (1771–1832). Edinburgh: A. Constable, 1820.

Jane Eyre by Charlotte Brontë (1816–55). London: Smith, Elder, 1847.

John Halifax, Gentleman by Dinah Maria [Mulock] Craik. London: Hurst and Blackett, 1856.

Kenelm Chillingly: His Adventures and Opinions by Edward Bulwer Lytton (1803–73). Edinburgh and London: W. Blackwood and Sons, 1873.

The Knickerbocker or *New York Monthly Magazine.* New York: 1833–65.

The Last of the Mortimers: A Story in Two Voices by Margaret Wilson Oliphant (1828–97). London: Hurst and Blackett, 1862.

Leighton Court; A Country House Story by Henry Kingsley. 2 vols. London: Macmillan, 1866.

Les Misérables by Victor Hugo (1802–65). Paris: Pagnerre, 1862. 1st ed.

The Life That Now Is, Sermons by Robert Collyer (1823–1912). Boston: Horace B. Fuller, 1871.

Lord and Master by Lillie Devereux Blake (1835–1913). New York: Sheldon, 1874.

Mademoiselle Mathilde by Henry Kingsley. London: Bradbury, Evans, 1868.

Magdalen Hepburn: A Story of the Scottish Reformation by Mrs. [Margaret] Oliphant. London: Hurst and Blackett, 1854.

Man and Wife by Wilkie Collins (1824–89). New York: Harper and Brothers, 1870.

Margaret and Her Bridesmaids by Julia Cecilia Collinson Stretton (1812–78). Boston: Loring, 1864.

Marjory Fleming: A Sketch; Being the Paper Entitled: "Pet Marjorie: A Story of Child-life Fifty Years Ago" by John Brown (1810–82). Edinburgh: Edmonston and Douglas, 1863.

Middlemarch: A Study of Provincial Life by George Eliot [Marian Evans] (1819–80). Edinburgh: W. Blackwood, 1871–72.

Midsummer Eve: A Fairy Tale of Love by Mrs. S. C. Hall (Anna Maria Fielding) (1800–81). London: Longman, Brown, Green, and Longmans, 1848.

Mopsa, the Fairy by Jean Ingelow (1820–97). London: Longman, Brown, Green, and Longmans, 1848.

Mosses from an Old Manse by Nathaniel Hawthorne, (1804–64). New York: Wiley and Putnam, 1846.

Mountain Adventures in Various Parts of the World; Selected from the Narratives of Celebrated Travelers. Introduction and additions by Joel Tyler Headley. New York: Scribner, 1872.

Mrs. Caudle's Curtain Lectures. Delivered during Thirty Years, by Mrs. Margaret Caudle, and Suffered by Job, Her Husband by "Punch" [Douglas William Jerrold] (1803–57). New York: E. Winchester, 1845. First published in *Punch* in 1845.

Mount Washington in Winter, or the Experience of a Scientific Expedition upon the Highest Mountain in New England, 1870–1871 by C. H. Hitchcock, J. H. Huntington, S. A. Nelson, A. F. Clough, H. A. Kimball, Theodore Smith, and L. L. Holden. Boston: Chick and Andrews, 1871.

My Wife and I; or Harry Henerson's History by Harriet Beecher Stowe (1811–96). New York: J. B. Ford, 1871.

Nature and Life; Sermons by Robert Collyer. Boston: Horace B. Fuller, 1867.

Neighbors' Wives by J[ohn] T. Trowbridge (1827–1916). Boston: Lee and Shepard, 1867.

The New Northwest. Portland, Oregon, 1871–87. Yearly.

The New York Ledger. New York, 1844–1903. Weekly.

The Newcombes: Memoirs of a Most Respectable Family by William Makepeace Thackeray (1811–63). London: Bradbury and Evans, 1853–55.

Nicholas Nickleby by Charles Dickens (1812–79). London: Chapman and Hall, [1838].

Off the Skelligs by Jean Ingelow (1820–97). London: H. S. King, 1872.

Old Margaret by Henry Kingsley. London: Tinsley Brothers., 1871.

Only a Girl: Or a Physician for the Soul by Wilhelmine (Birch) von Hillern (1836–1916). Translated from the German by Mrs. A. L. Wister (1830–1908). Philadephia: J. B. Lippincott, 1870.

Our Mutual Friend by Charles Dickens. London: Chapman and Hall, 1865.

Our Young Folks. Boston: James Osgood, 1865–73. Monthly.

Pamela: Or, Virtue Rewarded by Samuel Richardson (1689–1761). London: C. Rivington and J. Osborn, [1740].

Past and Present by Thomas Carlyle (1795–1881). London: Chapman and Hall, 1843.

Pendennis; His Fortunes and Misfortunes, His Friends and His Greatest Enemy by William Makepeace Thackeray. New York: T. Y. Crowell, [1850].

Petronel by Mrs. Florence Church Lean (1837–90). London: Frederick Wanee, [1870].

Phantastes: A Faerie Romance for Men and Women by George MacDonald. London: Smith, Elder, 1858.

The Pilot: A Tale of the Sea by James Fenimore Cooper (1789–1851). New York and London: D. Appleton, [1819].

Plutarch's Lives (many translations available).

The Poems of Ossian, Being a Literal Translation from the Original Gaelic into English . . . , collected and translated by James Macpherson (1736–96). Edinburgh: Printed for the Highland Society of Scotland, 1762.

The Princess and the Goblin by George MacDonald. Philadelphia: J. B. Lippincott, 1872.

Ravenshoe by Henry Kingsley. Cambridge: Macmillan, 1862.

Real Folks by Adeline Dutton Train Whitney (1824–1906). Boston: J. R. Osgood, [1871].

Reports and Realities: From the Sketch-book of a Manager of the Rosine Association. Philadelphia: Rosine Assoc., 1855.

The Ring and the Book by Robert Browning (1812–89). London: Smith, Elder, 1868–69.

The Romance of the Harem by Anna Leonowen (1834–1914). Boston: James Osgood, 1872.

Salem Chapel by Mrs. Margaret Oliphant. Edinburgh: W. Blackwood and Sons, 1863.

School Days at Rugby by Thomas Hughes (1822–96). Boston: Ticknor and Fields, 1857.

The Scouring of the White Horse or the Long Vacation Ramble of a London Clerk by Thomas Hughes (1822–96). Cambridge: Macmillan, 1859.

Scribner's Monthly. New York: Scribner, 1870–81.

A P P E N D I X   1

Selections from the Writings and Speeches of William Lloyd Garrison. Boston: R. F. Wallcut, 1852.

Shield; a Review of Moral and Social Hygiene. London: South Shields, 1870–86. Monthly.

Shirley, a Tale by Charlotte Brontë [Currer Bell, pseud.] (1819–55). 3 vols. London: Smith, Elder, 1849.

Sintram and His Companions; a Romance by Friedrich Heinrich Karl La Motte-Fouque (1777–1843). Translated by J. C. Hare. London: C. and J. Oliver, 1820.

Story of a Bad Boy by Thomas Bailey Aldrich (1836–1907). Boston: Fields and Osgood, 1869.

Stretton by Henry Kingsley. London: Tinsley Brothers, 1869.

The Surgeon's Daughter by Sir Walter Scott. London: Whitaker, 1833.

Tam O'Shanter: A Tale and Lament of Mary, Queen of Scots by Robert Burns (1759–96). London: J. Sharpe, 1824.

Tanglewood Tales for Girls and Boys, Being a Second Wonder-book by Nathaniel Hawthorne. Boston: Ticknor, Reed, and Fields, 1853.

Thief in the Night by Harriet Elizabeth Prescott Spofford (1835–1921). Boston: Roberts Brothers, 1872.

Three Little Spades by Anna Bartlett Warner (1827–1915). New York: Harper and Brothers, 1868.

Tom Brown at Oxford by Thomas Hughes. New York: Harper and Brothers, 1860.

Two College Friends by Frederick Wadsworth Loring (1848–71). Boston: Loring, [1871].

Ungava: A Tale of Esquimaux Land by Robert Michael Ballantyne (1825–94). London, New York: Thomas Nelson and Sons, [1857].

Vanity Fair by William Makepeace Thackeray. London: Bradbury and Evans, 1848.

Virginia: Or the Power of Grace by Mrs. Madeline Leslie, i.e. Harriet Newall Woods Baker (1815–93). Boston: H. Hoyt, [1862].

The Water Babies: A Fairy Tale for a Land-baby by Charles Kingsley. London and Cambridge: Macmillan, 1863.

The Water Witch by James Fenimore Cooper. London: H. Colburn and B. Bentley, 1830.

Westward Ho! or the Voyages and Adventures of Sir Amyas Leigh, Knight . . . , rendered into modern English by Charles Kingsley. Cambridge: Macmillan, 1845.

What She Could by Susan Warner (1819–85). London: J. Nisbet, 1870.

Wives and Daughters: An Every-day Story by Elizabeth Cleghorn Gaskell (1810–65). London: Smith, Elder, 1866.

Woman in White by Wilkie Collins. 3 vols. London: Sampson, Low, Son, 1860.

The Woman's Journal. Boston, 1870–1912. Weekly.

Yeast: A Problem by Charles Kingsley. London: J. W. Parker, 1851.

Zaidee: A Romance by Margaret Oliphant. Edinburgh and London: Blackwood, 1856.

Zerub Throop's Experiment by Mrs. Adeline Dutton Whitney. Boston: Loring, [1871].

A P P E N D I X 2

The Published Poems of
Alice Stone Blackwell, 1872–1874

PUSSY CAT

Pretty little Toby,
Lying in the sun!
Well he knows which easy chair
Is the softest one.

Well he knows the window
Warmest and most bright
Where he lies in lazy
Satisfied delight!

Lying warm and cosy,
On this summer day,
What cares he for Washington,
Or the U.S.A?

Little does he know or care
Why the cannons fire,
Happy there in easy chair,
Nothing to desire.

Woman's Journal, 22 February 1872, p. 1.

MOLLY AND THE BROOK

Wee Molly sits on a mossy stone
    With her feet in the brooklet's flow,
And this is the song the water sings
    Down where the rushes grow.

"I have left for the sea the purple hills
    And the banks where the alders sigh,
And the mossy roots of the forest trees
    I kiss, and pass them by.

"I have left the glens where the cardinal-flowers
    Their crimson spires upraise,
And the sunny slopes where the birch-leaves glance
    Through all the summer days.

"I pass them by and leave them all
    For the glory of the sea;
For the flashing surf and echoing rocks,
    And the bright waves dashing free.

"And rippling on and singing on,
    And laughing soft and low,
By bush and bank and bending tree
    I ever seaward go.

"But of all the pleasantest things I leave,
    The sweetest far is she,
The little sunbrowned maiden
    Who loves to play with me.

"I make my pools her looking-glass,
    My ripples kiss her feet,
The fairy barks she trusts to me
    I bear both safe and fleet.

"I love her well, and sing to her
    My sweetest melody;
But even for Molly stay I not
    My journey to the sea."

Our Young Folks 95 (November 1872): 695.

BIBLIOGRAPHY

PRIMARY SOURCES

Manuscripts

Library of Congress:
  Blackwell Family Papers
  National American Woman Suffrage Association Papers
Schlesinger Library
  Blackwell Family Papers

Newspapers and journals

Boston Daily Evening Transcript
Boston Daily Globe
Toledo Blade
Woman's Journal

Published material

Lasser, Carol, and Marlene Deahl Merrill, eds. *Friends and Sisters: Letters Between Lucy Stone and Antoinette Brown Blackwell, 1846–1893.* Urbana: University of Illinois Press, 1987.

Wheeler, Leslie, ed. *Loving Warriors: Selected Letters of Lucy Stone and Henry B. Blackwell, 1853 to 1893.* New York: Dial, 1981.

REFERENCE WORKS

Boston directories: 1872, 1873, 1874.

City of Boston (Platte maps): 1874.

The Compact Edition of the Oxford English Dictionary. New York: Oxford University Press, 1981.

Drabble, Margaret. *The Oxford Companion to English Literature.* 5th ed. Oxford: Oxford University Press, 1985.

Encyclopaedia Britannica. 11th ed. New York: Encyclopedia Britannica, 1911.

Freeman, William. *Dictionary of Fictional Characters.* Boston: The Writer, 1977.

James, Edward T., Janey Wilson James, and Paul S. Boyer, eds. *Notable American Women: A Biographical Dictionary.* 3 vols. Cambridge: Harvard University Press, 1971.

Johnson, Allen, ed. *Dictionary of American Biography.* New York: Scribner's, 1956.

Machennan, Malcolm. *A Pronouncing and Etymological Dictionary of the Gaelic Language.* Edinburgh: John Grant, 1915.

National Cyclopedia of American Biography. New York: James T. White, 1898.

Stephen, Sir Leslie, and Sir Sidney Lee. *Dictionary of National Biography.* London: 1885–1901. Reprint. Oxford: Oxford University Press, 1959–60.

SECONDARY SOURCES

Unpublished material

Burditt, Alice A. "Harrison Square As It Used To Be." Paper delivered at a meeting of Dorchester Historical Society, March 23, 1926.

"Fiftieth Anniversary of the Foundation of St. Mary's Parish, Dorchester: 1847–1897." Printed for the Parish, 1898.

[Floyd, Alice B.] *The History of The Parish of All Saints.* Dorchester, Mass.: Printed for the Parish, 1945.

Horn, Margo. "Family Ties: The Blackwells, a Study in the Dynamics of Family Life in Nineteenth-Century America." Ph.D. Diss., Tufts University, 1980.

King, Mary Fifield, compiler. "First Church in Dorchester: Memorabilia of Sixty Years (1859–1918)." Scrapbooks of Meeting House Hill, 1925.

Polito, Ronald. "A Directory of Boston Photographers, 1840–1900." Department of Art, University of Massachusetts at Boston, 1983.

Published books and articles

Abzug, Robert. *Passionate Liberator: Theodore Weld and the Dilemma of Reform.* New York: Oxford University Press, 1980.

Bacon, Edwin M. *King's Dictionary of Boston.* Cambridge, Mass.: Moses King, 1883.

Bartlett, J. Gardner. *Gregory Stone Genealogy: Ancestry and Descendants of Dea. Gregory Stone of Cambridge, Mass.,* Boston: Stone Family Assoc., 1918.

Beeton, Isabella. *Mrs. Beeton's Book of Household Management.* London: S. O. Beeton, 1861. Revised and enlarged edition. London: Chancellor Press, 1984.

Blackwell, Alice Stone. *Lucy Stone: Pioneer of Woman's Rights.* Boston: Little, Brown, 1930. Reprint. New York: Krause Reprint Co., 1971.

———. "To Henry B. Blackwell." In *What I Owe To My Father.* Sydney Strong, ed. New York: Henry Holt, 1931.

The Boston Almanac for the Year 1871. Boston: George Coolidge, 1871.

Boston Illustrated. Boston: James R. Osgood, 1872.

Boston Sights and Strangers Guide. Boston: J. Munroe, 1856.

Brown, Henry Collins. *Brownstone Fronts and Saratoga Trunks.* New York: E. P. Dutton, 1935.

Cazden, Elizabeth. *Antoinette Brown Blackwell: A Biography.* Old Westbury, N.Y.: Feminist Press, 1983.

Chase, Elibet Moore. "Chapel Hill–Chauncy Hall: An Historical Perspective." *The Chronicle,* publication of Chapel Hill–Chauncy Hall School, Fall 1987.

Cushing, Thomas. *Historical Sketch of Chauncy Hall School; With Catalogue of Teachers and Pupils.* Boston: David Clapp and Son, 1895.

Dorchester. Boston: The Boston 200 Corp., 1978.

Faderman, Lillian. *Surpassing the Love of Men: Love Between Women from the Renaissance to the Present.* New York: William Morrow, 1981.

Green, Martin. *The Problem of Boston: Some Readings in Cultural History.* New York: W. W. Norton, 1966.

Handlin, David P. *The American Home: Architecture and Society, 1815–1915.* Boston: Little, Brown, 1979.

Hays, Elinor Rice. *Morning Star: A Biography of Lucy Stone, 1818–1893.* New York: Harcourt, Brace and World, 1961.

_____. *Those Extraordinary Blackwells: The Story of a Journey to a Better World.* New York: Harcourt, Brace and World, 1967.

Horn, Margo. "'Sisters Worthy of Respect': Family Dynamics and Women's Roles in the Blackwell Family." *Journal of Family History* (Winter 1983): 367–82.

Johnson, Edgar. *Charles Dickens: His Tragedy and Triumph.* New York: Simon and Schuster, 1952.

Kay, Jane Holtz. *Lost Boston.* Boston: Houghton Mifflin, 1980.

Kidwell, Claudia. *Cutting a Fashionable Fit: Dressmakers' Drafting Systems in the United States.* Washington, D.C.: Smithsonian Publication, 1979.

Kidwell, Claudia, and Maggie Christman. *Suiting Everyone: The Democratization of Clothing in America.* Washington, D.C.: Smithsonian Publication, 1974.

Kirkland, Edward Chase. *Men, Cities and Transportation: A Study in New England History, 1820–1900.* 2 vols. Cambridge: Harvard University Press, 1948.

Krythe, Maymie. *Sampler of American Songs.* New York: Harper and Row, 1969.

Lasser, Carol. "'Let Us Be Sisters Forever': The Sororal Model of Nineteenth-Century Female Friendship." *Signs: Journal of Women in Culture and Society* 14, no. 1 (1988): 158–81.

Lerner, Gerda. *The Grimké Sisters from South Carolina.* New York: Schocken, 1971.

Meeks, Carrol. *The Railroad Station: An Architectural History.* New Haven: Yale University Press, 1956.

Merrill, Walter M. *Against Wind and Tide: A Biography of William Lloyd Garrison.* Cambridge: Harvard University Press, 1963.

Morgan, H. Wayne. *The Gilded Age.* Syracuse, N.Y.: Syracuse University Press, 1971.

Motz, Marilyn Ferris, and Pat Browne: *Making the American Home: Middle Class Women and Domestic Material Culture, 1840–1940.* Bowling Green, Ohio: Bowling Green University Popular Press, 1988.

New York Illustrated: A Pictorial Delineation of Street Scenes, Buildings, River Views, and Other Features of the Great Metropolis. New York: D. Appleton, 1882.

Orcutt, William Dana. *Good Old Dorchester: A Narrative History of the Town, 1630–1893.* Cambridge, Mass: John Wilson and Son, 1893.

Perkins, Robert F., Jr., William J. Gavin III, and Mary Margaret Shaughnessy, comps.

and eds. *The Boston Athenaeum Art Exhibition Index, 1827–1874.* Boston: Boston Athenaeum, 1980.

Quincy, Josiah. *The History of the Boston Atheneum.* Cambridge, Mass.: Metcalf, 1851.

Rossi, Alice. S., ed. *The Feminist Papers.* New York: Bantam, 1973.

Rossiter, Margaret. *Women Scientists in America: Struggles and Strategies to 1940.* Baltimore: Johns Hopkins University Press, 1982.

Rugoff, Milton. *The Beechers: An American Family in the Nineteenth Century.* New York: Harper and Row, 1981.

Sahli, Nancy. "Smashing: Women's Relationship Before the Fall." *Chrysalis* 8 (1979): 17–27.

Smith-Rosenberg, Carroll. "The Female World of Love and Ritual: Relations between Women in Nineteenth-Century America." *Signs: Journal of Women in Culture and Society* 1, no.1 (1975): 1–29.

Stites, Richard. *The Women's Liberation Movement in Russia: Feminism, Nihilism, and Bolshevism, 1860–1930.* Princeton, N.J.: Princeton University Press, 1978.

Strasser, Susan. *Never Done: A History of American Housework.* New York: Pantheon, 1982.

Swan, Mable Munson. *The Athenaeum Gallery, 1827–1873: The Boston Athenaeum as an Early Partron of Art.* Boston: Boston Athenaeum, 1940.

Tucci, Douglass Shand. *Built in Boston: City and Suburb, 1800–1950.* Boston: New York Graphic Society, 1978.

Warner, Sam B. *Streetcar Suburbs: The Process of Growth in Boston, 1870–1900.* Cambridge: Harvard University Press and MIT Press, 1962.

Whitehill, Walter Muir. *Boston: A Topographical History.* Cambridge: Harvard University Press, 1959.

———. *History of the Boston Public Library: A Centennial History.* Cambridge: Harvard University Press, 1956.

INDEX

Numbers in italics refer to illustrations. Only those school friends, teachers, and domestics who figure prominently in the journal are included in the index. Books are listed by title if they receive special comments in the journal (see appendix 1 for complete listing).

Reconstruction, 6
religion, 15–16, 19, 31, 35, 42, 58–59, 66*n*, 68–70, 74, 80, 103, 110, 132, 148, 159*n*, 161, 178, 198, 220, 221, 247. *See also* church(es)
Reports and Realities, 232
Republican Party, 131*n*, 192*n*, 230*n*, 245; woman suffrage supported by, 103, 111*n*, 122*n*
Restell, Madame (Ann Trow Lohman), 218
"Rhyme of the Duchess May" (Browning), 57, 70, 186
Rich, Frances L., 248
Rogers, Lily, 45
Romance of the Harem, The (Leonowen), 112, 145
Roosevelt, Eleanor, 246
"Root and Flower" (Collyer), 141
Rossetti, Christina, 63
Rossetti, Dante Gabriel, 63

Sacco, Nicola, 242
Safford, Mary Jane Blake, 133, 134, 141, 145, 146, 169, 171, 177
St. Louis, AWSA annual meeting in (1872), 125
St. Mary's Chapel, 126, 159, 163, 167, 168, 184, 191, 226*n*
St. Mary's Episcopal Church, 120*n*, 126*n*, 159
St. Patrick's Cathedral, New York, 218
St. Paul's Episcopal Church, 58, 59, *59*, 245
Santo Domingo, 49, 64, 107*n*
Savin Hill, 86, 92, *92*
Scott, Sir Walter, 17, 202; *The Antiquary*, 42–65 passim, 80, 93–109 passim; *Ivanhoe*, 27–37 passim; *The Surgeon's Daughter*, 192
Secor, Mary Belle, 94
Seneca Falls woman's rights convention (1848), 4
Sewall, Lucy Ellen, 63, 220, 223, 231
sewing, 62, 130, 131
Sex in Education (Clarke), 134*n*

Sherman, General William Tecumseh, 122
Shirley, A Tale (Brontë), 39
Siddons, Sarah Kemble, 54
slavery, 143–44
Smith, Oberlin, 92
Smith, Sarah, 192
Society of Natural History, *117*
Some Spanish-American Poets (Blackwell), 243
Somerville, N.J., 135, 214
Songs of Grief and Gladness (Blackwell), 243*n*
Songs of Russia (Blackwell), 243*n*
spelling matches, 62, 68
spiritual meetings, 198, 199–200
Spofford, Ainsworth, 49*n*
Spofford, Harriet Prescott, 110; *Thief in the Night*, 95
Spofford, Harry, 16, 49, 68–85 passim, 191*n*, 195
Squantum, 81, 89, 96, 179, 184, 188
Standish, Lorna, 100
Standish, Miles, 100
Stanton, Elizabeth Cady, 6, 122, 215*n*, 230*n*
Stanton, Harriet, 122
State House, 230 *231*, 245
Stewart, Alexander Turney, 218*n*
Stone, Bowman, 46*n*, 140, 149, 154, 185, 186
Stone, Lucy, 2, 3, *3*, 4–12, *5*, 14, 19*n*, 31, 34–35, 49, 52*n*, 57–58, 63, 67, 68*n*, 69, 73, 94*n*, 122*n*, 125, 137*n*, 168, 182*n*, 190*n*, 204, 215*n*, 245, 248; Alice's biography of, 144*n*, 244, 245; and Boston Tea Party centennial (1873), 211–12; on Charles Sumner and black suffrage, 230; death of, 239, 244; and Garner trial, 143–44; physical decline of, 180*n*, 239; wedding of, 135*n*; and *Woman's Journal*, 3, 43, 124*n*, 151*n*, 228, 237–38. See also *Woman's Journal, The*
Stone, Phebe, 46, 104, 158, 185, 186, 187
Stone, Samantha Robinson, 186*n*

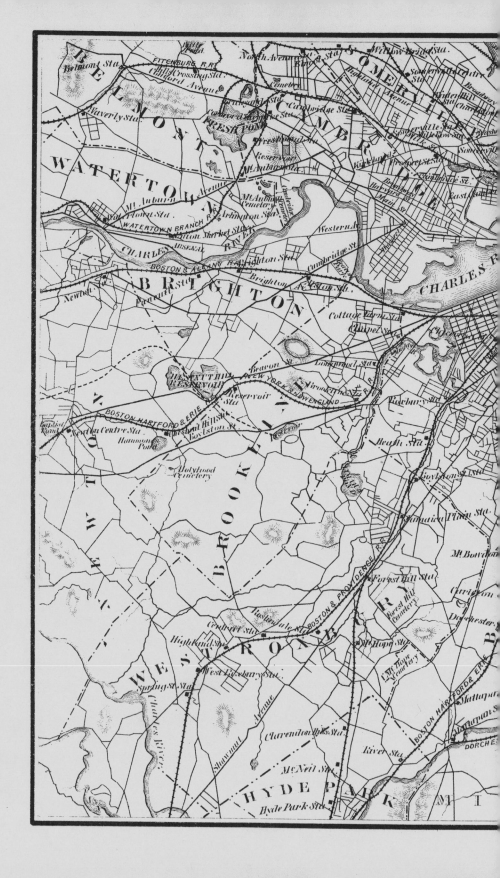